Thomas North's 1555 Travel Journal

Thomas North's 1555 Travel Journal

From Italy to Shakespeare

Dennis McCarthy and June Schlueter

FAIRLEIGH DICKINSON UNIVERSITY PRESS
Vancouver • Madison • Teaneck • Wroxton

Published by Fairleigh Dickinson University Press
Copublished by The Rowman & Littlefield Publishing Group, Inc.
4501 Forbes Boulevard, Suite 200, Lanham, Maryland 20706
www.rowman.com

6 Tinworth Street, London SE11 5AL, United Kingdom

Copyright © 2021 by the Rowman & Littlefield Publishing Group, Inc.

All rights reserved. No part of this book may be reproduced in any form or by any electronic or mechanical means, including information storage and retrieval systems, without written permission from the publisher, except by a reviewer who may quote passages in a review.

Fairleigh Dickinson University Press gratefully acknowledges the support received for scholarly publishing from the Friends of FDU Press.

British Library Cataloguing in Publication Information Available

Library of Congress Cataloging-in-Publication Data Available

Library of Congress Control Number: 2020949995

ISBN 978-1-68393-305-2 (cloth : alk. paper)
ISBN 978-1-68393-307-6 (pbk : alk. paper)
ISBN 978-1-68393-306-9 (electronic)

∞™ The paper used in this publication meets the minimum requirements of American National Standard for Information Sciences—Permanence of Paper for Printed Library Materials, ANSI/NISO Z39.48-1992.

In memory of
David Bevington
(1931–2019)

Contents

List of Illustrations		ix
Acknowledgments		xi
1	The Journey	1
2	The Journal and Its Author	11
3	From Italy to Shakespeare	27
4	Revisiting History: North's Sources—and Shakespeare's	41
5	*Henry VIII*: Transplanting a Marian History Play	63
6	*The Winter's Tale*: An Homage to Queen Mary	83
7	*The Winter's Tale* and Mantua	115
8	Further Thoughts on *The Winter's Tale*	139
Epilogue: The Lost Playwright		167
The Transcript		173
Index		229
About the Authors		241

List of Illustrations

Figure 1.1.	A modification of a Google Maps depiction that closely approximates the delegation's route from Calais to Rome, 27 February to 5 June. Map data © Google, GeoBasis-DE/BKG (©2009), Inst. Geogr. Nacional.	2
Figure 1.2.	A modification of a Google Maps depiction of the approximate route of the delegation's return trip from Rome through Austria and Germany to London, 20 June to 25 August. Map data © Google, GeoBasis-DE/BKG (©2009), Inst. Geogr. Nacional.	6
Figure 2.1.	Handwriting samples from the 1555 journal and North's legal letter.	19
Figure 3.1.	Page 1 results of a Google search for the juxtaposition of "after them" and "next them with." Each work quotes either Henry VIII or North's journal. The same is true with all other pages of results. A search of Google Books also reproduces these same results. Google and Google logo are registered trademarks of Google LLC, used with permission.	28
Figure 6.1.	The approximate domains of the brother Kings of Bohemia and Sicily. Modified from Katepanomegas / CC BY-SA (https://creativecommons.org/licenses/by-sa/3.0).	91

Figure 7.1.	The painted wax and papier-maché figures of tortured Catholics saved by the Virgin Mary, Santa Maria delle Grazie. Two statues of noblewomen appear above them, their hands in a prayer pose. Used with permission and modified after picture in "Le Grazie di Curtatone," Umano Errare (2016): https://www.dellumanoerrare.it/2016/04/07/le-grazie-di-curatone/.	116
Figure 7.2.	Giulio Romano's *Banchetto rustico* on the west wall of Sala di Psyche in Palazzo Te, depicting the pastoral wedding feast with Flora and her attendants. Above the depiction are three lunettes, each showing the story of Psyche's ordeal with Proserpina (Giulio Romano, 1526–28).	129
Figure 7.3.	Detail of Flora and the satyrs, the focus of the west wall of Sala di Psyche, Palazzo Te (Giulio Romano, 1526–28).	130
Figure 7.4.	Fresco on the east wall of Sala di Psyche, Palazzo Te, of Jupiter as half-serpent embracing Olympia while her husband, Philip of Macedon, tries to look on (Giulio Romano, 1526–28).	132
Figure 7.5.	South wall of Sala di Psyche, Palazzo Te, depicting the golden-haired Apollo, dressed as a shepherd, cavorting with mortal women. The elephant and camels have brought sacks of goods from the spice trade to the feast, and the Mediterranean is visible in the background (Giulio Romano, 1526–28).	134
Figure 8.1.	Four consecutive pages of North's *Plutarch's Lives* (1038–41). The various passages used for both *The Winter's Tale* and Greene's *Pandosto* have been highlighted. As shown, Greene and Shakespeare appear to have borrowed different halves of the same Plutarchan sea-story.	158
Figure 10.1.	First page of Thomas North's journal. Compliments of Lambeth Palace Library.	174

On the cover: Detail of Giulio Romano's *Banchetto rustico* on the west wall of Sala di Psyche, Palazzo Te, depicting the pastoral wedding feast with Flora and her attendants (Giulio Romano, 1526–28).

Acknowledgments

A number of special people and institutions deserve our gratitude. Chief among these is Lafayette College, June's home institution, which, in a critical way, enabled this project to proceed: then Dean of Libraries Neil McElroy gave Dennis access to Skillman Library's digital resources. Without this, we could not have realized the power of the technology tools that, we believe, will form the foundation of twenty-first century source study.

Colleagues and friends regularly provided encouragement. Three of June's—Emily Schneider, Leslie Muhlfelder, and Marilyn Kann—listened over lunches, numerous times; others—Eric Luhrs, Elaine Hallett, Lynn Van Dyke, and Ian Smith—commented on early drafts. Mary North Clow, a descendant of Roger North, Thomas's brother, and a scholar in her own right, graciously helped with our research, as did Michael Blanding, who directed our attention to relevant discoveries of his own.

We are both grateful to the staffs of the British Library, Lambeth Palace Library, and The Huntington Library, as well as Cambridge University, Oxford University, and the Grolier Club. Special thanks to Giles Mandelbrote, Librarian and Archivist at Lambeth Palace Library, who helped solve a number of questions concerning the manuscript. Thanks too to Alan Nelson, whose skill in reading sixteenth-century hand was key to deciphering a heavily edited paragraph in the journal.

We are both grateful to our respective partners, Lori McCarthy and Paul Schlueter, who exhibited Griselda-like patience and provided daily support. Paul deserves more than the usual spousal accolade, for it was his own online research that led to the WorldCat listing of a nineteenth-century copy of North's journal, a discovery that prompted the research that has now issued in this book. As always, Harry Keyishian and James Gifford at Fairleigh Dickinson University Press and Zachary Nycum and Ashleigh Cooke at Rowman & Littlefield were unfailingly helpful in seeing this work through to publication.

Finally, we thank our children, who, each in his or her own way, brings joy to our lives. And we thank one another for a relationship that has made working together a continuing pleasure.

Chapter One

The Journey

In 1553, when England's young King Edward VI died after only six and a half years in office, religion was once again in the forefront of England's national identity. In the contest for the throne waged by supporters of Mary Tudor and supporters of Lady Jane Grey, Mary prevailed, and the country found itself transitioning into the Catholicism that Mary's father, Henry VIII, had abjured. To celebrate the re-establishment of the Roman Catholic faith as England's official religion and to secure the nation's reconciliation with the pope, Mary and her new husband, Philip of Spain, sent an embassy to Rome.

Three ambassadors led the delegation: Thomas Thirlby, Bishop of Ely (*c.* 1506–1570); Anthony Browne, Viscount Montague (1552–1592); and Sir Edward Carne (*c.* 1500–1561)—the last to remain at the papal court as the resident ambassador. The embassy left London on 18 February 1555,[1] arrived in Dover on 23 February, crossed the Channel the same day, and left Calais four days later for the arduous journey to Rome. Although they spent two weeks with the pope as planned, by the time the ambassadors arrived in Rome on 5 June, the pope they had intended to see, Julius III, had died, as had Julius's successor, Marcellus II. Their visit, then, was with the newly installed Gian Pietro Carafa, Pope Paul IV, who, though known to hold sympathies with the French, ceremoniously received them.

All told, the journey to and from Rome lasted six months. The embassy's route through France—Calais, Amiens, Paris, Nevers, Lyon, Chambéry (see figure 1.1)[2]—included views of vineyards and orchards and visits to medieval castles, luxurious houses, and decimated towns, casualties of the last stages of the Hapsburg-Valois war, which began in 1494 and was then being fought between Emperor Charles V and King Henry II of France. In Luzarches, the travelers visited the recently built Château d'Écouen. They saw the walled town of Saint-Pierre, where the Justices sat, and in Moulins, the house of the

Duke of Bourbon, with its decorative gardens and conduits. There were alleged relics along the way: in Amiens, the head of St. John, enclosed in gold and jewels; in Saint-Denis, the head of St. Denis, a piece of the holy cross, a nail used in the crucifixion of Christ, and the finger of doubting Thomas. In Lyon, they saw the pillar to which Christ was bound and heard reminders that those who spoke evil would be burned in St. Anthony's fire. At Saint-Mathurin's, they met a holy man who had power to heal those suffering from madness. The king's crown they saw at Saint-Denis, set with an outsized ruby, undoubtedly impressed the ambassadors—as did the astronomical instrument, a kind of planetary clock devised by Orontius Finnaeus, which they saw in Paris. In Fontainebleau, they were received by Henry II, Catherine of Medici, and the adolescent Mary, Queen of Scots.

Figure 1.1. A modification of a Google Maps depiction that closely approximates the delegation's route from Calais to Rome, 27 February to 5 June.

One month after their departure from Calais, the delegates were facing the most treacherous part of their journey, the Alps. As the hills of Tarare and Lyon yielded to the mountains of Chambéry, the men found themselves navigating increasingly challenging—and dangerous—terrain. While climbing Mount d'Aiguebelette, one of the Englishmen, along with his horse, tumbled down the mountainside, fortunately escaping serious injury. Often, the entourage walked and rode between mountains, deafened by the powerful surge of the river and waterfalls that had been engorged by the melting snows of spring. As they traveled higher up the mountains, they started experiencing blinding blizzards with winds so furious they could barely remain upright. At one point, the delegates saw a man nearly drowned in the snow, eating snowballs for sustenance.

In a church in St. André, an old woman sat before a statue of the Virgin Mary, a dead child upon a board at her side. The woman explained that the child was stillborn and that she would be praying for fifteen days for the baby to return to life, or, failing that, praying s/he would start to bleed. If so, the child would be christened; if not, the body would be cast into the river. The men climbed the great Mount Cenis to La Chapelle de Transis, the Chapel of the Dead, housing some thousand skulls of those who died upon the mountain. The embassy itself lost no one, despite villagers' reports that Mount Cenis had claimed more than fifty souls in the preceding half year. Below, in Susa, they heard that four men had drowned in the snow at Mount Cenis that day, another five men just the week before, and another three men three weeks earlier. And they learned that on a nearby mountaintop, a Jewish worshiper had erected a chapel to Our Lady of the Snows. The delegates were undoubtedly relieved at their good fortune. Nonetheless, death staked a claim elsewhere: it was on their passage through the Alps that the ambassadors received news of the death of Pope Julius III.

In northern Italy, the Englishmen were repeatedly reminded of the costs and the proximity of the war. Turin, the largest town in Piedmont, on the river Po, had to be bypassed: with the emperor's troops stationed nearby, the gates could not be opened. In Rivoli, there were daily skirmishes; so too in Asti, where a scout nearly killed one of the delegation; and in other towns, the damage was massive. Those towns that escaped destruction—Novalesa, Susa, and Saint-Georges, for example—made monthly payments to the French king.

Asti was the first town of Emperor Charles V. Now, town after town—Alessandria, Voghera, Tortona, Pavia—welcomed them with escorts and ceremonial shots, some evidently believing the ambassadors were in Italy to broker a peace with France. Not far from wealthy Milan, the Englishmen were guests at one of the best houses in Europe, La Certosa di Pavia, once belonging to the first Duke of Milan. They visited the duke's white marble tomb and admired the ivory altar, the cloister, the woodcuts, and the garden. They visited a hospital as well, one of many, staffed with 500 nurses; a separate facility with 365 rooms stood outside the town, reserved for those sick with the plague.

After spending six days in Milan, the company journeyed to Lodi, Piacenza, Cremona, and Canneto, into the dukedom of Mantua. They passed gardens, meadows, pastures, lines of poplars, and fat cows, crossing the Po several times, as well as the river Oglio. In Aquanegra, they saw men in a processional whipping themselves with chains. In Mantua, they visited the chapel of Santa Maria delle Grazie (Our Lady of Mantua), the Palazzo Ducale, and the Palazzo Te, all three decorated with the works of Renaissance artist Giulio Romano. There, they saw elaborate frescoes and exquisite lifelike works of wax. The Duke of Mantua, Guglielmo Gonzaga, feasted and entertained the ambassadors, introducing them to others in the Gonzaga family. In the duchess's jewel house, they were shown rich gems, a unicorn's horn (perhaps a narwhal tusk or rhinoceros horn), and, nearby, a tiger. Such luxuries were present in other towns as well, and, throughout the dukedom, no expense was spared in welcoming them.

In Ferrara, Prince Alphonso II d'Este met with the Englishmen and took them to the duke's house, which was richly furnished in marble and jasper stone. They enjoyed an elaborate feast in the ducal palace where they were lodged, and they were shown the thriving town, as well as a camel and a tortoise. The duke himself arrived late in their stay, having missed their arrival because he was in Rome for the induction of Pope Marcellus II. Thirty miles later, having arrived in the pope's dominions, the ambassadors heard the astonishing news that Pope Marcellus II had died. He had served as head of the Roman Catholic Church for twenty-two days.

The train continued to Bologna, where they stayed for thirteen days and saw more relics: Saint Dominic, the founder of the Dominican Order, in his sarcophagus; the mummified body of Saint Catherine, sitting on a golden throne; and a piece of the crown of thorns. In Imola, across the river Reno, the company split, the Bishop of Ely and Viscount Montague going to Florence, Sir Edward Carne, along with most of the train, continuing through the region of La Romagna. It would be eleven days before they regrouped in Perugia to continue their mission.

When the company split, Carne and the train advanced toward Rome. In each town where they tarried, they were greeted warmly and stayed in the palace. On 19 May, the travelers reached the dukedom of Urbino. There the Duke of Urbino let his young son, Francesco Maria II della Rovere, then only six years old, greet the Englishmen and lead them to their lodgings. They would soon meet the duchess, Vittoria Farnese, and her alluring "troop of ladies." As the music of virginals, lutes, and viols began to play, the women danced, and the young Prince Francesco urged the Englishmen to join them. The duchess then invited them to a banquet provided by the duke.

On 22 May, the entourage passed the last ducal town and proceeded to Perugia, where they quickly learned that the townspeople were sympathetically aligned with the French. Celebrations of the investment of the new pope were well underway, with bonfires and fireworks, drums, trumpets, and volleys of shot. The Englishmen were not happy with their lodgings in an abbey and even refused a massive present of capons, rabbits, rams, lambs, a veal, and thirty-two sacks of barley that the pope's vice legate sent by way of recompense. They were similarly displeased in Spoleto, where the people were notorious for murder and sodomy. (One wonders why they remained there for five days!) Their spirits were undoubtedly lifted just outside La Prima Porta, where they were guests at the house of the late Pope Julius III, a house filled with excavated treasures of old Rome. There, the three ambassadors were met by a procession of noblemen and clergymen sent by the pope to escort them into Rome.

Led by 1,000 horses and mules, trumpets and drums before them, the escort of bishops, cardinals' pledges, officers of the papal court, and the pope's guard conveyed the train to the palace where they would lodge.

On 10 June, the pope summoned the ambassadors to court. Clad in a rich cope, a costly miter upon his head, Pope Paul IV sat in the consistory on a high chair, surrounded by the cardinals and bishops. When the Englishmen arrived, the Bishop of Ely delivered an oration to the pope. The speech apparently pleased him, for he invited the visitors to kiss his crimson slipper and blessed them all.

On 12 June, they saw the pope at evensong, where he was attended by a procession of his household officers and the cardinals, with crosses and pillars carried before them. The pope, held high in a crimson velvet chair carried by sixteen men, blessed those along the way. The next day, the pope went to the chapel of St. Peter to say Mass, after which he and his many attendants—friars, officers of the court, priests and the chorus, bishops, cardinals, and others—withdrew in ceremonial procession. The pope was kept cool and free of pesky insects by fans of peacock tails. Behind him were sixty-four horsemen, armed and appointed.

On 16 June, at the palace of St. Mark, the ambassadors enjoyed a final dinner with the pope. As a farewell gesture, the pope gave a gold cross to the Bishop of Ely and a table diamond with a ring to Lord Montague. Bonfires and peals of ordnance celebrated England's reconciliation with the church of Rome. The delegation completed their two-week stay in Rome with more

Catholic relics: the table used for the Last Supper, the stairs Christ climbed to be heard before Pilate, Christ's crown of thorns, and, as seemed to be quite common, a nail from the crucifix.³

The ambassadors' return to England followed a different route, through Austria and Germany. From Rome, they retraced their steps to Urbino, Bologna, and Verona. But at Verona, instead of heading west to Milan and through the Alps to France, they continued north, crossing the mountains to Austria (Innsbruck), then through Germany (Mittenwald, Augsburg, and Mainz) before veering west to Brussels and, finally, to Calais (see figure 1.2).

Figure 1.2. A modification of a Google Maps depiction of the approximate route of the delegation's return trip from Rome through Austria and Germany to London, 20 June to 25 August.

In northern Italy, in Urbino, the delegation saw the grave of Polydore Vergil, who had died weeks earlier; they passed through the strait between Mantua and Trento, paying a toll that apparently was not used to repair highways and bridges; and they dined at the house of the Cardinal of Trent, where they saw two ostriches and the preserved body of a child allegedly martyred by the Jews. In Trento, on 12 July, the lords who had tarried in Rome caught up with the rest, and they prepared for the passage through the Alps. This was not so grueling as the trek from France: the train took the Brenner Pass, which, during the summer, though surrounded by cloud-covered mountains, provided a less punishing way across the Italian border. Used by the ancient Romans and others before them, and still active today, the passage is, at its highest, only 4,500 feet. On the far side of the passage stands Innsbruck.

The delegation arrived in Innsbruck on 16 July. They spent time in the old town, where they saw brass statues of various royal members of the House of Austria, along with water mills that ground both corn and malt. Three days later, in Seefeld, the last town in Tyrol, they saw remnants of a miracle believed to have taken place in 1384. At Easter, an arrogant local knight stood rather than kneeled before the altar and demanded a larger piece of the Host for Communion. In punishment for his blasphemy, the earth opened up beneath his feet, intending to swallow him. The man clapped his right hand on the altar, leaving an impression that was still visible when the Englishmen stopped there in 1555. When the communicant repented, the ground became firm again, and, later, the Host that had been offered to him began to bleed. Some still visit this chapel today, where the imprint of his hand on the altar may still be seen.

The men travelled through the small town of Mittenwald, the first in the dukedom of Bavaria, to Oberammergau, a village in southern Germany, where they saw the Blackfriars' Abbey Ettal. They continued to Schongau, near Landsberg am Lech, where the Bishop of Ely overtook Lord Montague. Apparently, Thirlby had remained in Rome an additional thirteen days after Montague and all but six men in the train departed.

At Augsburg, where there was a balance of Catholic and Protestant churches, the *Burgermeister* sent the ambassadors twenty trout and sixty gallons of wine. Ferdinand I, brother to Charles V and King of Bohemia, Hungary, and the Holy Roman Empire, was also in Augsburg, petitioning the Germans for aid in the fight against the Ottomans. The Turkish fleet, led by Turgut Re'is, had just invaded Calabria at the southern tip of Italy. This would also be the year the Peace of Augsburg would be signed, which granted the rulers of states within the Holy Roman Empire the right to choose the religion for their realm. On 25 July, the company lay in Dillingen at the house of the Cardinal of Augusta, then passed through Heidenheim, where they saw the Duke of Württemberg's castle: the duke was one of the great Protestant princes of Germany.

In Göppingen, they saw the baths of mountain water; in Cannstatt, a free town, they tasted Neckar wines. They proceeded through the duchy of Württemberg to the territory of Frederick II, the County Palatine, and saw the town—Bretten—where Philip Melanchthon was born. They avoided Speyer, which was suffering an outbreak of the plague.

The company rode on to the double-walled free town of Worms; to Mainz, where the printing press was invented; to several more towns along the Rhine, known for their Rhenish wine; and to Sankt Goar, the first town of the landgrave. They passed through other towns as well, including Koblenz and Bonn, and on 5 August arrived in the free town of Cologne, where they saw the majestic Cathedral, a nunnery housing highborn women, and the relics of the three kings and the 11,000 virgins who had allegedly been killed along with St. Ursula.

A few miles after Cologne, they were in the duchy of Jülich. The Englishmen dined in Aachen, where Charlemagne was buried and where each new emperor receives the first of his three crowns. (The order is the iron crown in Aachen, the lead crown in Milan, and the gold crown in Rome.) In the Low Countries, they first passed through Maastricht, then on to Leuven and Brussels. In Brussels, they entered the court of Emperor Charles V, where they met Edward Courtenay, Earl of Devon, who was great-grandson to Edward IV and considered a threat to the Tudor dynasty; and Sir John Mason, who had replaced Thirlby as ambassador to the emperor. Charles V lived alone in a house in the park, which is where he met with the lords. The train remained in Brussels for thirteen days before advancing to Ghent, the first and chief city of Flanders, where the emperor was born. The town, which hosted 400 windmills, was protected by 60,000 fighting men.

They passed through Bruges, with its 132 bridges, and on to Ostend. Just beyond Nieuwpoort, the men were back in Calais, where the company stayed on 20 August, before sailing across the English Channel to Dover. They proceeded to Canterbury, then Dartford, and finally reached London on 25 August.

NOTES

1. "February the 18th [1554/55], the Lord Viscount Mountague, and Thirlby Bishop of Ely, with divers others in their company, passed through London with seven score horse, being appointed ambassadors to the pope; to thank his holiness, as was pretended, for his great clemency to the realm, but, as was thought more truly, to treat about the restoration of abbeys." John Strype, *Ecclesiastical Memorials;*

Relating Chiefly to Religion, and Its Reformation, under the Reigns of King Henry VIII. King Edward VI. and Queen Mary the First: with the Appendixes Containing the Original Papers, Records, &c. In Seven Volumes. Volume the Fourth. Containing the Events That Occurred during the Reign of Queen Mary the First (1721; London: Printed for Samuel Bagster, 1816), 346.

2. In his 1656 *Voyage et Description d'Italie*, Pierre Duval identifies eight such routes through France, noting that surviving travel journals suggest a preference for Mount Cenis, the route the Marian delegation chose. Pierre Du Val, *Le voyage et la description d'Italie* . . . (Paris: Clouzier, 1656), 7–12. At least since the ninth century, it was customary for abbots of Westminster to travel to Rome to have the pope confirm their positions. The abbots took one of three routes: (1) northern France to Burgundy, the upper Rhone Valley, then over Mount Cenis or the Great St. Bernard Pass and into the Po Valley; (2) through Flanders, up the Rhine Valley, and across the Brenner Pass to Trento and Verona; and (3) northern France to Lausanne and Brig and over the Simplon Pass. Each had its dangers. See William Wallace, "Dangerous Journey," *Westminster Abbey Review* Summer 2018, 40–46.

3. The delegation's return departure date is confirmed by John Strype, *Ecclesiastical Memorials*, 363.

Chapter Two

The Journal and Its Author

Geographically and chronologically, we have a detailed account of the embassy to and from Rome in a travel journal that records the where and the when of the excursion along with considerable commentary on the places the company passed through, the wonders they saw, and the experiences they had. Entitled "The Jorney of the Queenes Ambassadours unto Roome Anno. 1555. The Reverend father in God the Bisshoppe of Ely, and Vicownt Montagu then Ambassadors: who set out of Calleis in picardy on Wednesday being Ash-Wednesday the 27. of February a° predicto," the manuscript is now housed in Lambeth Palace Library in London. It was purchased on 2 December 2015, when the collection of the recently deceased American book collector Robert S. Pirie was up for auction at Sotheby's, New York. The lot, no. 798, sold for $43,750.[1]

In 1778, a transcript of a portion of the travel journal appeared in *Miscellaneous State Papers. From 1501 to 1726*.[2] The editor was Philip Yorke, 2nd Lord Hardwicke (1720–1790), who transcribed a number of miscellaneous state papers held by the British Library (then known as the British Museum Library). The transcript is listed in the 1794 *Catalogue of the Manuscripts in the Possession of the Earl of Hardwicke* as "Journey of the Queen's Ambassadors to Rome, the Bp. of Ely and Viscount Montague" (Vol. 97, no. 101).[3] At the head of the transcript, Hardwicke inserted this parenthetical note:

> This Journal . . . contains many curious particulars of the face of the country, the appearance of the great towns, and the customs of Italy at that time. Some minutiæ and inaccuracies must be overlooked. This is the last embassy which went from England to pay public homage to the See of Rome. Lord Castlemain, sent by King James, could only address the Pope in the name of his Master, and of the English Catholics; not that of the nation.[4]

Hardwicke omitted the return portion of the trip, through Austria and Germany, ending the published narrative in Trento. "The rest of the journey homewards," he explained, "is omitted as not material."⁵

The journey received additional attention from Rawdon Brown, who in 1877 published a letter from Cardinal Pole to Pope Julius III dated 10 March 1555. In it, Pole stresses the Catholic *bona fides* of the three main figures in the delegation, which was already en route. He was, of course, intent on assuring the pope that the three were devout Roman Catholics, committed to the reconciliation of England and Rome. The letter reads:

> The youngest of them, and who is the chief person of the embassy [Anthony Browne, Viscount Montague], gave such proof of his piety heretofore in his youth, that when after his father's death, on succeeding to his inheritance, he had to take the usual oath according to the words of the statute, which constituted the King supreme head of the Church in his kingdom, his voice suddenly failed him, nor for some time could he utter a word . . ., which caused him to be so suspected by the persons then in authority that he narrowly escaped the loss both of life and property . . . Some years afterwards he was, moreover, imprisoned on account of religion . . . His colleague, the Bishop of Ely [Thomas Thirlby], in those troublous times when the abrogation of the mass was discussed, opposed that measure, both in public and private; and had he not been absent on an embassy to the Emperor he would have been cast into prison, like so many others of his episcopal brethren. He is a good jurist, and an able negotiator. The third, Sir Edward Carne, is "*Eques auratus*," as they call him, and an able lawyer, and like his other colleagues is supposed to be well inclined towards the Catholic religion and piety . . .; of yore when King Henry commenced being schismatic, he sent him to Rome as Excusator, and to inform the Pope of the danger of rebellion in case of his refusal to consent to the divorce. At present, the piety of Queen Mary and King Philip induces them to appoint him as their resident ambassador at Rome as a witness of the cessation of the schism, and of the true and due obedience of this kingdom to the Pope and the Apostolic See. . . .⁶

A second letter concerning the journey also survives and was sold, as lot 556, at the same 2015 auction as the travel journal. This, too, is a letter of introduction, signed by Mary and Philip, dated February 1554/5, and addressed to Cosimo I de' Medici, 2nd Duke of Florence (and, from 1569, Grand Duke of Tuscany). On their way to Rome, the royal ambassadors were planning to deliver good wishes to the duke, a gesture intended to secure his loyalty. But when Pope Julius died, his successor's anti-Spanish position intruded on the plan.

In 1910, C. M. Antony reprinted Cardinal Pole's letter, as well as portions of the journal, in "The Last National Embassy to Rome." The two-part essay, which appeared in *The Month: A Catholic Magazine*, is a condensed, mostly paraphrased account of the journal.[7] Similarly, in 1964, T. F. Shirley published *Thomas Thirlby: Tudor Bishop*, which includes a chapter, "The Path to Rome," that recaps the journey.[8]

Information on the journal's earliest provenance has proved elusive. We know that two early modern manuscripts of the journal exist: the Lambeth Palace Library manuscript (MS 5076) and a copy from the late sixteenth or early seventeenth century in the British Library (Harley 252, fols 62–102). We also know that a transcript of a portion of the journal appeared in *Miscellaneous State Papers* in 1778. And we know that the Huntington Library in San Marino, California, holds a nineteenth-century handwritten transcript, catalogued as "The booke and diare of the ambassadors jorney to Rome" (HM 81033). Edwin Francis Gay (1867–1946), a Harvard economist who spent the last decade of his life in a research position at the Huntington, donated the transcript to the library in October 1937. On the cover of the transcript is a note indicating its derivation: "From the Harleian MS. 252. Fol. 49." In that same hand, on a cover sheet, is a quotation from John Stowe's commentary on the journey in *The Annals of England* (1592):

    A.D. 1555.
The 18. of Februarie Thomas Thurleby bishop of Ely, and Anthonie Lord Montecuto with other, tooke this journey towards Rome, ambassadors from the king and queene.
                Stow's Annals
                edit. 1592 p. 1061

We do not know who wrote either note. Although Gay is a likely suspect, the hand is not his. Nor was he responsible for another note, on a separate sheet, in the same hand as the transcript, which reads "Phillipps MS 24316." Both notes provide information on provenance: one indicating that this nineteenth-century Huntington transcript was a copy of the British Library copy, the other providing the manuscript number for the transcript when it was in the possession of Thomas Phillipps (1792–1872), the celebrated nineteenth-century collector.

The Huntington transcript was in Phillipps' collection until at least 1872, when it appeared in the handwritten probate inventory compiled by Edward A. Bond of the British Museum Library.[9] We do not know when it passed from Phillipps to Gay or whether there were other custodians in between. But we do know that Phillipps, who owned some 60,000 manuscripts, held both the nineteenth-century Huntington transcript and the manuscript now in Lambeth Palace Library.

The known custodial history of the Lambeth Palace Library manuscript begins in 1836, when bookseller Thomas Thorpe listed the document in his *Catalogue of Upwards of Fourteen Hundred Manuscripts, Upon Vellum and Paper* (no. 832).[10] Thorpe had acquired it in February 1836 at Part 11, Day 7, of R. H. Evans' auction of the immense library of Richard Heber (1773–1833). Thorpe owned the manuscript for only a few months before Phillipps made a block purchase from him and, in 1837, listed the document in *Catalogus Librorum Manuscriptorum in Bibliotheca D. Thomæ Phillipps, Bart.* (no. 9013), the inventory of the manuscripts in his collection.[11] On 26 June 1967, the American collector Robert S. Pirie (1934–2015) acquired the manuscript at a Sotheby's auction, through Bernard Quaritch (Lot 754).[12] Finally, in December 2015, at a Sotheby's auction of the books and manuscripts in Pirie's estate, Lambeth Palace Library purchased the document. Thorpe's extended description of the journal in his 1836 sale catalogue characterizes the document as "The Original Manuscript."

The British Library copy of the journal may be traced to the lifetime of Sir Simonds D'Ewes (1602–1650).[13] In 1704, Robert Harley, 1st Earl of Oxford and Mortimer (1661–1724) purchased some 600 manuscripts, including the 1555 journal, from the D'Ewes estate for £500.[14] In 1724, when Robert Harley died, the library passed to his son; at Edward Harley's death in 1741, the now expanded collection went to the 2nd Earl's wife and daughter— Henrietta Cavendish Harley (née Holles), Countess of Oxford and Mortimer (1694–1755) and Lady Margaret Cavendish Bentinck (née Harley), Duchess of Portland (1715–85), widow and daughter, respectively. The women sold the books of the library shortly after Harley's death. But they held on to the manuscripts until 1753, when, in order to keep intact the 7,660-item collection of manuscripts and make the collection generally accessible, they sold it to the British Museum for a mere £10,000.[15] Below is the (untangled) custodial history of the two manuscripts:

Lambeth Palace Library Manuscript: MS 5076

1836 Bookseller Thomas Thorpe purchases the journal at R. H. Evans' auction of the library of Richard Heber.
1836 Thomas Thorpe lists the journal in his *Catalogue of Upwards of Fourteen Hundred Manuscripts*.
1837 Thomas Phillipps, having purchased the journal from Thorpe, lists the item in his *Catalogus Librorum Manuscriptorum*.[16]
1967 Robert S. Pirie purchases the journal at a Sotheby's auction.
2015 Lambeth Palace Library purchases the journal at Sotheby's auction of the Pirie estate.
2020 The manuscript is in Lambeth Palace Library under shelfmark MS 5076.

British Library Manuscript: Harley 252, fols 62–102

- *c.* 1625–50 The journal is in the possession of Sir Simonds D'Ewes (1602–1650).
- 1704 Robert Harley, 1st Earl of Oxford and Mortimer (1661–1724) purchases 600 manuscripts, including the journal, from the D'Ewes estate.
- 1753 The British Museum Library purchases some 7,660 manuscripts from the widow and daughter of Edward Harley, 2nd Earl of Oxford and Mortimer (1689–1741), who left them the library that his father, the 1st Earl (1661–1724), had assembled and that he (Edward) had strengthened.
- 1759 The journal is listed in the British Museum Library's *Catalogue of the Harleian Collection.*[17]
- 1778 A transcript of a portion of the journal is published in *Miscellaneous State Papers. From 1501 to 1726.*[18]
- 1794 The transcript of a portion of the journal is listed in *Catalogue of the Manuscripts in the Possession of the Earl of Hardwicke* (Vol. 97, no. 101).
- 1808 The journal is listed in the new edition of the British Museum Library's *Catalogue of the Harleian Collection.*[19]
- 2020 The manuscript is in the British Library under shelfmark Harley 252, fols 62–102.

But which of the two manuscripts is the earlier? Despite the elusive provenance of the Lambeth Palace Library manuscript prior to 1836, that document clearly has priority. Two hands are involved in Harley 252; both appear to be late sixteenth century or early seventeenth. By contrast, MS 5076 is in a single, earlier secretary hand, consistent with the time of the journey. Indeed, the evidence strongly suggests that the Lambeth Palace Library manuscript is the original, first-draft compilation of travel notes. The level of detail in the journal makes it likely that the journalist recorded much of the information now in the journal as he traveled, but the presence of several comments concerning post-journey events confirms that he first assembled this information into the Lambeth Palace Library manuscript after he was back in England, sometime between 1555 and 1558. MS 5076 also includes later corrections and edits, in the journalist's own hand, that may be early Elizabethan, perhaps 1558–59. Harley 252 closely follows the Lambeth Palace Library manuscript, reproducing only the text that survived the edits, ignoring the lines that were crossed out, and introducing only incidental differences. The British Library copyist makes a few silent corrections but generally retains the spelling of towns and rivers in the original, which, despite the journalist's edits, are still often erroneous. There are only two substantive departures from the original: distances between towns, monetary values, and other numbers occasionally do not match those in MS 5076, and the British Library manuscript does not have marginalia.

The Lambeth Palace Library manuscript (MS 5076) consists of fifty-seven pages plus blanks, measuring *c.* 12.20 × 8.07 inches [*c.* 310 × 205 mm]; these are bound in nineteenth-century green morocco gilt with gilt edges. A few of the early folios are incorrectly bound: specifically, bound pages 10 and 9 should be 3 and 4; bound pages 3 through 8 should be 5 through 10. The manuscript proper is in sixteenth-century secretary hand, with place names in italic; marginalia are also in italic and written in the same hand as the place names. The Lambeth Palace Library manuscript may be viewed at Lambeth Palace Library in London or online at http://images.lambethpalacelibrary.org.uk/luna/servlet/s/r9qik9.

The British Library manuscript (Harley 252, fols 62–102)[20] measures *c.* 11.02 × 6.69 inches [*c.* 280 × 170 mm]; it is bound in mottled paneled leather gilt in a composite volume of seventy leaves of state tracts and loose papers. The manuscript is in two late sixteenth-century or early seventeenth-century secretary hands, with place names in italic and no marginal notes. The British Library manuscript is not online but may be viewed in the Manuscripts Reading Room at The British Library in London.

THE AUTHOR

The identity of the author of the 1555 journal has been of interest at least since 1759, when the cataloger of the Harleian Collection noted that the journal was "Written by one of that Bishop's [i.e., Ely's] Servants, who seems to have had no great Faith in Popish Miracles," a comment that was repeated in the 1808 edition of the *Catalogue*. In 1778, when the partial transcript of the manuscript was published, the editor of that volume, Philip Yorke, 2nd Lord Hardwicke, inserted a preliminary note that begins: "This journal, though not writ by one of the most distinguished persons in the train of the Ambassadors . . ." In 1910, Antony, adding speculation to a number of comments in the journal, provided a profile of the journalist, styling him "this mediæval Pepys":

> The sublime pageant of colour and sound [at High Mass at St. Peter's] seems to have sobered this mediæval Pepys. He declines modestly to write any description of Rome itself, the antiquities of which, he tells us, have been "truly and notably set forth" by one William Turner.[21] We take leave of him with regret and gratitude, with which is mingled a feeling almost of affection. But for this diary of his—kept perhaps for his wife or mother at home—we should have no details of a journey so important historically, so fraught with human interest. That he was a brave man is abundantly evident, in spite of his climbing Mont Cenis by

the help of his horse's tail; that he was tender-hearted, enthusiastic, and highly susceptible is even more clear. But what strikes us most in reading his long, but never dull narrative is the extraordinary number of tiny, picturesque details which his journalistic mind appreciated so intensely. Who else has told us of the "tiger" at Mantua, and the Cardinal of Pisa's long-suffering ostrich? Had he lived in our own day he would certainly have been foreign correspondent to a well-known morning paper. . . .[22]

All appear to have been curious, but none offered a proposal for who the journalist might be.

That the journal remained anonymous as long as it did may be explained not by the absence of evidence but by its obscurity. Had scholars been researching the journal, they would have discovered that the little-known probate inventory of book collector Thomas Phillipps, drawn up after his death in 1872, included "The booke & Diarie of the Ambassadors to Rome, Sir Thos. Northe his travels, from Harl. MS" (Item 24316). Since only two copies of that inventory are known to exist, one at the Bodleian in Oxford and one at the Grolier Club in New York, it is not surprising that no one came upon it. But there was a second opportunity in and after 1937, when the Huntington Library acquired the nineteenth-century transcript, for its catalogue entry also attributed authorship to Sir Thomas North (1535–1603 or later).[23]

But both attributions reference the nineteenth-century transcript. Were the two early manuscripts also associated with North? We were in for a surprise when investigative journalist and author Michael Blanding, who is writing a book on our research, informed us that he perused the British Library manuscript and made a discovery: the *Sammelband* catalogued as Harley 252, which contains numerous documents as well as the journal, includes a leaf bound after the end of the journal, following a single unrelated sheet on beasts. Though largely blank, the page is important. For rather like a modern-day half-title page, it states, in late sixteenth- or early seventeenth-century hand, "The Booke ^and diare^ of the Ambassadors Jorney to Rome Sr Thomas North his travels."[24] Though the asterisk on the page—fol. 74*—indicates that it was not bound at the same time as the journal, this misplaced sheet, which may once have been an outer front cover or wrapper for the manuscript,[25] lends strength to the claim that the author was North.

There are other reasons as well to attribute authorship to Thomas North. He was certainly capable of the prose responsible for the journal's appeal. Though not quite twenty when the delegation left London in February 1555, he was only two years away from the publication of his first major translation, into English, of a French translation of Antonio de Guevara's *Dial of Princes* (1557), a work published in France. In the years that followed, he would publish three more: Anton Francesco Doni's Italian translation of *The Moral Philosophy of Doni* (1570); James Amyot's French translation of Plutarch's *The Lives of the Noble Grecians and Romanes* (*Plutarch's Lives*, 1579/80); and Simon Goulart's French translation of Cornelius Nepos' *The Lives of Epaminondas, of Philip of Macedon, of Dionysius the Elder, and of Octavius Cæsar Augustus* . . . (1602).[26]

Moreover, digital research tools indicate that terms used in the journal and in North's translation of *Plutarch's Lives* are unique. In the sixteenth century, for example, there was no English term for *canal* or *levee*, so North, in his 16 August entry, invented his own: a "river . . . **forced by men's hands**" (i.e., man-made). North also uses this expression in *Plutarch's Lives* when referring to an artificial isthmus: "He went to see this Isle of Pharos . . . a little above the mouth of the **river** of Nylus, called Canobia, howbeit it is now joined unto firm **land**, being **forced by man's hand**" (736). A search of the Early English Books Online (EEBO) database confirms that *Plutarch's Lives* is the only work in the database that includes this expression.[27] The search would have also resulted in North's journal had it been in the database.

Throughout the journal, the journalist also had the habit of emphasizing allusions to rivers in the margin and then exclusively using the Latin abbreviation for river: *fl.* or occasionally *flu.*, which derives from *flumen* or *fluvius*. On the very first folio of the travel diary, the journalist mentions passing by the river Som[m]e, and in the margin we find "Som[m]e fl." As far as we can tell, the only author in the EEBO database who had this peculiar habit was North, whose margins of his *Plutarch's Lives* frequently include the names of the rivers followed by the abbreviation "fl." or occasionally "flu."

Finally, North's handwriting secures his authorship. The Cambridge University library holds the 1582 edition of *The Dial of Princes* once owned by North (Adv. D. 14. 4). On the volume's final page is North's handwritten inscription of ownership: "29 Marche 1591. Price—5s.," followed by his bold signature, ending with a conventional "*manu propria*" (in his own hand) flourish.[28] Throughout *The Dial* are marginal annotations that match the italic hand used in the narrative to indicate the names of towns. Even more telling are the similarities in secretary hand, made visible in a comparison of an autograph letter by North held by the British Library (Add. MS 12497). As the samples in figure 2.1 reveal, although thirty years intervene between the letter and the journal, it is strikingly clear that the journal hand (left facsimile) and the letter hand (right facsimile) are the same.

The "anonymous author," then, is clearly Thomas North. We know this not only because both the British Library and the Huntington copies identify him as the author but also because the journal is clearly in his hand; moreover, it includes at least two Northern idiosyncrasies: "forced by men's hands" and the placement of Latin abbreviations in the margins to indicate rivers.

	Travel Journal	North's Legal Letter
praying	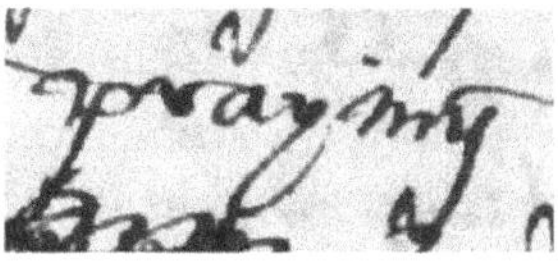	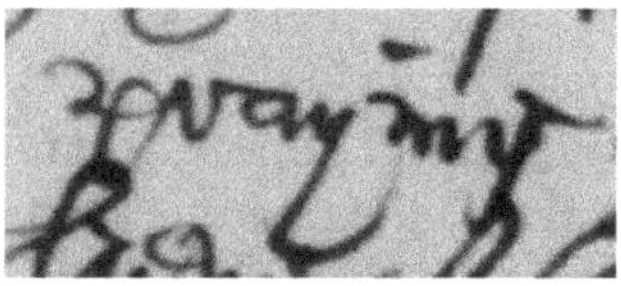
first	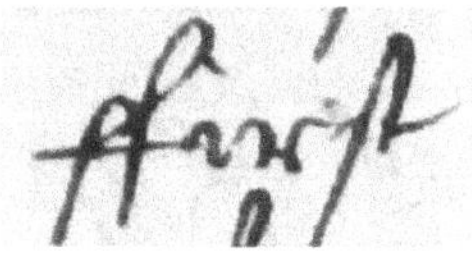	
commoditie	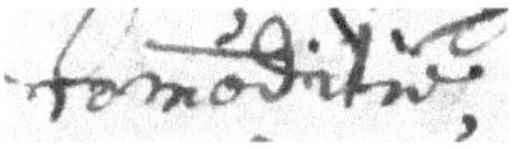	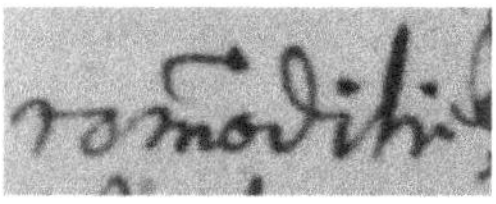
with an		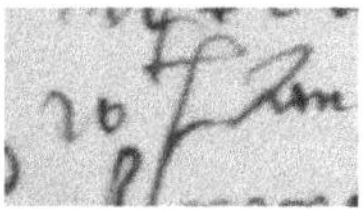
the same.		
if there be	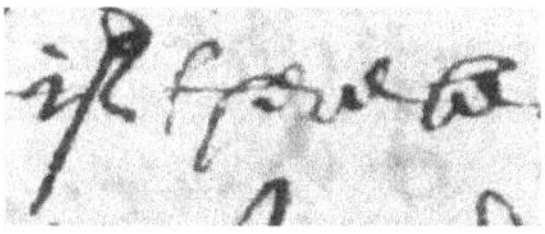	
downe		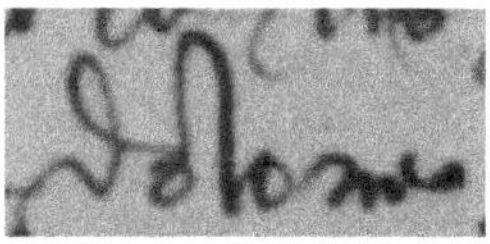
officers	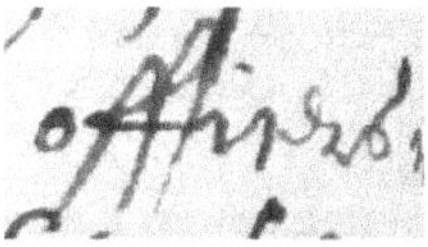	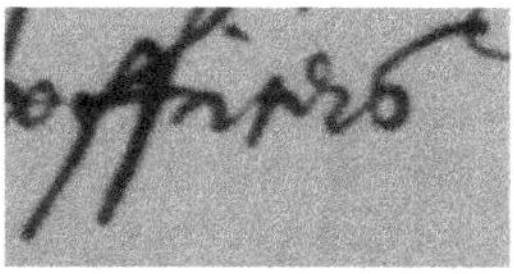
the Queene		

Figure 2.1. Handwriting samples from the 1555 journal and North's legal letter.

Interestingly, although throughout the journal North refers to himself in the first person, in the 7 April entry, when he describes the Italian scout's coming upon him with a pistol, crying "*Chi Viva*" ("Who goes there?"), he uses the third person. This description of his near-death experience contains the most densely edited lines of the narrative, and it seems as if he was having a difficult time deciding what he should call himself, whether "my L[ord] Northes son," which he crosses out twice, or "the Bisshoppe of Elyes page." Why he switches from the first person here is unclear. Perhaps the reason is that for most other entries, North was primarily acting as a witness—a reporter of the events that he was seeing. In the 7 April entry, he is the subject, so he may have felt it important to identify himself as the one who was nearly killed. It is also possible that he wanted, for some reason, to avoid being identified as the journalist.

We are indebted to Alan H. Nelson for the transcription of these lines from that entry:

Diplomatic text (*italicized text is interlinear*)
men of armes met the Lordes, and brought them to the Towne
       ^ *reioycing*
with great ^ ~~Reioysing~~, and they so corvetted their great horses,
that some of them horse and man lay in the dytches: and when
we came to the towne, they gave the Lordes a great volley of
                                    shott
small shotte, small and some great ordinance ^ of the walles. As we were
my L. Northes younger sonne and my Lorde of (blank) & ~~my L. Northes sonne~~,
coming nere the Towne, M. Thomas North ^ ~~the Bisshoppe of~~
      ^ *~~was in danger And my L. Northes soone was in~~*
Elyes page ^) ~~And Lyke to have been slayne by a skowte of the towne~~
In dawnger ^ *to have ben slayne by a skowte*
~~being vpon him ere he was ware~~, sent to discover the Lordes
      who being ypon him ere he was ware, with his pistoll
coming) ~~offering his pistol to his brest, crying vpon the sodeyn~~
in his hand cried: wherevpon he answering
^ ~~Chi Viua: But he answering presently that~~ they were Englishmen,
      ^ *wheled about and* ~~about and galloped awaye~~
the horseman ^ ~~turned his horse from him and did him no hurte~~
      away
so left him, galloping ^ ~~back agayne~~ to bring newes of the Lordes
away from him
coming.
Left margin: Mr North in / danger of / kylling.
Left margin: ~~Cried~~ in Italian / Chi viua

By way of summary, we offer the following observations about the Lambeth Palace Library manuscript and its author:

- It is clear from the nature and consistency of the handwriting, both in secretary and italic, including the document's corrections, marginal comments, and interlineations, that one person was responsible for the entirety of the text.
- The journalist did not write the extant journal in its entirety while on his trip but compiled it after his return to England. We know this because he occasionally includes information that post-dates the entry. Consider the line on 8 March: "I saw in Paris the wonderful instrument of Orontius *then alive*." Orontius Finnaeus [Oronce Finé] did not die until five months afterward, 8 August 1555. As the 8 March entry occurs at the beginning of the journal, and "then alive" is not an interlineation or correction, this means the 8 March entry and (based on layout) all the entries that follow had to have been written after Orontius's death. Also note the line that ends the section describing the embassy's entry into the pope's dominions: "Pope Marcellus Secundus was *then alive*" (29 April), confirming again that he is writing the entry after that date. Although some of the detail in certain passages suggests the journalist likely took notes while on his trip, he almost certainly compiled those notes into the extant journal after he returned home.
- The journalist wrote the extant journal within three years and three months of his return, as evidenced by a number of entries that are plainly Marian. For example, he refers to "King Philip of Spain (now our king)" (22 April), a comment that would cease being true on the day of Mary's death, 17 November 1558. He also refers to Paul IV as the pope "that now is" (19–21 April). Paul IV would die 18 August 1559.
- At least one of the journalist's later corrections appears to have occurred during the reign of Elizabeth. In the 28 March entry, the journalist originally had referred to one of his fellow travelers as "Master Whight, (sonne to Master Whight one of the masters of the requests)." He had to have written this original line during the reign of Queen Mary, for Whight (Thomas White) served as master of requests until her death. At some later time, he crossed out the line following the word Master and replaced it with "White (whose father was master of the requests to Queen Mary)."

We offer the following summary of the evidence supporting our claim that the journalist was Thomas North:

- The late sixteenth- or early seventeenth-century British Library manuscript, the nineteenth-century Huntington Library transcript, and the 1872 probate inventory of Thomas Phillipps all attribute authorship to North.

- Certain peculiar terms used in the journal also appear in North's translation of *Plutarch's Lives*—and in no other surviving early modern English text.
- North, like the journalist, was a page for the Bishop of Ely, and the journal confirms he accompanied the embassy to Rome.
- The known examples of North's italic hand (his marginalia in *The Dial*) and his secretary hand (the letter in the British Library) match both the italic and secretary hand in the journal.

To scholars interested in early modern manuscripts, our analysis of this 1555 travel journal and publication of the transcript may seem the end of the story. But scholars interested in early modern drama—particularly Shakespeareans—are bound to be intrigued by the identification of the journal's author as Thomas North. For Shakespeareans have long known that North's translation of *Plutarch's Lives* was a major source for Shakespeare's Roman plays—*Julius Caesar*, *Antony and Cleopatra*, *Coriolanus*—and that in those plays the playwright subsumed many of North's passages with little change. In 1895, George Wyndham, an editor of *Plutarch's Lives*, wrote: "Shakespeare, the first poet of all time, borrowed three plays almost wholly from North." He also had a high opinion of North's writing abilities: "Of good English prose there is much, but of the world's greatest books in great English prose there are not many. Here is one, worthy to stand with Malory's *Morte d'Arthur* on either side of the English Bible."[29] C. F. Tucker Brooke, also an editor of *Plutarch's Lives*, agreed, writing that many of the most memorable speeches in the Roman tragedies, "all of which rank among the special treasures of Shakespearean poetry, come straight and essentially unaltered out of North."[30] Might North's journal also have been a source? In the chapters that follow, we explore the relationship between the journal and two of Shakespeare's late plays, *Henry VIII* and *The Winter's Tale*, revealing the story suggested in our furtive subtitle, "From Italy to Shakespeare."

NOTES

1. See http://www.sothebys.com/en/auctions/ecatalogue/lot.798.html/2015/property-collection-robert-s-pirie-books-manuscripts-n09391.
2. *Miscellaneous State Papers. From 1501 to 1726. In Two Volumes*. Vol. I (London: W. Strahan; and T. Cadell, 1778), 62–102.
3. Privately printed, 1794.
4. *Miscellaneous State Papers. From 1501 to 1726*. Vol. I, 62.
5. *Miscellaneous State Papers. From 1501 to 1726*. Vol. I, 102.
6. *Calendar of State Papers and Manuscripts, Relating to English Affairs, in the Archives and Collections of Venice, and in Other Libraries of Northern Italy, Volume*

6. *Part I. 1556–1558*, ed. Rawdon Brown (London: Longman & Co. / Also, Oxford: Parker & Co., Cambridge: Macmillan & Co., Edinburgh: A. & C. Black, and Dublin: A. Thom, 1877), 16–17. (Ellipses indicate that the original Latin, which the translator provided, is omitted.)

7. C. M. Antony, "The Last National Embassy to Rome," *The Month: A Catholic Magazine* 116, no. 554 (July–December 1910), I, 46–55; II, 144–45.

8. T. F. Shirley, *Thomas Thirlby: Tudor Bishop* (London: S.P.C.K., 1964), 142–56.

9. The Grolier Club holds unpublished manuscript copies of the probate inventory in the Horblit Phillipps Collection, Phillipps Collection Cat. 13 and Cat. 14, compiled in 1872 by Edward A. Bond of the British Museum. The journal is item 24316 (Cat. 13 extends the list of Phillipps' manuscripts to no. 26179, the second to no. 26365). (The Bodleian holds a second handwritten copy of Cat. 13 [MS Phillipps-Robinson e.466].) Phillipps, then, owned both the Lambeth Palace Library manuscript and the nineteenth-century transcript.

10. Thomas Thorpe, *Catalogue of Upwards of Fourteen Hundred Manuscripts, upon Vellum and Paper, Collected in This and Other Countries, Forming, It Is Presumed, the Most Important and Interesting Collection Ever Offered for Sale, Particularly Rich in English, Irish and Scotish History, from the Conquest to the Present Time* (London: Thomas Thorpe, 1836), no. 832. The item appears, in small caps, as "Mary (Queen).—Journal of the Journey of Queen Mary's Ambassadors, T. Thirlby, Bishop of Ely, and Viscount Montague, to Rome, and Back to England, in 1555, the Original Manuscript, folio, 8*l*. 18*s*. 6*d*." The description begins: "An extremely curious, interesting, and valuable volume, commencing,—Observations on their Arrival at Calais, the first of which is that of King Henry the Eighth having destroyed the abbey of Sandyforde, &c." It then highlights twenty-six moments recorded in the journal, in no particular order.

11. *Catalogus Librorum Manuscriptorum in Bibliotheca D. Thomae Phillipps, Bart.* (Typis Medio-Montanis, 1837), no. 9013.

12. See http://www.sothebys.com/en/auctions/ecatalogue/lot.798.html/2015/property-collection-robert-s-pirie-books-manuscripts-n09391.

13. See Cyril Ernest Wright, *Fontes Harleiani: A Study of the Sources of the Harleian Collection of Manuscripts Preserved in the Department of Manuscripts in the British Museum* (London: The Trustees of the British Museum, 1972), 376, and Andrew G. Watson, *The Library of Sir Simonds D'Ewes* (London: The Trustees of the British Museum, 1966), 322. In 1624–25, D'Ewes had made a substantial purchase from Henry Savile of Banke, followed by another from the estate of John Dee, who died in *c.* 1609, and a third from the estate of Ralph Starkey, who died in 1628. See J. Sears McGee, *An Industrious Mind: The Worlds of Sir Simonds D'Ewes* (Stanford: Stanford University Press, 2015), 163–64.

14. The purchase price of D'Ewes library is cited in the website for Sotheby's: Property from the Collection of Robert S Pirie Volumes I & II: Books and Manuscripts, New York, 02 Dec 2015, 10:00 AM, N09391. http://www.sothebys.com/en/auctions/2015/property-collection-robert-s-pirie-books-manuscripts-n09391.html.

15. See https://www.bl.uk/collection-guides/harley-manuscripts.

16. In Phillipps' catalogue of his manuscript library, no. 8539 begins the list of items that he places under this heading: "Thorpe MSS. 1836 / From the Libraries of Lord de Clifford, Sir Rob. Southwell, Sir G. Naylor, Dr. Adam Clark, Earl Stamford, Sir J. Sebright, Lord Guilford, John & Ric. Towneley, J. Bindley, Isaac Reed, Dr. Askew, Lord Langueville, &c."

17. *A Catalogue of the Harleian Collection of Manuscripts, Purchased by Authority of Parliament, for the Use of the Publick; and Preserved in the British Museum. Published by Order of the Trustees.* Vol. I. (London: Printed by Dryden Leach, And Sold by L. Davis and C. Reymers, 1759), no. 252.15, fol. 49. The manuscript is among the items in no. 252, "*A Collection of Tracts, and Loose Papers, bound up together.*"

18. Philip Yorke, 2nd Earl of Hardwicke (1720–1790), the editor, provided transcripts of manuscripts and noted his source in the margin alongside the 1555 journal—"Harleian Lib. 252.15"—and on the Contents page (viii)—"From the Harleian Collection." In 1794, *Catalogue of Manuscripts in the Possession of the Earl of Hardwicke* revealed that the earl still held the transcript. On p. 26, the following appears: "101. . . . Journey of the Queen's Ambassadors to Rome, the Bp. of Ely and Viscount Montague—1555."

19. *A Catalogue of the Harleian Collection of Manuscripts, in the British Museum. With Indexes of Persons, Places, and Matters.* Vol. I. (Printed by Command of His Majesty King George III. In Pursuance of an Address of the House of Commons of Great Britain, 1808), 80, no. 252.15, fol. 49. As in the 1759 edition, it identifies the manuscript as being among the items in no. 252, "*A Collection of Tracts, and Loose Papers, bound up together.*"

20. Although the catalogue entry for Harley 252 indicates fols 62–102, the folio numbers on the manuscript are 49–73v.

21. Antony is mistaken here. The relevant entry correctly cites William Thomas.

22. C. M. Antony, "The Last National Embassy to Rome, II," 144–45.

23. For North's birth date, see *The English Historical Review* 37 (1922): 565–66.

24. This reference to "Sr Thomas North" must post-date North's knighthood, which did not occur until the 1580s or early 1590s.

25. We are grateful to Giles Mandelbrote, Librarian and Archivist, Lambeth Palace Library, for this observation. Mandelbrote notes that the leaf "has been mounted and guarded and is out of sequence, so appears now as a single leaf of paper, but it looks to me as though it was originally the same size and type of paper as the rest of the manuscript."

26. Below are the full citations for North's four translations. **The Dial**: Anthony of Guevara, *The Diall of Princes. Compiled by the reverend father in God, Don Anthony of Guevara, Bysshop of Guadix. Preacher and Chronicler, to Charles the fyft Emperoar of Rome.* Englysshed oute of the Frenche, by Thomas North, second sonne of the Lorde North. Ryght necessary and pleasant, to all gentylmen and others whiche are lovers of virtue (Anno. 1557, Imprinted at London by John Wayland). Because the 1557 edition in EEBO is not searchable, quotations follow the 1619 edition: Antonio de Guevara, *Archontorologion, or The Diall of Princes: Containing The Golden and Famous Booke of Marcus Aurelivs, Sometime Emperour of Rome.*

Declaring What Excellency consisteth in a Prince that is a good Christian: And what evils attend on him that is a cruell Tirant. Written By the Reverend Father in God, Don Antonio of Guevara, Lord Bishop of Guadix; Preacher and Chronicler to the late mighty Emperour Charles the fift. First translated out of French by Thomas North, Sonne to Sir Edward North, Lord North of Kirthling: And lately reperused, and corrected from many gross imperfections. With addition of a Fourth Booke, stiled by the Name of The fauoured Courtier (London: Bernard Alsop, 1619); **Doni**: Anton Francesco Doni, *The Morall Philosophie of Doni: drawn out of the aunctient writers. A work first compiled in the Indian tongue, and afterwards reduced into divers other languages: and now lastly englished out of Italian by Thomas North, Brother to the right Honorable Sir Roger North Knight, Lorde North of Kyrtheling* (London: Henry Denham, 1570); **Plutarch's Lives**: Plutarch, *The Lives of the Noble Grecians and Romanes, Compared together by that grave learned Philosopher and Historiographer, Plutark of Chæronea: Translated out of Greek into French by James Amyot, Abbot of Bellozane, Bishop of Auxerre, one of the Kings privy counsel, and great Amner of Fraunce, and out of French into English, by Thomas North* (London: Thomas Vautroullier dwelling in the Black Friers by Ludgate, 1579[/80]); **Nepos' Lives**: Cornelius Nepos, *The Lives of Epaminondas, of Philip of Macedon, of Dionysius the Elder, and of Octavius Cæsar Augustus: Collected out of good Authors. Also the lives of nine excellent Chieftaines of warre, taken out of Latine from Emylius Probus, by S. G. S. By whom also are added the lives of Plutarch and of Seneca: Gathered together, disposed, and enriched as the others. And now translated into English by Sir Thomas North Knight* (London: Richard Field, 1602). Throughout, we cite from these editions and give page numbers parenthetically.

27. The Early English Books Online digital database contains over 146,000 printed works (more than 60,000 of which are searchable) published in English between 1470 and 1700, comprising an estimated two million-plus pages and nearly a billion words. Launched in 1998, EEBO became part of ProQuest in 2020.

28. For a discussion of North's annotations in *The Dial*, see Kelly A. Quinn, "Sir Thomas North's Marginalia in His *Dial of Princes*," *The Papers of the Bibliographical Society of America* 94.2 (2000): 283–87.

29. George Wyndham, Introduction to *Plutarch's Lives of the Noble Grecians and Romans, Englished by Sir Thomas North, Anno 1579*, ed. George Wyndham (London: David Nutt, 1895), lxxxviii, ci.

30. C. F. Tucker Brooke, Introduction to *Shakespeare's Plutarch, Vol. 2 Containing the Main Sources of "Antony and Cleopatra" and of "Coriolanus"* (New York: Duffield & Company, 1909), ix–xi.

Chapter Three

From Italy to Shakespeare

As with our 2018 book, *A Brief Discourse of Rebellion and Rebels by George North: A Newly Uncovered Manuscript Source for Shakespeare's Plays*,[1] this study underscores the remarkable impact that digital technologies can have on literary research. Scholars of today have many new tools at their disposal and can, within just a few seconds, discover and access information that would have been impossible to find in previous centuries. Plagiarism software tools such as WCopyfind[2] and massive searchable databases like Early English Books Online (EEBO), Google, and Google Books now grant researchers new-found powers, placing seemingly omniscient information retrieval systems at our fingertips.

As an illustration, let us say a scholar wanted to track down potential source material for certain passages in the Shakespeare canon. One fruitful method would be to search through EEBO and Google Books for peculiar phrases and verbal juxtapositions from that Shakespearean passage to see whether a prior text also includes this same language in a similar context or while making the same peculiar point. As able scholars have been exploring Shakespeare's inspirations for centuries, such efforts would, of course, frequently uncover sources that are already well known. If you wanted to use EEBO to look for the source for the visitation of Caesar's ghost to Brutus in *Julius Caesar*, a search for the ghost's phrase "thy evil spirit," followed by a careful study of the context of the sixteenth-century results, would soon lead you to the very work and passage—*Plutarch's Lives*, 1072—that served as a source. While this is old news, these search engines can also reveal something new.

For example, if you wanted to find all the sources for the unusually elaborate stage directions that describe Cardinals Wolsey and Campeius's procession into Blackfriars for Queen Katherine's trial in *Henry VIII* (2.4.0.s.d.), you might search EEBO for other works that also include the people in attendance or the ceremonial items the marchers are holding. Or you might notice that the playwright uses peculiar introductory adverbial phrases to introduce the rows: *after them*, *next them with*, *then*. Of course, *next them with* is what is especially distinctive. Is it possible that Shakespeare picked up this verbal quirk while borrowing some of the elements from an earlier depiction of a similar procession? If you searched the EEBO database for all texts that also juxtapose these adverbial phrases—specifically looking for *after them* within twenty words of *next them with*—you would find no results other than the First Folio version of *Henry VIII* (1623). If you searched the 130 trillion webpages of Google and the 25 million-plus texts of Google Books for any works (or webpages) that place the phrase *after them* within twenty words of *next them with*, again you would notice that nearly every result is an edition

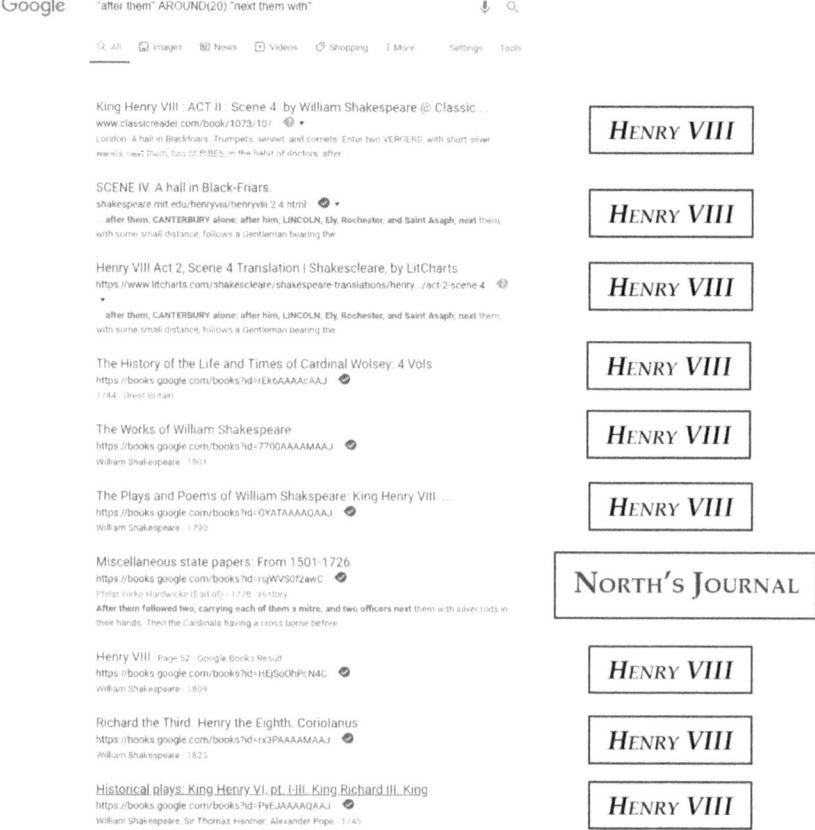

Figure 3.1. Page 1 results of a Google search for the juxtaposition of "after them" and "next them with."

of *Henry VIII* or is quoting *Henry VIII*—every result, that is, except one (see figure 3.1).[3]

Figure 3.1 shows Google's first page for this search, and all the rest of the pages also quote *Henry VIII*. The only other result is a 1778 collection of English political texts, *Miscellaneous State Papers*, which published excerpts from North's 1555 journal of his trip to Rome.[4] A search of Google Books yields these same results: North's journal and Shakespeare's *Henry VIII*.

When we examine the context of the phrases in North's travel journal, we discover something intriguing. As these shared pair of adverbial phrases—*after them* and *next them with*—contain no content words, the enveloping sentences could be referring to literally anything. Yet North's journal places them in the exact same context as does the stage direction in *Henry VIII*. Both passages are describing processions involving cardinals, and in each case the cardinals have both *crosses* and *pillars borne before* them. Both also detail the distinctive seating arrangements of a *consistory*—or, even more specifically, a papal *consistory*, which is a formal meeting of the pope with the College of Cardinals. Its peculiar set-up places the pope in a very high chair, situated in the center of a raised platform, with bishops and cardinals sitting on lower benches on either side of him.

Here is the relevant stage direction in *Henry VIII*, in which a procession of cardinals enters into Queen Katherine's trial court, which is arranged like a consistory:

> Enter **two** Vergers, **with** short **silver** wands;
> **next them two** Scribes, in the habit of doctors;
> **AFTER THEM** the [Arch]bishop of Canterbury alone;
> after him the Bishops of Lincoln, Ely, Rochester, and Saint Asaph;
> **NEXT THEM, WITH** some small distance, **follows** a Gentleman **bearing** . . . a **cardinal's** hat;
> **THEN two** Priests, **bearing each a silver cross**; . . .
> **THEN** two Gentlemen **bearing two** great **silver pillars**;
> **AFTER THEM**, side by side, the two **Cardinals**;
> two Noblemen with the sword and mace. The King takes place under the cloth of state;
> The two **Cardinals sit under** him as judges. . . .
> **The Bishops** place themselves on each side **the court**, in manner of a **consistory**;
> below **them**, the Scribes. The Lords **sit next the Bishops**. (2.4.0.s.d.)

An earlier stage direction describing a mini-procession just for Wolsey entering alone reads: "**Cardinal** Wolsey, the purse **borne before him**" (1.1.114.s.d.).[5]

30   Chapter Three

On 10 and 12 June 1555, the twenty-year-old Thomas North had an opportunity that was rare for an Englishman. He was able to visit Rome and see the pope and the College of Cardinals sitting in a formal meeting, a consistory, then watch a papal procession that included those same cardinals. Since his journal entry for 11 June was merely one sentence in length, the relevant descriptions of the procession and consistory appear in essentially successive paragraphs—fewer than 600 words in total. The parallels between these June entries in North's journal and the stage directions in *Henry VIII* are conspicuous:

first, the officers of his household, being a great number, **before him**, all in scarlet gowns;

AFTER THEM followed two, <u>carrying **each** of them a miter [bishop's hat]</u>, and two officers
NEXT THEM WITH silver rods in their hands;
THEN the **cardinals**, having **a cross borne before them**, and every **cardinal** his **several pillar borne** next **before him**self;
AFTER THEM cometh the pope's holiness (12 June)

The lords repair to the court . . . The pope **sat** in the conclave (or **consistory**), where he was chosen in a great **high** chair . . . **The cardinals sat** upon benches within the rails, round about the pope's holiness, **the bishops underneath them**, and the pope's servants lay upon the ground. (10 June, including marginal comment marked by asterisks)

Table 3.1 lays out the isolated correspondences.

Not only are these the only two known works accessible on the internet through either Google or EEBO that juxtapose *after them* with *next them with*; both also continue their lists with *then* and *after them* and use them to introduce the rows of cardinal processions. In the opening lines, both refer to *two officers* (or *vergers*) *with silver rods* (or *wands*) in their hands, and men carrying a cardinal's or bishop's hat. North introduces the next row with *then* and notes the *cross borne before* the *cardinals* and the *several pillar* too. Likewise, the playwright also switches to *then* to introduce those *bearing each a silver cross* and *great silver pillars* before *cardinals*. Though in 2.4 the playwright stays with the present tense of *borne* (*bearing*), in an earlier stage direction he even writes: "Enter *Cardinal* Wolsey, the purse *borne before him*" (1.1.114.s.d.)—again matching the words of the journal: "*cardinals*, having a *cross borne before them*" (12 June).

As is clear from these distinctive parallels, a Google search of still other elements from this stage direction would have also led to North's journal.[6] But perhaps the most remarkable correspondence is that both the journalist

Table 3.1.

Isolated Correspondences	
North's Journal 10 and 12 June	*Henry VIII* 2.4.0.s.d.
after them next them with then after them	after them next them with then . . . then after them
two officers . . . with **silver** <u>rods</u>	two Vergers, **with** short **silver** <u>wands</u>
followed two, carry**ing each** of them **a**	follows . . . two Priests, bear**ing each a**
Carry**ing** . . . **a** <u>miter</u> [bishop's hat]	bear**ing** . . . **a** <u>cardinal's hat</u>;
then the cardinals, having **a cross borne** before **them**, and every **cardinal** his several **pillar borne** . . .	**then** two Priests, **bearing each a silver cross** . . . **then** two Gentlemen **bearing** two great silver **pillars**; after **them** . . . the two **Cardinals**
the **court** . . . **consistory** . . . the **cardinals** sat . . . the **bishops under**neath	the **court** . . . **consistory** . . . The two **Cardinals** sit **under** . . . the **Bishops**
the **cardinals**, having **a cross borne before** them	**Cardinal** Wolsey, the purse **borne before** him —1.1.114.s.d.

and the playwright also describe the seating arrangements of a *consistory*, stressing the lone high chair in the center with the cardinals and bishops sitting below and on either side.

In *Henry VIII*, the juxtaposition of this coronation-like religious procession with similar descriptions of a consistory was ahistorical, an apparent invention of the playwright: there was no such parade into Katherine's consistory-like courtroom. So, not surprisingly, both an EEBO and a Google search for other similar descriptions involving *cross, pillar, cardinal*, and *consistory*, even extending the proximity search to 100 words, produces no other results.[7] These are, after all, two different events that are rarely ever witnessed together unless one just happens to be in Rome and have personal access to a recently elected pope. As with the phrasing *after them* and *next them with*, we find a tight combination of these descriptions only in North's journal and this stage direction for *Henry VIII*. Clearly, these passages are related.

Upon uncovering these links, the *Henry VIII* scholar who then read the rest of North's journal would soon discover still other entries that seemed to inspire other scenes in the play. One need not use plagiarism software to find these parallels; they are conspicuous. What is more, the playwright not only seems to borrow language from North's corresponding journal entries but also modifies the actual history of events so that they more closely resemble North's experiences.

With more research into North's writings from that time period, the scholar would also find parallels connecting *Henry VIII* to North's first translation, *The Dial of Princes* (1557, 2nd edn. 1568). For example, later in this same trial scene, Wolsey refers to the *whole consistory of Rome*. The cardinal does this in an exchange in which he defends himself to Henry VIII against accusations that he has spoken maliciously about the queen. The wording of this passage clearly links to a similar one in North's *Dial of Princes*. As shown in table 3.2, in each work a man defends himself to a monarch over claims that he has spoken ill of someone else. Each passage refers to the wicked ***heart*** and ***spleen*** of a hateful gossiper and ends with the same appeal to a ruler, ad-

Table 3.2.

North's *Dial of Princes*	*Henry VIII*

his breath stink, his **spleen** stopped, and his body faint and feeble with age, and all the parts thereof consumed save only the **heart** and **tongue** . . . What evil the wretched **heart** thinketh in that crooked and miserable age that doth that accursed tongue with all celerity utter . . .
 	
Truly **sir** . . . **I never** uttered or devised **word that might be to the prejudice of** any.
—714
	Katherine: . . . You're meek and humble-mouthed;
	    . . . but your **heart**
	Is crammed with arrogancy, **spleen**, and pride. . . .
	Wolsey: . . . Most gracious **sir**,
	In humblest manner I require Your Highness
	. . . to declare . . .
	    whether **ever I**
	Did broach this business to Your Highness, or . . . spake one the least **word that might**
	Be to the prejudice of her present state
	—2.4.105–108, 141–52

dressing him as "sir" and using the same unique eight-word word-string that occurs nowhere else in either EEBO or Google.

The passages share ***spleen, heart, tongue*** (***mouth***), and an eleven-word grouping, eight of them in a string, both by elderly gentlemen defending themselves against accusations they have slandered others. The remarkable correspondence is this string:

> *The Dial*: Truly **sir** . . . **I never** uttered or devised **word that might be to the prejudice of** any
>
> *Henry VIII*: gracious **sir** . . . **ever I** . . . spake . . . **word that might / Be to the prejudice of** her

It is important to be clear here: it is very probable that no one else in the history of the English language has ever used the eight-word line "word that might be to the prejudice of" without quoting *Henry VIII* or *The Dial of Princes*. It occurs nowhere else in EEBO, Google, or Google Books, and indeed Grammarly plagiarism software will red-flag shared word-strings of eight words or longer. It is at about this length where most word-strings represent a unique utterance, originating only once in history. And then any recurrence of that same word-string descends from that original line. Someone has read or heard it before and is using it again.

This is all part of the subject of forensic linguistics, a science that made the news during the 2016 United States presidential election when reporters were eager to determine whether Melania Trump's GOP convention address was partly indebted to a suspiciously similar speech given by Michelle Obama in 2008. The Trump campaign originally denied it, claiming that the resemblances involved commonplaces and were coincidental. But it was the specific wording that mattered, and the two speeches shared an identical sixteen-word word-string. As columnist Megan McArdle pointed out, even seven-word word-strings are often likely to be unique:

> Writers know that it's unlikely to hit on someone else's words as closely as Melania Trump's speech copied Michelle Obama's. As my friend Terry Teachout once pointed out to me, highlighting as few as seven words of your own writing, and searching them in Google surrounded by quotation marks, which restrict the search to exact matches, is likely to produce exactly one hit: your work. And I'm not talking about elaborate sentences; I'm talking about boring fragments like "And I'm not talking about elaborate sentences." That search returned no hits when I searched it Monday morning, and will return exactly one after this column is published.[8]

Similarly, following the publication in 1995 of the Unabomber's 35,000-word manifesto, FBI profiler James Fitzgerald compared phrases in that text with phrases in letters written by Ted Kaczynski. The verbal parallels he found—all written in the service of identical, convoluted anti-technology arguments—helped identify Kaczynski as the Unabomber, leading to a warrant to search his cabin and, eventually, to his conviction. Forensic linguistics is a science and can establish incontestable links between texts in a way similar to the certainty achieved by DNA or fingerprint analyses.

Still, we do not need this much proof to establish the authenticity of a source passage. Shakespeare scholars have long known that an unusual word or phrase in an identical context is often enough to secure a playwright's debt. As a case in point, while there are many possible inspirations for the casket subplot in *The Merchant of Venice*, one particular version of the tale that appeared in Richard Robinson's translation of *Gesta Romanorum*[9] includes the rare word "insculpt" in reference to a casket. As Kenneth Muir notes, Morocco also uses "insculpt" in the analogous scene in *The Merchant of Venice*, and as the word is "used nowhere else by Shakespeare—it is fairly certain that this is the version he used."[10] Likewise, there are many renditions of the tale of *Romeo and Juliet* that pre-date Shakespeare, but it is only in Arthur Brooke's poem on the subject that we find an allusion to Romeo's poison as "speeding gear."[11] As Shakespeare's Romeo also uses this same peculiar expression in reference to the poison—and since no other known version of the tragic tale includes this phrase—scholars agree Brooke's poem was a source. But, of course, neither *insculpt* nor *speeding gear* is unique to these stories. Both Google and Google Books confirm myriad independent usages of this language. The point is that by stressing the uniqueness of these links connecting North to *Henry VIII*, especially given the use of unique language in identical contexts, we are showing how far we have exceeded any rational criteria for establishing a source passage. For many of the shared lines, phrases, and groupings connecting North to *Henry VIII* and *The Winter's Tale* do not just occur once in the Shakespeare canon or once in every thousand books or even once in a million books, but once in the known history of the English language.

Shakespeare's work on *The Winter's Tale* and *Henry VIII* near the end of his career is well known. The playwright first wrote *The Winter's Tale* in 1610, reworking a storyline, characters, and passages that were first *published* in Robert Greene's *Pandosto: The Triumph of Time* (1585).[12] When Shakespeare adapted the tale, he kept the two main settings of Sicily and Bohemia, but he switched them around, making the main villain the King of Sicily rather than the King of Bohemia. As Jonathan Bate has pointed out, he likely did this for prudential reasons. In 1610, James I was on friendly terms with Rudolf II, King of Bohemia, and Shakespeare would have certainly wanted to avoid offending the king and his powerful ally. Meanwhile, the King of Sicily was Philip III, the son of England's notorious Spanish nemesis, Philip

II. Using a Sicilian king to portray the jealous tyrant of *The Winter's Tale* was a safer choice.

Three years later, Shakespeare would work with John Fletcher on *Henry VIII*, often relying, whether directly or indirectly, on historical accounts that originally appeared in Edward Hall's *Union of the Two Noble and Illustre Families of Lancaster and York* (1548)[13] and George Cavendish's unpublished manuscript, *The Life of Wolsey* (1554–56).[14] Here too, the playwrights made sure to flatter King James by prophesying in the final scene prosperity for England under his reign. This basic story about the origins of both *Henry VIII* and *The Winter's Tale* is conventional and correct.

But it is important to stress that, as editors have long known, the characters and stories of these two plays were not an original product of Shakespeare's imagination. Rather, scholars agree that Shakespeare—and Fletcher too—had old source texts that they closely followed while they wrote. And it is only this particular aspect of the origin of these plays—the source material—that now requires reexamination. For as will become increasingly clear, the only explanation for all of the connections to North is that he wrote early versions of *The Winter's Tale* and *Henry VIII*, borrowing extensively from both his experiences and his own writings. More than fifty years later, Shakespeare (and Fletcher) would then adapt these early plays of North for the King's Men.

Scholars have long been aware that, in the words of Giorgio Melchiori, Shakespeare was "an expert at remakes of old plays for the Chamberlain's/ King's Men."[15] We know this for many reasons, including the fact that researchers have discovered allusions to seemingly "Shakespearean" plays that significantly pre-date the time that Shakespeare could have written them. This and other evidence have led many editors to accept Shakespeare's reliance on old dramas for *Hamlet*, *The Merchant of Venice*, *Timon of Athens*, *The Taming of the Shrew*, *1 Henry IV*, *2 Henry IV*, *Henry V*, *The Two Gentlemen of Verona*, *King John*, *King Lear*, and *Much Ado About Nothing*. C. A. Greer even suggests "the possibility, if not probability, that Shakespeare had a source play for most if not all of his plays."[16] The question of exactly how many of Shakespeare's plays were adaptations will not be addressed here, but we will indeed seek to prove that this list must now include both *Henry VIII* and *The Winter's Tale*.

One way in which we will confirm North's original authorship of the *Henry VIII* source play is through a careful study of passages from the various historical texts that North used to craft his journal, which, in many cases, turn out to be the same historical source texts and passages that were used for important scenes in *Henry VIII*. As we will show, it was North who carefully studied Cavendish's *Life of Wolsey* and Hall's *Union* and used them for his journal. It was North who then borrowed from these same texts—even from the same passages—when writing *Henry VIII*, also embellishing these scenes with the striking images of his trip to Italy. He also used the fabulous wonders he encountered in Italy for *The Winter's Tale*, decorating the play with passages from both his journal and *The Dial*.

The discovery of the circumstances of North's penning of *Henry VIII* and *The Winter's Tale* helps increase our understanding of both plays. The North family history—particularly the circumstances of Edward, 1st Lord North, Thomas's father—helps explain why the main storyline of the first four acts of *Henry VIII* focuses on the extravagance and demise of Cardinal Wolsey. The blatant Catholicism of both *Henry VIII* and *The Winter's Tale* also makes sense for plays originally written during the reign of Queen Mary, as does the focus on and deification of Mary's mother, Katherine. The old-fashioned qualities of the play are also consistent with this earlier chronology. Jay L. Halio, an editor of *Henry VIII*, sees in the falls of Katherine and Wolsey "a throwback to the *de casibus* tradition of medieval tragedy, as in Chaucer's 'Monk's Tale' or later in *The Mirror for Magistrates*."[17] Its seminal sources, Hall's *Union* (1548) and Cavendish's *Life of Wolsey* (1554–56), are early Tudor too.

Similarly, *The Winter's Tale* frequently relies on a medley of English and continental sources that date between 1544 and 1557. This includes *Amadis de Grecia* (1546–1548), *Florisel de Niquea* (1552), *Rogel de Grecia* (1554), Pierre de Ronsard's poem *L'Alouette* in *Nouvelle Continuation des Amours* (1556), John Heywood's *The Play of the Four P's* (1544), the anonymous *Respublica* (1553), John Brende's English translation of *The History of Quintus Curtius* (1553), and George Ferrers' "The Fall of Robert Tresilian" in *A Memorial of Such Princes* (1554).[18] But why would Shakespeare, writing in 1610, become so focused on English and continental literature originally written in such a remote and narrow period of time? Plausible reasons are difficult to imagine. However, a reliance on these sources does make sense if North was the original author of the play in 1556–57.

Perhaps most significantly, as we shall see in Chapters 6, 7, and 8, North's journal also gives us a new perspective on *The Winter's Tale*, for all of the play's mysterious and wondrous exotica, from its strange settings to its striking visuals, derive from North's trip to Rome and the circumstances surrounding them. This includes the far-flung settings of Bohemia and Sicily and the kings that rule them; a Catholic trickster trying to con crowds with fake relics; a very honest Camillo; a pastoral feast with the goddess Flora handing out flowers; Apollo dressed as a shepherd; and a dance of satyrs. Indeed, everything that makes *The Winter's Tale* seem dreamlike and otherworldly comes from North's remarkable journey. We even find the origins of the lifelike statue of Giulio Romano, the only Renaissance artist mentioned by name in the canon, as well as the scene of Perdita kneeling and praying before the saintly statue of her dead mother, Hermione, just moments before she comes back to life. Finally, North's journal confirms that *The Winter's Tale* is an historical allegory and the story that it relates is true.

NOTES

1. Dennis McCarthy and June Schlueter, *A Brief Discourse of Rebellion and Rebels by George North*: *A Newly Uncovered Manuscript Source for Shakespeare's Plays* (Cambridge: D. S. Brewer in association with the British Library, 2018).

2. WCopyfind, an open source plagiarism software program, is distributed by Lou Bloomfield of the University of Virginia.

3. Both EEBO and Google have their own Boolean operators to allow searches for a particular word or phrase that is near another word or phrase. EEBO uses NEAR, Google AROUND—both typed in all-caps. The default size of the grouping is ten words, but this can be changed in EEBO by adding a period and number to the operator. So typing in *ham* NEAR.20 *eggs* to the EEBO search bar will yield all works that place *ham* within twenty words of *eggs*. Similarly, EEBO's Boolean operator FBY allows the researcher to search for words or phrases *followed by* other words or phrases. Again, the size of the search can be modified. A similar search can be used in Google, except one must use AROUND and place the number in parentheses: *ham* AROUND(20) *eggs*. In Google, you have to add quotation marks for searches of phrases, e.g., "*after them*" AROUND(20) "*next them with*." In 2020, the technology company ProQuest took over the old EEBO platform, so new operators may now be required.

4. At times, a 1910 issue of the Catholic journal *The Month* appears among the first-page Google results, but this too is quoting North's journal.

5. Throughout this study, quotations from Shakespeare's plays follow *The Complete Works of Shakespeare*, 7th ed., ed. David Bevington (Boston: Pearson, 2013).

6. A Google search for *cardinal* AROUND(20) "*next them with*" also leads to both *Henry VIII* and excerpts from North's journal. This too is unique. Likewise, typing *cardinals* "*borne before*" *pillar cross* into the Google search field—with no Boolean operators so that the results include all works that include those four elements— would lead to North's journal and *Henry VIII* in the first page of results. But while this last grouping is rare, it is not unique.

7. In EEBO, a search for *cross* NEAR.100 *pillar* NEAR.100 *cardinal* NEAR.100 *consistory* yields no results other than *Henry VIII*. The same is true for a Google search of *cross* AROUND(100) *pillar* AROUND(100) *cardinal* AROUND(100) *consistory*. This query on Google does not produce North's journal because the excerpt published in *State Papers* omits North's word "consistory."

8. Megan McArdle, "Melania's speech confirms fears of Trump campaign's incompetence," *Bloomberg View* 19 July 2016: https://www.chicagotribune.com/opinion/commentary/ct-melania-trump-speech-plagiarism-20160719-story.html.

9. *A Record of auncient Histories, intituled in Latin: Gesta Romanorum . . . Now newly perused and corrected by R. Robinson, Citizen of London* (London: Thomas Est, 1595). Robinson's translation was published in 1577, but "insculpt" first appeared in this second edition.

10. Kenneth Muir, *The Sources of Shakespeare's Plays* (New Haven: Yale University Press, 1978), 89.

11. [Arthur Brooke], *The Tragicall Historye of Romeus and Iuliet, written first in Italian by Bandell, and nowe in Englishe by Ar. Br.* (London: Richardi Tottelli, 1562).

12. The 1585 edition of Greene's *Pandosto*, published under the title *Triumph of Time*, is lost. The date of the first extant edition of Greene's *Pandosto* is 1588. See Lori Humphrey Newcomb, *Reading Popular Romance in Early Modern England* (New York: Columbia University Press, 2002), 56.

13. Edward Hall, *The vnion of the two noble and illustre fameli128 of Lancastre [and] Yorke, beeyng long in continual discension for the croune of this noble realme with all the actes done in bothe the tymes of the princes, bothe of the one linage and of the other, beginnyng at the tyme of kyng Henry the fowerth, the first aucthor of this deuision, and so successiuely proceadyng to the reigne of the high and prudent prince kyng Henry the eight, the vndubitate flower and very heire of both the sayd linages* (London: Richard Grafton, 1548). This book is commonly referred to as Hall's *Chronicle*, presumably due to the later success of Holinshed's *Chronicles* (1577; 1587). But this is technically incorrect as *Chronicle* appears nowhere in Hall's title.

14. See notes to Chapter 4 for information on the text(s) of *The Life of Wolsey* that we use. Although nearly all editions of *Henry VIII* cite Holinshed's *Chronicles* (1587) as the primary source for much of the play and especially the acts devoted to the falls of Wolsey and Katherine, many scholars, past and present, have shown that the *seminal* source for a number of the passages on Wolsey and Katherine was Cavendish's manuscript. As we will show in Chapter 5, *Henry VIII* also includes many details from *The Life of Wolsey* that are absent in Holinshed, Stowe's *Annals* (1592), and all other published chronicles, suggesting that Wolsey was the direct source for this dramatic material. We also find a similar story with Hall's *Union*: that it was the direct source for certain material in *Henry VIII*.

15. *The Second Part of King Henry IV*, ed. Giorgio Melchiori (Cambridge: Cambridge University Press, 2007), 10.

16. C. A. Greer, "A Lost Play in the Case of *Richard II*," *Notes and Queries* 197 (1952): 24–25.

17. Jay L. Halio, Introduction to *King Henry VIII or All Is True*, ed. Jay L. Halio (Oxford: Oxford University Press, 2000), 25.

18. Many discussions of the sources for *The Winter's Tale* include mention of the continental *Amadis* adventures—*Amadis de Grecia* (1546–48), *Florisel de Niquea* (1552), *Rogel de Grecia* (1554)—which would be translated from Spanish into French in the late 1540s and 1550s. For a longer discussion, see E. A. J. Honigmann,

"Secondary Sources for *The Winter's Tale*," *Philological Quarterly* 34 (1955): 27–38; for Pierre de Ronsard's poem *L'Alouette* (1556), see Sidney Lee, *The French Renaissance in England: An Account of the Literary Relations of England and France in the Sixteenth Century* (New York: Charles Scribner's Sons, 1910), 245; for John Heywood's *The Play of the Four P's* (1544), see William Elton, "Two Shakespearean Parallels," *The Shakespeare Association Bulletin* 22.3 (1947): 115–16; for the anonymous *Respublica* (1553), see Soji Iwasaki, "*Veritas Filia Temporis* and Shakespeare," *English Literary Renaissance* 3.2 (1973): 249–63; 251; for John Brende's English translation of *The History of Quintus Curtius* (1553), see J. H. P. Pafford, ed., *The Winter's Tale* (London: The New Arden Shakespeare, 1963), 137n; and for George Ferrers' "The Fall of Robert Tresilian" in *A Memorial of Such Princes* (1554), see Andrew J. Power, "'Not weighing well the end': Shakespeare's Use of The Mirror for Magistrates in *The Winter's Tale*, I.II.258," *Notes and Queries* 58.2 (2011): 266–67. Much of this will be discussed in greater detail in Chapters 6, 7, and 8.

Chapter Four

Revisiting History
North's Sources—and Shakespeare's

As many of the entries make evident, North's journal is not just a collection of spontaneous observations; it is also the product of careful research. Curious about the source of North's knowledge, we searched EEBO to uncover the tomes that the young traveler had studied to help him craft his entries. Once we identified one of North's source texts, we then used plagiarism software, specifically WCopyfind, to locate any other potential borrowings. The textual background to North's journal has now become clear.

Before the young Englishman compiled his notes into the extant travel journal, he studied George Cavendish's *Life of Wolsey* (1554–56)[1] and pored over chapters on Henry VIII in Edward Hall's *Union* (1548), presumably to understand the political events and geopolitical relationships that made the embassy to Rome necessary. He also searched for relevant information in William Thomas's *History of Italy* (1549).[2] So just as one might find borrowings from *The Sibley Guide to Birds* in the journal of a birdwatcher, loans from Thomas, Hall, and Cavendish populate North's travel journal.

Frequently, North found these history texts useful in helping him add certain details about various cities or events. Table 4.1 shows North's use of Thomas's *History of Italy* to help him describe Milan, both the Duomo and its inhabitants. An EEBO search confirms that the match is unique.[3]

Notice that while the studious North clearly borrowed from Thomas, the young journalist also added his own details. He has discovered that the marble in the Duomo comes from nearby Lake Como, and he has seen the women of Milan and noticed that they wear the gold chain mentioned by Thomas about their "*neck or middle*."

The information North shared on Pope Paul III and his son Pier Luigi also derives from Thomas's *History of Italy* (table 4.2). An EEBO search confirms the uniqueness of the borrowing.[4]

Table 4.1.

William Thomas's *History of Italy*	North's Journal 11–17 April
Nevertheless the Duomo of Milan (being their Cathedral **church**) **is** one of the rarest works of **our time**, built **all of fine marble** . . . most men doubt whether ever it would **be finished** or not: though it **have** . . . a number of workmen **daily laboring** theron. —188v–189	The **church is** an huge thing, **all of white marble**, growing [i.e. naturally occurring] within their own duchy at a place called Lago di Como [Lake Como] . . . but it is not likely to **be finished** in **our time**, notwithstanding they have **daily** 100 **laborers** a work upon it . . .
There is almost no craftsman's **wife** in Milan that hath not her gown of silk and her **chain of gold**. —188v	there is almost no artificer's **wife** but she weareth **a chain of gold** about her neck or middle.

Table 4.2.

William Thomas's *History of Italy*	North's Journal 19–21 April
The estate of Placentia [**Piacenza**] and **Parma** . . . But **Paul** the third, now bishop of the same, **a Roman** of nation, **of the house of Farnesi**, to increase **his own** family, found the mean to separate these two cities with their territories from the churches' dominion: and to give it unto **his own son** named **Peter Aluigi**, **creating** him **Duke** thereof —212v–213	This town did belong to the church of Rome, **Paul**us Tertius being **a Roman born, and of the** noble **house of the Farnesi** and pope, who, willing to advance **his own** blood, **created his son Peter Aluigi** [Pier Luigi Farnese], **Duke of Piacenza and Parma** . . .

Table 4.3.

William Thomas's *History of Italy*	North's Journal 12 June
the Cardinals . . . to come to Saint Peters must pass **Pont Sant' Angelo**, where is an old order, that **when so ever any Cardinal passe**th **the bridge**, there is a **piece of ordnance shot off** in **the castle**: for an honor that the Bishop is bound to observe towards **his brethren**. —37	**The cardinals** . . . ever as they came over the bridge of **St. Angelo**, whether it were one, 2, or 3 **cardinals** together, so many as they were, so many **pieces of ordnance were shot off the castle** for an honor that the pope is bound to observe to his well-beloved **brethren**, **when-so-ever** they **pass the bridge** . . .

When in Rome, North could see cardinals coming over the bridge of Saint Angelo to visit the English delegation at the court of the pope. Once again, he turned to Thomas for help with the details (table 4.3). EEBO again confirms the obligation.[5]

CAVENDISH'S *LIFE OF WOLSEY*

North used Cavendish's *Life of Wolsey* and Hall's *Union* in the same way: to help him with his descriptions of striking and peculiar events. As North discovered, these texts do more than just record history; they also provide an insider's view of certain royal ceremonies, especially grand international banquets and the composition of regal processions. In other words, besides historical context, these two works gave the young journalist the language, knowledge, and framework necessary to detail the lavishness of the celebrations and ceremonies that impressed him on his trip.

Cavendish's *Life of Wolsey* was never published during either North's or Shakespeare's lifetime. But North could have acquired a manuscript copy through any number of connections, including, and perhaps most obviously, Thomas Thirlby, Bishop of Ely. Cavendish was the gentleman usher of Thomas Wolsey, and Bishop Thirlby had certainly known the cardinal. It is interesting that Thirlby lived for a time and died at Lambeth Palace and was buried at Lambeth church, as Lambeth Palace Library now holds two different manuscript copies of Cavendish's *Life of Wolsey* as well as North's own manuscript of his journal.

We cannot confirm whether North had *The Life of Wolsey* so early as to bring it with him on the journey to Italy, but he necessarily had carefully studied the manuscript by the time he compiled and rewrote his travel notes into the journal that is extant today. The date of the biographical manuscript is sometimes set at 1558, but various scholars have pointed out that that was simply the signed date of Cavendish's final draft, perhaps in preparation for possible publication. Currently, fifty-three manuscript copies of *The Life of Wolsey* are known to scholars, but many if not most of them exclude details and corrections found in Cavendish's last reworking and so appear to derive from an earlier version.[6] Internal evidence suggests that Cavendish produced the original during the middle part of Mary's reign. His reference to King Philip as "now our sovereign lord" (34) provides a *terminus a quo* of 25 July 1554, the date of Philip's marriage to Mary, and another reference to Philip's father, Charles V, as "the emperor . . . that now reigneth" (34)[7] sets a *terminus ad quem* at some point near 15 January 1556, when Charles officially completed his abdication. Copies of the manuscript then "spread rapidly,"[8] particularly among Catholics.

The reasons for Thomas North's interest in *The Life of Wolsey* are not hard to find. For one, his father, Edward, 1st Lord North (*c.* 1504–1564), had written two long epic poems about Cardinal Wolsey. The first—"The Ruin of a Realm" (1523)—blamed the cardinal's pride and extravagance for depleting the wealth of the nation and for corrupting other prelates and nobles. This nearly cost Edward his life. The formal charge brought against him in February 1524 was "complicity" in a Coventry taxation rebellion led by schoolmaster Francis Philip. Philip's group was furious with a recent commission devised by Cardinal Wolsey—a taxation on their wealth—and they planned on robbing one of the king's tax collectors, using the money to raise a small army and take over the nearby castle of Killingworth. From there, they would wage war against King Henry VIII.

It seems likely that the reason North stood trial with them is that these rebels were in possession of a copy of his poem, and that the cardinal partly blamed its author for inciting them. If so, it would not have taken the cardinal's henchmen long to figure out who had written the provocative work. At the end of the poem, Edward North had placed a three-stanza coda under the title "The Author," and the first letter of each of the first twelve lines comprise an acrostic spelling out *Edwarde North*.

All the leaders of the rebellion were executed, but Edward North escaped with his life and was sent to prison. While there, North wrote another poem apologizing to the cardinal for his earlier "book," overly praising him for all his virtues, and begging him for mercy. He also crafted another acrostic into this poem, this time spelling out "God Preserve Thomas Lord Legate and Cardinal."[9] The future Lord North would receive a pardon in January of 1525 and would then begin his extraordinary rise in the court of Henry VIII after the fall and death of Wolsey in 1530. Evidently, Edward's authorship of an anti-Wolsey poem no longer hurt his reputation once the king and others uncovered many of the same examples of the cardinal's corruption. Perhaps it should come as no surprise that essentially all of these same faults described by Edward North in his poem—devouring the wealth of the realm with the appetite of a wolf, wearing overly expensive garb, riding a mule, sending the confiscated English tax revenue to friends in Rome to earn special honors, organizing the Field of the Cloth of Gold in which the pages wore gowns of gold, having a heart filled with pride, profiting from extortion and simony, etc.—are the same ones affecting Wolsey in *Henry VIII*.[10]

Thomas North's interest in *The Life of Wolsey* would also have been stimulated by the manuscript's important background information on Henry VIII's marriage matter, which is what ultimately necessitated the delegation's trip to Rome. The king's desire to divorce his queen, Katherine of Aragon, led to the Protestant reformation and the English split with the pope. When Mary rose to power in 1553, she immediately worked to return the country to Roman Catholicism, and North's journey marked the official reunification with Rome. The traveler clearly did his homework, especially studying Hall's and Cavendish's accounts. Thus, as with William Thomas's text, the ghosts of these early Tudor histories frequently haunt his journal.

North's fellow travelers had also played important roles in Henry VIII's annulment. Thirlby, North's lord and master at the time, rose to prominence during the controversy and in 1533 went on an embassy "to France to explain the King's matrimonial adjustment."[11] Edward Carne, one of two other ambassadors in North's train, had been Henry's legal representative in the matter in Rome from 1530 to 1533. Henry had sent the Oxford-educated Welsh negotiator to Pope Clement VII as his excusator and tasked him with the effort to delay their proceedings on the marriage question. Carne skillfully managed to do just that, staying in Rome and frustrating the papal court with various legal maneuvers for three years.

William Benet, a doctor of civil law, joined Carne in his legal efforts, arriving in "Rome on 16 June 1531, while a special legatine court of Cardinals Wolsey and [Lorenzo] Campeggi had begun to hear the marriage suit in England."[12] Benet also helped stall proceedings and worked for a change of venue from Rome to England. As L. E. Hunt notes, such delays "first gave Henry the opportunity to plunder Europe's universities for arguments favourable to his cause, and secondly afforded the king more time to prepare England for the break with Rome."[13]

In April 1533, after the fall of the Catholic Cardinal Wolsey and rise of the reform-minded Thomas Cranmer, the English Parliament officially broke with Rome with its passage of the Restraint of Appeals, which prevented all possible English efforts to enlist rulings by the pope and made the king and privy council the supreme judge of all matters in England, religious or political. The next month, Cranmer's court annulled the marriage between Henry VIII and Katherine. That summer, Carne and Benet began their journey home, but Benet did not make it back to England. He died in the northern Italian town of Susa, at the foot of the Alps.

In 1555, Carne traveled with North and the train back to Rome to mend the resulting split. As the train rode through Susa, North underscored the death of Carne's fellow ambassador, writing in his journal, "Doctor Benet, sometime Archdeacon of Salisbury and ambassador from King Henry the eighth to the pope, lieth buried in Susa" (3, 4 April). For an eleven-day stretch in May, Thirlby and Lord Montague departed from the group to visit Florence while North traveled with Carne from Bononia (Bologna) to Perugia. At some point, Carne may have told the young writer about his role in the divorce and his travels with Benet.

Other Henrician elements also appear in North's journal. In his first entry on their journey from Calais to Boulogne, North stresses that this was the region conquered by Henry VIII. He also alludes to the 1525 Italian conflicts between Emperor Charles V and Pope Clement, which had important repercussions in England. As Jay L. Halio observes in the Oxford edition of *Henry VIII*, "Perhaps the most significant events of all, having a direct bearing on Henry's efforts to obtain an annulment of his marriage to Katherine from the pope, occurred in 1525: Charles V's conquest of papal Italy, the Sack of Rome, and the capture of Pope Clement VII."[14]

Cavendish also describes this conflict, particularly the battle just outside of Pavia, led by Charles III, Duke of Bourbon, who was fighting for the emperor against Francis I, King of France, who had united forces with the pope. Cavendish credits Wolsey with encouraging Henry VIII to help Bourbon and the emperor but points out that by 1525 England had secretly switched allegiance to France.

Cavendish writes that after Bourbon had taken the Italian town of Pavia, the King of France "encamped him wondrous strongly, intending to **enclose** the duke within this town" (38).[15] The besieged Bourbon waited patiently in Pavia for money from a now unsympathetic England, and, with no aid coming and his troops weakened from hunger, the desperate duke rallied his soldiers into one last fight. Bourbon told his men that it would be better to fight than be executed—better "to sell our lives most dearly rather than to be murdered like *beasts*" (40). He then led a surprise attack at night on the surrounding French forces, breaching their enclosed camp, annihilating the enemy, and even capturing Francis I. Cavendish describes how "**the duke had obtained the field and the French king taken prisoner**, his men slain, and his tents robbed and **spoiled** . . ." (41). Bourbon blamed Wolsey's influence for England's shift in alliances, and the incident ended up emboldening the cardinal's enemies at home.

In traveling from Pavia to Milan, North comments on the same battle, then thirty years old, and does so in Cavendish's language: "By the way we saw **the field** where **the French king** was **taken prisoner**" (11–17 April). North then notes that the fight had taken place within a large walled garden created by the late fourteenth-century Duke of Milan, Gian Galeazzo Visconti:

> Betwixt Pavia and the Charterhouse, **the duke enclosed** a piece of ground with a great high wall, four square and 15 miles in compass about. This he called his garden, having within it divers several enclosures for bears, wild boars, red and fallow deer, wolves, and all other kind of **beasts** of venery; which garden, at the battle when **the French king was taken prisoner**, was **spoiled** by divers breaches that he had made into the same. (11–17 April)

EEBO again confirms that the shared language is unique.[16]

Earlier, we noted how North used Thomas's *History of Italy* to provide additional information on the cardinals' crossing the bridge of St. Angelo. In precisely the same way, North turned to two different passages in *The Life of Wolsey* to help him describe a large procession of cardinals in Rome and the seating arrangements of a consistory. Table 4.4 juxtaposes the parallel passages in North's journal and Cavendish's *Life of Wolsey*.[17] And, as we shall see, it is not a coincidence that these are the same passages used for the related stage direction in *Henry VIII*.

Table 4.4.

Cavendish's Description of Cardinal Wolsey's Procession and Consistory-like Court	North's Journal 10–12 June, the Cardinals in Procession and Consistory in Rome
And as soon as he was <u>entered **into** his **chamber of presence**, where there was daily **attending upon** him</u>, as well noble men of this realm, and other worthy gentlemen, as gentlemen of his own family; his <u>two great **crosses** were there **attending**, to be **borne before him**: **Then cried** the gentlemen ushers, **going before him** bare headed, and said: "On before, my Lords and **Masters**, on before. Make way for my Lord's Grace."</u> **Thus** went he down through the hall with a sergeant of arms **before him** bearing a great mace of **silver**, and **two** gentlemen **carrying** of **two** great **pillars** of **silver**; and when he came to the hall door, then his mule stood trapped all in **crimson velvet**, with a saddle of the same, and gilt stirrups. Then was there attending upon him, when he was mounted, **his two cross** bearers, **and his pillar** bearers, in like case, upon great horses trapped **all in** fine **scarlet**. Then marched he forwarder with a train of noblemen and gentlemen, having his foot-men four in **number** <u>about **him**, **bearing each of them** a</u> gilt poll-axe **in their hands**: and **thus** <u>passed</u> he forth until he came to **Westminster** Hall door. —38–40	After dinner the Lords went to visit other **cardinals** which lay in the pope's court, and so <u>went up **to the chamber of presence** to wait **upon**</u> the pope, that came out to even-song. . . . he went in this manner towards the chapel to evensong, **attended upon** as follows: first, the officers of his household, being a great **number, before him, all in scarlet** gowns; *after them followed* **two, carrying each of them a** miter, and **two** officers *next them with* **silver** rods <u>**in their hands**; then</u> the **cardinals**, <u>having a cross borne before</u> them, and every cardinal his several **pillar borne next before him**self; after them cometh the pope's holiness in a chair of **crimson velvet** wrought with gold, . . . having 16 more spare men waiting upon the chair. **Thus** <u>going to the chapel, two servants going before him crying</u> still *Abasso! Abasso!* <u>(which is to **say**, kneel down, **masters**)</u> —12 June

(continued)

Table 4.4. (*continued*)

Cavendish's Description of Cardinal Wolsey's Procession and Consistory-like Court	North's Journal 10–12 June, the Cardinals in Procession and Consistory in Rome
And then in the Black Friars a certain place was there appointed most convenient for the King and Queen's **repair to the court** . . . whereas <u>sat these two</u> **Cardinals** for judges in the same. Now I will set you out the manner and order of the said court. First, there was a court planted with tables and **benches, in manner of a consistory,** one seat raised **higher** for the judges to **sit** in than the other were. Then as it were <u>in the midst of</u> the said judges, aloft above them three degrees **high**, was a cloth of estate hanged, with a **chair** royal **under** the same, wherein <u>sat</u> the King; and besides him, some distance from him, **sat** the Queen; and **under** the judges feet **sat** the scribes. . . . Then before the King and the judges, with the court, sat the Archbishop of Canterbury Warham, and all the other **Bishops**. —124–26	The lords **repair to the court** and audience with the pope; the pope's receiving of the lords in the conclave, <u>sitting in state</u>, **the cardinals** about him as in our Parliament house <u>at</u> **Westm(inste)r**. —10 June margin The pope **sat** in the conclave (or **consistory**), <u>where he was chosen in a great</u> **high chair** . . . **The cardinals sat** upon **benches**, within the rails, <u>round about the pope's holiness</u>, **the bishops underneath** them, and the pope's servants lay upon the ground. —10 June
Isolated Correspondences	
[**Cardinal** Wolsey] entered **into** his **chamber of presence,** where there was daily **attending upon** him [**Cardinal, into** his **chamber of presence, attending upon**]	**cardinals** . . . went up **to the chamber of presence** to wait **upon** the pope . . . **attended upon** as follows [**cardinals, to the chamber of presence, attended upon**]
bearing **each of them** a gilt poll-axe **in their hands**	carrying **each of them** a miter . . . **in their hands**
all in fine scarlet . . . number about him	number, before him, all in scarlet
Then **cried** <u>the gentlemen ushers,</u> **going before him** bare headed, and said: "On before, my Lords and **Masters**, on before. Make way for my Lord's Grace." **Thus** <u>went</u> he down through the hall [**cried** the gentleman ushers **going before him** . . . **Masters; Thus went**]	**Thus** <u>going</u> to the chapel, <u>two servants</u> **going before him crying** still *Abasso! Abasso!* (which is to say, kneel down, **masters**) . . . [**Thus** going . . . servants **going before him crying** . . . **masters**]

Table 4.4. (*continued*)

Cavendish's Description of Cardinal Wolsey's Procession and Consistory-like Court	North's Journal 10–12 June, the Cardinals in Procession and Consistory in Rome
[**Cardinal**] his two great **crosses** were there attending, to be **borne before him** . . . and two gentlemen carrying of two great **pillars** of silver . . . **his** mule stood trapped all **in crimson velvet**, with a saddle of the same. [**Cardinal-crosses-borne before** him, **pillars of silver, in crimson velvet**]	**cardinals**, having **a cross borne before them**, and every **cardinal** his several pillar borne next before himself . . . in a chair of crimson velvet . . . [**cardinal**s-**cross borne before** them, his several **pillar, in** . . . **crimson velvet**]
repair to the court	**repair to the court**
sat these two **Cardinals** . . . **benches in** manner of a consistory	the cardinals sat upon benches . . . in the conclave (or consistory)
one seat raised **higher** . . . **high** . . . **chair** . . . under . . . the other **Bishops**	in a great **high chair** . . . the bishops underneath

As shown in Table 4.4, North has used Cavendish's manuscript as a template for (and perhaps reminder of) the related details of the events he witnessed in Rome.[18] In the first extract, Cavendish describes Cardinal Wolsey's march to and from Westminster, which clearly influenced North's own description of the procession of cardinals. For example, North reuses "chamber of presence," which is soon followed by the echo "attended upon" (12 June).

Cavendish also emphasizes the cardinal's grandiosity by noting that the ushers preceding him could address their superiors and command them to take heed: "Then **cried** the gentlemen ushers, **going before him** . . . 'On before, my Lords and **Masters**, on before. Make way . . .' **Thus** went . . ." (38–39). The point is that Wolsey was so powerful that his ushers in front of him could give orders to their superiors. North here was clearly following Cavendish's language, describing the servants preceding the pope to make exactly this same point ("Thus . . . servants going before him crying . . . kneel down, masters). Indeed, Cavendish's influence was such that North actually modified the translation of the servants' cry. While Abasso is merely a bidding to kneel, North gratuitously transformed it into "kneel down, **masters**" (12 June), echoing Wolsey's ushers and emphasizing that these servants can also command their masters. A search for this verbal juxtaposition—*thus, going before him, crying, masters*—in any database—EEBO, Google, or Google Books—yields only Cavendish's *Life of Wolsey* and works that include excerpts of North's journal.[19]

North, following Cavendish, also made sure to record all the ceremonial objects carried by the marchers and the material upon which the pope sat, again using the same language. For example, Cavendish describes the *Cardinal* . . . "**crosses** . . . **borne before them**" and "**two** great **pillars**" and Wolsey sitting on the mule, "trapped all **in crimson velvet**" (39). Likewise, North stresses the *cardinals* as having a "**cross borne before them**"—and then the "several **pillar**"—and then the pope sitting "**in** a chair of **crimson velvet**" (12 June). Once again, these groups of parallels are unique to Cavendish and North according to EEBO, Google, and Google Books.[20]

In the second extract, Cavendish describes the court for Katherine's trial, which Wolsey was overseeing. And just as Cavendish compares the seating arrangement for the English proceeding to its Roman counterpart—a consistory—North likewise compares the seating arrangement of a consistory to its English political counterpart, the Parliament house at Westminster. (Westminster was also the destination of Wolsey's procession.) North and Cavendish both begin by stressing the repair to the court and then describe the same set-up of the chamber: with a high chair—raised above the others—surrounded by benches, with cardinals and bishops about and some who sat directly under(neath) the high chair. Once again, EEBO records no other examples.[21]

So far, we have shown how each of various sets of borrowings confirms North's debt to *The Life of Wolsey*. But we can also establish a connection by just focusing on the shared word-strings in North's journal: *going before him*, *repair to the court*, *chamber of presence*, *attended upon*, *all in scarlet*, *a cross . . . borne before*, *each of them a . . . in their hands*. Each one occurs in precisely the same circumstances in both manuscripts. For example, nowhere else does North write *repair to the court* in the journal—or, for that matter, in any of his translations. Yet he observes that the lords *repair to the court* in the margin next to the entry on the seating arrangements of the consistory, taking the phrase from Cavendish's own discussion of seating arrangements *in the manner of a consistory*.

Importantly, while these two passages—the descriptions of the procession and the consistory—are widely separated in Cavendish's *Life of Wolsey* (38–40, 124–26), North uses them together in his journal. And, astonishingly, so too does the playwright for the opening stage directions in *Henry VIII* 2.4. The dramatist even reproduces a combination of the exact same lines from Cavendish. So we find in *Henry VIII*—just as we have in North's journal—a detailed description of a religious procession before cardinals, with the bearing of the crosses and pillars, combined with a consistory-like setting. Table 4.5 compares the stage direction in *Henry VIII* with these two passages in The Life of Wolsey.[22]

Table 4.5.

Cavendish's *Life of Wolsey*	*Henry VIII*
his two great **crosses** were there attending, to be borne before him: Then cried the **gentlemen ushers**, going before him **bare-headed**, and said: "On before, my Lords and Masters, on before. Make way for my Lord's Grace." Thus went he down through the hall with <u>a Sergeant of arms</u> before him <u>bearing</u> a great **mace of silver**, and **two gentlemen** carrying of **two great pillars of silver**; and when he . . . . . . whereas <u>sat these two</u> **Cardinals** for judges in the same. Now I will set you out the manner and order of the said court. First, there was a court planted with tables and <u>benches,</u> **in manner of a consistory**, <u>one seat raised</u> **higher** for **the judges** to **sit** in than the other were. Then as it were <u>in the midst of</u> the said judges, aloft above them three degrees **high**, was **a cloth of estate** hanged, with a **chair** royal **under** the same, wherein **sat the King**; and besides him, some distance from him, **sat** the Queen; and **under** the judges feet **sat the scribes** —38–39, 126	**then two** Priests, **bearing each a silver cross; then a gentleman usher, bareheaded**, accompanied with <u>a Sergeant at Arms bearing a silver mace</u>; then **two gentlemen** bearing **two great silver pillars**; after them, side by side, the two **Cardinals** [Cardinal Wolsey and Cardinal Campeius]; two Noblemen with the sword and **mace**. The King takes place **under the cloth of state**; the two **Cardinals sit under him** as **judges**. The Queen takes place some distance from the King. **The Bishops** place themselves on each side the court, **in manner of a consistory; below them the Scribes**. The Lords sit next **the Bishops**. The rest of the attendants stand in convenient order about the stage. —2.4.0.s.d.

The playwright, seeking historical accuracy, takes the substance from Cavendish and often quotes the same lines that influenced North: *the two . . . bearing each a silver cross; then a gentleman usher bareheaded . . .; two great silver pillars; Cardinal[s] . . . sit under him; the Bishops on each side of the court in the manner of a consistory; below them, the Scribes.* All these same lines that clearly informed North in his writing of the journal are quoted or paraphrased in the stage direction.

But, again, this exact event did not really happen. There was no such elaborate procession into Katherine's trial. Yet, as North was well aware, the extravagant Cardinal Wolsey did in fact recreate such Romish processions in his march to Westminster in the early 1520s, years before Katherine's trial in June 1529. In *The Life of Wolsey*, Cavendish relates these two striking images—the cardinal's procession and Katherine's trial—in widely separated passages, one near the beginning of the manuscript, the other near the end. And North, the playwright, *knew* about these two passages because he had also borrowed from them when he reworked his 10–12 June entries in his journal, helping him relate the corresponding arrangement of the pope's consistory and the cardinals' procession. So when North was writing his 12 June journal entry, or perhaps sometime just before, he reread Cavendish's description of Wolsey's procession to help him relate the cardinals' procession he saw in Rome, frequently borrowing Cavendish's language. Likewise, for the 10 June entry, North flipped to the end of Cavendish's manuscript to use the arrangement of Katherine's consistory-like court trial to help him describe the papal consistory in Rome. It was North's journal, not Cavendish's *Life of Wolsey* or any other historical chronicle, that juxtaposed the scenes of the consistory and the procession of cardinals—just as they are juxtaposed in *Henry VIII*. Similarly, it was only North's journal that refers to two officers with silver rods in their hands, which was the inspiration for the two vergers with silver wands in *Henry VIII*. The stage direction also contains North's own idiosyncratic phrasing from the journal, including the introductory phrases *after them*, *next them with*, *then*, and *after them*, which are not similarly juxtaposed anywhere else in EEBO, Google, and Google Books.

Nor are these the only instances in which the play borrows from *both* North's entries and the very same source texts that North used to write those entries. As we shall see in Chapter 5, the young traveler would also use two widely separated passages from *The Life of Wolsey* to help him describe the extraordinary international banquet he experienced at the court of the Duke of Urbino. And, once again, the playwright combines these same passages for the banquet scene in *Henry VIII*. Moreover, the dramatist once again modifies the scene so that it more accurately reflects the Italian festivities that North had enjoyed. The result is that reading various entries throughout the journal gives the surreal impression that North, in 1555, somehow managed to experience the most spectacular events of Shakespeare and Fletcher's *Henry VIII*.

Even assuming Shakespeare and Fletcher somehow got hold of the unpublished travelogue—and for some reason wanted to reproduce its visuals—we are stuck with the even more important question of "How?" How, without the use of digital technologies, would either have been able to determine what source passages the young journalist had used for his entries—some of which include a mix of widely separated elements—so that they could then make sure to conflate these same passages in their play? They couldn't. It was North who had carefully studied these scenes in Cavendish's *Life of Wolsey* and Hall's *Union*. It was North who, when writing about the fall of Wolsey in the play, conflated the language and visuals of his own journal with the historical events he was staging. And it is North's play, now lost, that is the missing link between his journal and the *Henry VIII* play that Shakespeare and Fletcher co-authored in 1613.

HALL'S *UNION*

Another important work that North studied was Edward Hall's *Union*. Specifically, North found Hall's descriptions of the lavishness of Anne Boleyn's coronation useful for his own entries on the glamorous duchesses and their entourages whom he met on his way to Rome. Anne also had a lovely coterie attending her and also greeted guests in grand and ornately decorated rooms, often to the sound of beautiful music. North also used Hall's description of the coronation to help him flesh out the rest of the papal parade in Rome. Table 4.6 shows how closely North has followed the historian—and, with

Table 4.6.

Edward Hall's Passage on Anne's Coronation, Later Quoted in *Henry VIII* ccxv–ccxvi	North's Journal Entries	EEBO/ Google Results
was such several solemn **instruments,** that it seemed to be an **heavenly noise,** and was much regarded and praised: and beside this the said conduit ran wine Claret and Red all the afternoon. So she with all her company and the mayor rode forth . . . till she came **to Westminster** Hall, **which was richly hanged.** . . . she was **set in a rich chair** . . . and so she was **brought to Westminster** Hall, and so to her **withdrawing chamber.**	The **heavenly noise** that was there, as well with strange **instruments** of music, as otherwise I cannot declare . . . —28 April . . . **brought** him <u>up to his lodging,</u> **which was** very **richly hanged.** . . . After dinner the duchess, his mother [Vittoria Farnese], sent for all the gentlemen of our train, into a **withdrawing chamber,** where <u>we found her</u> **sitting in a rich chair**, the prince her son standing by her, and a great number of **ladies** and gentlewomen sitting about her . . . —19 May	1. Unique (16th century EEBO) 2. Unique (in EEBO and Google)
[heavenly noise-instruments; which was richly hanged, ladies, set in a rich chair, brought-to, withdrawing chamber]	[heavenly noise-instruments; which was very richly hanged, ladies, sitting in a rich chair, brought-to, withdrawing chamber]	

(continued)

54   Chapter Four

Table 4.6. (*continued*)

Edward Hall's Passage on Anne's Coronation, Later Quoted in *Henry VIII* ccxv–ccxvi	North's Journal Entries	EEBO/ Google Results
and then came in the King's **chapel** and the monks of **Westminster** all **in rich copes** and many **bishops** and abbots in **copes and miters** which went into the midst of the hall . . . which was **railed on** both sides to the **high** altar of **Westminster** . . . [**Westminster, bishops, rich copes and** . . . **copes and miters high, railed on**]	The pope sat in the conclave (or consistory), where he was chosen in a great **high** chair, having a very **rich cope** upon him **and** a **miter** of a wonderful price upon his head. The place where he sat was **railed in** . . . **the bishops** underneath them [Margin:] . . . as in our Parliament house at **Westm(inste)r**: —10 June and margin [**Westminster, bishops, rich cope upon him and a miter high, railed in**]	3. Unique (in EEBO and Google)
the officers of arms appointed the order accustomed: **First** went gentlemen . . . **in** their cloaks of **scarlet. After them** . . . the king's chapel and the monks solemnly **singing** with procession, **then** came abbots and **bishops mitered** —ccxv–ccxvi [**the officers of** . . . **first In** . . . **scarlet after them the** king's **chapel, singing, then** . . . **bishops mitered**]	**first, the officers of** his household . . . all **in scarlet** gowns; **after them** . . . the priests and **singing** men of **the** pope's **chapel**; **then bishops**, to the number of 58, all of them having **miters** —12, 13 June [**first the officers of, in scarlet** . . . **after them, the** pope's **chapel, singing, then bishops** . . . **miters**]	4. Unique (in EEBO)

one minor exception, he even does so in the same order. As the third column indicates, essentially all the verbal resemblances are unique in EEBO—and often in Google too.[23]

As is clear, Hall's description of Anne Boleyn's coronation and North's journal share an extensive series of unique parallels. Hall's passage also reveals what led North to liken the Roman arrangement to such official gatherings at **Westm(inste)r**. He read the identical description of Westminster in Hall's *Union* and so makes this point in the margin (10 June).

Significantly, these very same passages from Hall's *Union* that North used for his journal were also then used for the stage direction and descriptions of

Anne's coronation in *Henry VIII* (4.1.36.1–36.25; 57–81). Moreover, the dramatist once again modified the scene in order to reflect North's experiences. Specifically, the playwright, for reasons that no scholar has yet been able to explain, strangely turns the English women watching Queen Anne's coronation into the raucous, costumed women of an Italian carnival (4.1.57–81). Again, this is ahistorical, something that no other chronicle has suggested. And, again, questions arise: Why would John Fletcher (the scene is commonly ascribed to him) or Shakespeare—neither of whom is thought to have traveled to continental Europe—invent such a thing? Where would they have seen or even read about an Italian carnival? But when we turn to North's journal, we find that the young traveler did indeed witness carnivalesque spectators at a procession at Asti and expressed amazement at the costumed women. And in the carnivalesque description in *Henry VIII*, the playwright even echoes the language of the journal. Once again, the only reasonable explanation for this peculiar Italianate addition is that Shakespeare and Fletcher were adapting an early play by North.

In summary, just before North started working on his entries that began on 28 April and continued to 13 June—entries that began with grand entertainments hosted by gracious duchesses and their captivating entourages and ended with the eye-catching and theatrical processions of the pope—he turned to Hall's description of the coronation of Anne Boleyn at Westminster (ccxv–ccxvi), Cavendish's detailing of the procession of Cardinal Wolsey to and from Westminster (38–40), Cavendish's depiction of the consistory-like court at Blackfriars for Katherine's divorce (124–26), and Cavendish's description of royal entertainments with Anne and her beautiful waiting women (43–47, 116).[24] North then modelled his own descriptions of Italian ceremony on theirs, and sometime afterward he used these very same passages, at times *verbatim*, to describe the corresponding historical moments in *Henry VIII*. Table 4.7 lists the source passages that influenced North's journal.

We have also discovered that North used *The Life of Wolsey* for more than just his journal. He also borrowed from one of its passages—a warning to youth entering the service of a king—when he translated *The Moral Philosophy of Doni* (1570). This latter work comprises a series of ancient Indian beast fables that had been translated into Italian by Anton Francesco Doni. But at one point in the story, North came across a situation in Doni's text (30) that reminded him of a similar scene described in Cavendish's *Life of Wolsey* (179–82).[25] So North stopped following Doni's words and added his own dialogue to this scene that clearly derives from Cavendish's manuscript. Thus, North, perhaps having perused *The Life of Wolsey* again, was still showing signs of its influence some thirteen to fifteen years after writing his journal.

Table 4.7.

Subject	Source Passage	North's Journal
Cardinals crossing the bridge of St. Angelo	*History of Italy* 37v	12 June
The women and Duomo of Milan	*History of Italy* 188v–189	12–17 April
Paul III and Pier Luigi	*History of Italy* 212v–214	19–21 April
Royal entourage/chamber/coronation	Hall's *Union* ccxv–ccxvi	28 April, 19 May, 12 June
Cardinals' procession	*Life of Wolsey* 38–40	10–12 June
Battle of Pavia	*Life of Wolsey* 69–71	11–12 April
International banquet	*Life of Wolsey* 43–47	16–19 May
International banquet	*Life of Wolsey* 116	16–19 May
Consistory	*Life of Wolsey* 124–26	10–12 June

Table 4.8.

Subject	Seminal Source Text	North's Use of Historical Source Text	Conflation of Source Passages with North's Experiences
Cardinals' procession and consistory court	*Life of Wolsey* 38–40 *Life of Wolsey* 124–26	North's journal 10–12 June	*Henry VIII* 2.4.1–20 (Shakespeare)
International banquet with foreign ambassadors meeting heavenly troop of ladies	*Life of Wolsey* 43–47 *Life of Wolsey* 116	North's journal 16–19 May	*Henry VIII* 1.4.50.s.d.–77.s.d. (Fletcher)
Anne's entourage/chamber/coronation/female spectators of Italian carnival	Hall's *Union* ccxv–ccxvi	North's journal 7 April, 28 April, 19 May, 12 June	*Henry VIII* 4.1.36.1–36.25, 57–81 (Fletcher)

But the most remarkable thing about this list is that nearly all the source passages from Hall and Cavendish that North used in crafting his journal are the very same source passages that inspired some of the most memorable scenes of *Henry VIII*. The only exception is Cavendish's description of the battle of Pavia. The rest—the description from Hall's *Union* and the four other scenes in *The Life of Wolsey*—is known to have been closely reproduced in Shakespeare and Fletcher's play. Even the passage that North recalled when working on *Doni* was used in the play (3.2.367–459). And, as noted, as North worked on his journal, he would occasionally conflate the source passages that were widely separated in *The Life of Wolsey*—and so too did the playwright combine these same disjunct source passages into a single stage direction or scene (table 4.8).

As Shakespeare and Fletcher could not have possibly known the exact combination of source passages that North used, Table 4.8 admits no reasonable explanation other than that they were adapting an early play by North.

NOTES

1. More than fifty copies of Cavendish's manuscript now exist, and each includes minor textual variations. These verbal discrepancies have then leaked into various published versions of Cavendish's manuscript, depending on the editor's choice of manuscript. We have relied primarily on two published versions of Cavendish's text. The first is *The Life and Death of Cardinal Wolsey. Written by George Cavendish, Illustrated with Portraits by Holbein* (Boston and New York: Houghton Mifflin, 1905). This follows an edition first published by S. W. Singer in 1815 with some corrections later added by F. S. Ellis. The other edition we use is *The Life of Cardinal Wolsey. By George Cavendish, His Gentleman Usher*, ed. John Holmes (London: Rivingtons, 1852). This version presents the manuscript that is now held at Lambeth Palace Library (MS 179). This manuscript has a subscription at the end indicating this was the very copy owned by the historian John Stowe, and Holmes clarifies that "Stowe's manuscript was made the groundwork of the present edition" (x). Holmes also consulted Stowe's *Annals*, as well as other copies of the manuscript, including another one held at Lambeth Palace Library (MS 250). Our choice on which publication to quote—Holmes' or Singer's—depends on which one we believed more accurately depicted that early copy of the mid-1550s version that North used.

2. William Thomas, *The historie of Italie, a boke excedyng profitable to be redde: Because it intreateth of the astate of many and diuers common weales, how thei haue ben, & now be gouerned* (London: Thomas Berthelet, 1549).

3. An EEBO search for *there is almost no* NEAR.20 *chain of gold* yields no results other than *The History of Italy*. It would also result in North's journal if it were in the database.

4. An EEBO search just for *Roman* FBY *house* FBY *Farnesi* results only in *The History of Italy*.

5. Just an EEBO search for all works that include both *for an honour that* AND *is bound to observe* yields only *The History of Italy*.

6. Quoting A. S. G. Edwards: "The popularity of the Life in the sixteenth and seventeenth centuries is demonstrated by the more than thirty manuscripts that have survived. In spite of their number, all these derive from a textual tradition differing from that of Cavendish's [final] holograph manuscript, which contains a long, unique passage describing a boar hunt in France." This same passage also contains an allusion to a defamatory French book written about Wolsey's intentions in France—also missing in most other copies. See A. S. G. Edwards, "Cavendish, George (*b.* 1494, *d.* in or before 1562?)," *Oxford Dictionary of National Biography* (Oxford: Oxford University Press, 2019); online edn, January 2014: http://doi-org.ezproxy.lafayette.edu/10.1093/ref:odnb/4933.

Nigel Mortimer favorably quotes Edwards' contention "that the dating of the completion of the autograph manuscript (BL MS Egerton 2402) as 24 June 1558 is the date of Cavendish's fair copy, rather than a date for the completion of his composition of the work." Nigel Mortimer, *John Lydgate's Fall of Princes: Narrative Tragedy in Its Literary and Political Contexts* (Oxford: Clarendon Press, 2005), 261n143. Mike Pincombe agrees and suggests that many of Cavendish's *de casibus* poems that introduced the biography in some manuscripts were complete and in circulation by 1554 and especially influenced William Baldwin and the poets of *Mirror for Magistrates* (1554). Mike Pincombe, "A Place in the Shade: George Cavendish and *De Casibus* Tragedy," in *The Oxford Handbook of Tudor Literature, 1485–1603*, ed. Mike Pincombe and Cathy Shrank (Oxford: Oxford University Press, 2009), 372–88; 374.

7. *The Life of Cardinal Wolsey. By George Cavendish, His Gentleman Usher*, ed. John Holmes.

8. D. B. C., who wrote for *The Dublin Review* at the beginning of the twentieth century, collected valuable information on the original dates of composition: "Cavendish speaks of Charles V. as 'the Emperor that now reigneth.' Now, Charles resigned the last of his possessions (Castille, Aragon, and Sicily) January 15th, 1556. The book must therefore have been written between July 25th, 1554, and this date. It spread rapidly in MS. Shakespeare has used it largely in his *Henry VIII.*, and taken two of his finest scenes from it (Act II., scene iv.; and Act III., scene i.)." Other evidence also suggests that many copies of the manuscript do indeed derive from Cavendish's earlier drafts. For example, many of the copies refer to "Mr. Ratcliffe, who was son and heir to the Lord Fitzwalter, and *now* earl of Sussex" (Holmes 102). As the Earl of Sussex died on 17 February 1557, these copies would have to derive from an edition written prior to that date. Yet in Cavendish's holograph, he has apparently corrected the description of Lord Fitzwalter to "and *after* Earl of Sussex." Thus, those copies that include "now earl of Sussex" must have derived from versions of Cavendish's manuscript written during the middle of Mary's reign. See D. B. C., Review of *The Life and Death of Thomas Wolsey . . .*, ed. Grace H. M. Simpson," *The Dublin Review* July 1901, 444–45; 444.

9. Both of these poems appear in different sections of *Ballads from Manuscripts*. Unfortunately, the editor did not realize "Ruin of a Realm" was also by Edward North, despite the acrostic. Furnivall also divided North's later, apologetic poem into two parts: "The Complaynte of Northe to the Cardnall Wolsey" and "By Northe to the Same Cardnall. Part II. The Praise of Wolsey." See Frederick J. Furnivall, ed., *Ballads from Manuscripts. Vol. 1. Ballads on the Condition of England in Henry VIII's and Edward VI's Reigns . . .* (London: Taylor and Co., 1868–72), 152–66, 336–39.

10. We are grateful to investigative journalist Michael Blanding for alerting us to Edward North's poems. It was he who correctly connected these poems to the 1523 tax rebellion and associated them with North's 1524 stint in prison.

11. C. S. Knighton, "Thirlby, Thomas (*c*. 1500–1570)," *Oxford Dictionary of National Biography* (Oxford: Oxford University Press, 2019); online edn. September 2015: http://doi-org.ezproxy.lafayette.edu/10.1093/ref:odnb/27184.

12. F. Donald Logan, "Benet, William (*d*. 1553)," *Oxford Dictionary of National Biography* (Oxford: Oxford University Press, 2019); online edn. January 2008: https://doi-org.ezproxy.lafayette.edu/10.1093/ref:odnb/2090.

13. L. E. Hunt, "Carne, Sir Edward (*c*. 1496–1561)," *Oxford Dictionary of National Biography* (Oxford: Oxford University Press, 2019); online edn, January 2008: https://doi-org.ezproxy.lafayette.edu/10.1093/ref:odnb/4712.

14. Jay L. Halio, Introduction to *King Henry VIII, or All is True*, ed. Jay L. Halio (Oxford: Oxford University Press, 2000), 14.

15. *The Life and Death of Cardinal Wolsey. Written by George Cavendish, Illustrated with Portraits by Holbein.*

16. This includes at least two elements unique in EEBO. First, an EEBO search for *the field* FBY *the French king* FBY *taken* yields only the seventeenth-century published rendition of Cavendish's *Life of Wolsey* (1641). See [George Cavendish], *The Negotiations of Thomas Woolsey, The Great Cardinall of England, Containing his life and Death . . . Composed by one of his owne Seruants, being his Gentleman-Vsher* (London: William Sheeres, 1641). This was a relatively low quality reproduction, filled with numerous errors and deletions, which is why we chose to quote from the editions of Holmes and Singer. Second, an EEBO search for *the French king* FBY *taken* FBY *spoiled* (with variant forms unchecked) again yields no results other than Cavendish's *Life of Wolsey*. Both searches would have also resulted in North's journal had it been in the database. Other echoes include *the duke*, *beast*, and *enclose*(*d*), and both North and Cavendish are describing the same battle.

17. *The Life of Cardinal Wolsey. By George Cavendish, His Gentleman Usher*, ed. John Holmes. While scholars agree that Cavendish's manuscript is the *seminal* source for the stage direction in *Henry VIII*, many today assume that Shakespeare and/or Fletcher got it from an intermediary, whether Holinshed (1587) or Stowe (1592). In the next chapter, we show that this assumption is false, but, even more importantly, the assumption is not relevant to the argument here. Either way, it remains a fact that North's journal entries are still plainly borrowing from the original and seminal source passages for some of the most striking scenes in *Henry VIII*. For the texts of Holinshed's *Chronicles* and Stowe's *Annals*, see Raphaell Holinshed, *The First and second volumes of Chronicles, comprising 1 The description and historie of England,*

2 The description and historie of Ireland, 3 The description and historie of Scotland: First collected and published by Raphaell Holinshed, William Harrison, and others . . . by John Hooker aliàs Vowell Gent. and others (London: [Henry Denham], 1587); John Stow[e], *The Annales of England faithfully collected out of the most autenticall Authors, Records, and other Monuments of Antiquitie, from the first inhabitation vntill this present yeere 1592. By Iohn Stow citizen of London* (London: Ralfe Newbery, 1592).

18. Janette Dillon, in her analysis of Cavendish's and Stowe's treatment of this stage direction, uses a slightly modified version of Cavendish's *Life and Death of Cardinal Wolsey*, ed. Richard S. Sylvester, EETS 243 (Oxford, 1959), 78–79, and so is led to believe the description of the "consistory"-like court, especially with its central seat raised higher than the others, was an interpolation by Stowe and did not occur in the original manuscript. Quoting Dillon: "Cavendish does not comment here on the physical layout of the court . . . Stowe, however, was not following Cavendish absolutely precisely, because Cavendish nowhere mentions the location of the throne . . . Holinshed follows Stowe's deviation from Cavendish's wording by adding the important detail that the King's seat was 'in the midst of the said judges aloft above them three degrees high'. Shakespeare, though he does not specify where the chair of estate should be, by implication follows Holinshed/Stowe in placing it centrally above the judges." In fact, many manuscript versions of Cavendish—including the document used by Stowe, which is still extant and was used in Holmes' edition of 1852 (see 125–27)—do indeed include the layout of the consistory and the high placement of the chair in the center. It is clear that for these passages, Stowe was following Cavendish *verbatim*. North also relied on a similarly worded copy. See Janette Dillon, "The Trials of Queen Katherine in *Henry VIII*," *Shakespeare Survey 63* (2010): 149–61; 151–52. See also *The Life of Cardinal Wolsey. By George Cavendish, His Gentleman Usher*, ed. John Holmes, Preface.

19. Just an EEBO search for *cry* NEAR *going before him* NEAR *masters*—without adding all of the shared details—yields only the first known publication of excerpts from Cavendish's manuscript in 1641. Of course, it would also result in North's journal if it were in the database. Also, a Google and Google Books search for *thus* AROUND(50) "*going before him*" AROUND(50) *crying* AROUND(50) *masters* produces only works quoting *The Life of Wolsey* or North's journal. North also continues to show influence from Thomas's *History of Italy* in this particular section, clearly using his "*Abasso*," but with the encompassing sentence North has opted for the almost exact wording of Cavendish, including *going before him* and *masters*. For the rest of North's passage, he exclusively follows Cavendish with the *cross-borne before* and the detailed description of the *consistory*, which is not mentioned by Thomas.

20. A search of EEBO for *cross* NEAR.50 *borne before* NEAR.50 *pillar* NEAR.50 *crimson velvet* provides no results as this particular description was modified in the first published version of Cavendish's manuscript (1641). A search of both Google and Google Books for *cross* AROUND(50) "*borne before*" AROUND(50) *pillar* AROUND(50) "*crimson velvet*" yields only works quoting *The Life of Wolsey* or North's journal.

21. An EEBO search for *cardinals* NEAR *sat** NEAR.50 *benches* NEAR.50 *consistory* produces only Cavendish's *Life of Wolsey*.

22. *The Life of Cardinal Wolsey. By George Cavendish, His Gentleman Usher*, ed. John Holmes.

23. 1. As EEBO confirms, *heavenly noise* NEAR.20 *instruments* appears nowhere else in the sixteenth century—except for Hall and quotations of Hall by Holinshed and Stowe. The search would also result in North's journal were it in the database.

2. No other works in EEBO include both *which was richly hanged* (or *which was* FBY *richly hanged*) and *in a rich chair* except Hall (or Holinshed and Stowe quoting Hall). When we search Google for *"in a rich chair"* AND *"which was"* AROUND(10) *"richly hanged,"* the only result is the excerpt of North's journal in *Miscellaneous State Papers*. Evidently, Hall's *Union* is not yet fully searchable on Google. On top of this, and surprisingly, even just the phrase "withdrawing chamber" was remarkably rare. According to EEBO, the earliest work to include the phrase was Hall's *Union* (1548). The next time "withdrawing chamber" appears on EEBO is in 1570, when North uses it twice in *Doni*, but that is North's phrase—not Doni's—and the translator used it in the same way as Hall, referring to the room where the king and others retire. "Withdrawing chamber" then appears in Stowe (1580), who is quoting Hall. North and Hall bring all these phrases together in a description of the chamber of a royal woman, sitting with her waiting women around her, followed by a fabulous coronation-like procession, described row-by-row with much of the same language.

3. An EEBO search for *rich cope* FBY.50 *miter* FBY.50 *railed* yields no results other than Hall. Of course, the search would also result in North's journal had it been in the database. Meanwhile, a Google search for *"rich cope"* AROUND(50) *miter* AROUND(50) *railed* yields no results other than North's journal—as Hall's *Union* is not yet searchable.

4. An EEBO search for just a few of the resemblances—*chapel* NEAR.20 *singing* NEAR.20 *bishops* NEAR.20 *miter*—yields no results but Hall—and Holinshed and Stowe quoting Hall.

24. *The Life of Cardinal Wolsey. By George Cavendish, His Gentleman Usher*, ed. John Holmes.

25. *The Life and Death of Cardinal Wolsey. Written by George Cavendish, Illustrated with Portraits by Holbein.*

Chapter Five

Henry VIII
Transplanting a Marian History Play

As we have seen, Thomas North's fascination with history began early. His 1555 journal confirms that he frequently consulted Edward Hall's *Union* (1548) and George Cavendish's unpublished manuscript, *The Life of Wolsey* (1554–56). He likely studied these texts to understand the political events behind Henry VIII's divorce of Katherine and England's resulting break with Rome—events that had made the current embassy necessary. Then he returned to them for help in relating the spectacle of banquets and parades he enjoyed during his stays throughout Italy.

North's research on Henry VIII's "great matter" and Cavendish's *Life of Wolsey* also led him to write what was likely his first play, *Henry VIII*, focusing on the falls of Queen Katherine and Cardinal Wolsey. He soon followed this with *The Winter's Tale*, an historical allegory on the same subject. Importantly, North would adorn these plays with the most striking and fabulous images of his trip to Rome.

Presumably, North hoped that his portrayal of Katherine as a noble and saintly martyr would please not only Bishop Thirlby, who led the embassy to Rome, but also Queen Mary, Katherine's Catholic daughter. From 1556 through the early 1560s, North was at Lincoln's Inn, a venue attractive to Catholic playwrights, printers, and "the surviving progeny of the 'Thomas More circle.'"[1] Naturally, they would also be amenable to works supporting Katherine's innocence. The nephew of Catholic playwright John Heywood, Stephen Heywood, would become master of revels at Lincoln's Inn in 1557, one year after North's stint as master of revels there. And in the Preface to his translation of *Thyestes* (1560), John's son, Jasper Heywood, would compliment North's gifts as a writer of tragedy.[2] This same John Heywood wrote *The Spider and the Fly* (1556), a Catholic allegory idealizing the return of Queen Mary, and *The Play of the Four P's*,[3] a source for *The Winter's Tale*.

This in turn is consistent with the general outlook of *The Winter's Tale* and *Henry VIII*, in which Catholic sympathies are everywhere evident. Susan Frye, commenting on *Henry VIII*, writes: "Katherine's female sovereignty acquires a religious valence through her subsequent martyr-like death . . . this courtly death-masque tribute slows the play's action to pay homage to the queen everyone remembers as Catholic."[4] Ruth Vanita describes Katherine's deathbed dream as evocative of the Assumption of the Virgin Mary, suggesting that Shakespeare may have found the bravery to stage it in the Jacobean era due to James's closeted Catholic sympathies as son to Mary, Queen of Scots:

> Katherine's deathbed vision is entirely the invention of the dramatist. In this vision, enacted on stage and then described by Katherine to her servants, she is encircled by personages clothed in white and gold who repeatedly hold a garland over her head. This image of coronation at death derives from what Warner describes as "one of western Christendom's favourite themes," Mary's coronation as Queen of Heaven after her death: "It switched the moment of Mary's triumph from the Incarnation to the Assumption." The idea of the Assumption of Mary was originated by a woman, Elizabeth of Schonau, and came under very special attack during the Reformation. It was the subject of whole plays in the Corpus Christi cycles. These plays were excised from the York cycle in the early 1560s, and other cycles were similarly censored . . .
>
> Shakespeare's pageant gets around such bans by focusing not on Mary but on a Catholic queen, in a play presented to the son of another persecuted Catholic queen. Images of the Assumption were under particular attack in Protestant England.[5]

Still, the final act shows undeniably Protestant sympathies. As Gordon McMullan observes, "Twentieth-century 'topical' critics . . . tended to place a great deal of weight on the final scene—and in particular on Cranmer's prophecy—to support the argument that *Henry VIII* projects a future for English Protestantism under James."[6]

These extreme variations in religious perspective of certain scenes are the result of the different eras in which they were written. North first wrote about the falls of Wolsey and Katherine, especially 1.4, 2.2, 2.4, 3.1, and parts of 3.2, 4.1, and 4.2, in the 1550s, during the reign of Queen Mary. Much of this final act, with its gestures toward Protestantism, was added more than half a century later, when Shakespeare and Fletcher adapted the play, putting in elements supportive of Queen Elizabeth and King James. This mixture of the sensibilities of two very different periods of English history explains the play's contrasting religious perspectives.

A similar schism is also apparent in the antiquated style of the early acts, which contrast markedly with the Jacobean references of Act 5. Although *Henry VIII* was Shakespeare's last history play, Jay L. Halio sees its first acts as "a throwback to the *de casibus* tradition of medieval tragedy."[7] The phrase *de casibus* derives from Boccaccio's *De Casibus Virorum Illustrium*, which focuses on the fall of nobility. In early Tudor England, *de casibus* literature typically included a tragic and morally instructive monologue by the ruined prince or, in the case of Henry VIII, cardinal and queen. Thomas Betteridge makes a similar point about Shakespeare's last history play: "At one level this is a reflection of the datedness of *Henry VIII*. The extent to which it looks back to the *De Casibus* tradition that Shakespeare had long since turned his back on."[8] In his important work on the development of *de casibus* literature in sixteenth-century England, Paul Vincent Budra not only marks the Wolsey and Katherine scenes in *Henry VIII* as a return to this earlier design but credits Cavendish, the biographer of Wolsey, as the one who introduced this tragic style, particularly the first-person laments, to English literature.[9]

The result of Shakespeare and Fletcher's later efforts to reconstruct this Marian history play in Protestant England was thematic and stylistic incoherence in a markedly disjointed work. Numerous scholars may be quoted to this effect, but perhaps it was James Spedding, the very scholar who was the first to recognize the hand of John Fletcher in *Henry VIII*, who wrote most persuasively on the subject. He pointed out that, while the acts on Wolsey and Katherine work together nicely and provide sufficient material for a full play, the fifth act seems to come out of nowhere. He stresses that this act introduces new major characters, focuses on a new storyline, and differs greatly in tone from the preceding acts. To Spedding, the attachment of this final act seems a jarring irrelevancy:

> The greater part of the fifth act . . . is occupied with matters in which we have not been prepared to take any interest by what went before . . . The scenes in the gallery and council-chamber . . . are utterly irrelevant to the business of the play; for what have we to do with the quarrel between Gardiner and Cranmer? Nothing in the play is explained by it, nothing depends on it.
>
> With the fate of Wolsey, again, in whom our second interest centres the business of this last act does not connect itself any more than with that of Queen Katherine. The fate of Wolsey would have made a noble subject for a tragedy in itself, and might very well have been combined with the tragedy of Katherine; but, as an introduction to the festive solemnity with which the play concludes, the one seems to be as inappropriate as the other.[10]

This is consistent with our contention: the fifth act was a post-Marian addition to a work that North wrote in the mid 1550s, not long after he returned from his trip to Italy.

Because North took the same passages from Hall and Cavendish that he had borrowed for his journal and reused them in the play, his involvement in

Henry VIII is both easy to discern and difficult to dispute. Wanting to augment the story with the most extraordinary images of his life, North recreated many of the scenes he had witnessed in Italy. Hence *Henry VIII* includes parallel descriptions of fabulous processions, strange scenes of carnival, grand international dances with impossibly beautiful gentlewomen, and solemn proceedings in a consistory-like courtroom. Indeed, the reason *Henry VIII* is often summarized as "a sumptuous spectacle of pomp and ceremony"[11] is that North's trip to Rome was "a sumptuous spectacle of pomp and ceremony," and so he reproduced the same visuals. True, these scenes are also quasi-historical, but North modified them so that they more accurately reflected his experiences.

On 19 May 1555, a few weeks before they reached Rome, the English embassy stopped at Pesaro on the Adriatic and enjoyed a glamorous international dance and banquet at the seaside villa of Guidobaldo II della Rovere, Duke of Urbino. Della Rovere's wife, the beautiful Duchess Vittoria Farnese, and her stunning entourage made an enduring impression on North, and he wrote about them in glorious detail in his journal. He also, as one might expect, tried to recreate something like the fabulous Pesaro reception in *Henry VIII*.

At this point in the trip, North was riding with the train of ambassador Edward Carne. Four days earlier, at Bononia [Bologna], the Bishop of Ely, Lord Montague, and a smaller group had left their fellow travelers for a side-trip to Florence. As revealed in the letter to Cosimo I de' Medici, the delegation had intended to greet the 2nd Duke of Florence on its way to Rome. But with the change in papal power and the siege of Siena having only recently come to an uncomfortable end, they may have decided it would be wiser to visit with a smaller embassy. Hence Carne, North, and the reduced train continued toward Pesaro.

On 15 May, the Carne embassy received a welcoming salute from the town of Faenza with "**trumpets and drums**," and then, in Forli, they were welcomed with "**shot discharged**." But Thomas particularly enjoyed the reception in Pesaro. It began with the duke and duchess's young son, Francesco Maria, then only six years old, greeting the visiting embassy in a charming and formal manner:

> The young prince . . . was determined to have met the **ambassador** [Carne] . . . he met with him at the stairs' foot of the hall and then **received him very honorably** and brought him up to his lodging, **which was very richly hanged**, and there we were notably feasted, all at the duke's charges. . . . the **duchess**, his mother, sent for all the gentlemen of our **train**, into a **withdrawing chamber**, where we found her sitting **in a rich chair**, the prince her son standing by her

and **a great number of ladies and gentlewomen sitting about her**. After we had all done our humble duties unto **her grace**, as many of us **as could speak Italian or French** went to entertain **these ladies** and gentlewomen. The rest of us that **had no language to entertain them with yet sat down amongst them to behold** (as *spectatores formarum*) **the glory of their surpassing beauties**. **This heavenly angelical troop of ladies** being thus accommodated and we greatly **graced** by their honorable **presence**, on the sudden we were presented with the music of the virginals, lute, and viol. Then the young prince stepped forth and took one of his play-fellows by the hand and danced the pavane with him and afterwards a galliard, which being ended the prince entreated our gentlemen that could **dance** to take out a **lady** or gentlewoman to **dance** withal; and so they did. **The dancing ended, a great banquet was made for us**, which ended we departed out of **the chamber** and there left the duchess with her ladies. (19 May)

North's phrase *spectatores formarum* (i.e., spectators or connoisseurs of form) often appears in *elegantes formarum spectatores* (i.e., admirers of beauty). His point was that, as foreign guests to the banquet, those other men of his train who could not speak the language of *this heavenly angelical troop of ladies*—North himself was fluent in both Italian and French—could at least be allowed into their *presence* as admirers of beauty and simply view them. This distinctive description of an international celebration with foreign ambassadors being entertained by beautiful ladies, with a dance and a banquet, should seem familiar, as this scene, with many of the same particulars and language, is replicated in *Henry VIII* 1.4:

        Drum and trumpet. Chambers **discharged** ...

Servant: A noble **troop of** strangers,
For so they seem. They've left their barge and landed,
And hither make, as great **ambassadors**
From foreign **princes**.
Wolsey: Good Lord Chamberlain,
Go, give 'em welcome; you **can speak the French tongue**;
And pray **receive 'em nobly** and conduct 'em
Into our **presence**, where **this heaven of beauty**
Shall shine at full upon them. . . .
Chamberlain: Because they [the visitors] **speak no** English, thus they prayed
To tell **Your Grace** that, having heard by fame
Of this so noble and so fair assembly
This night to meet here, they could do no less,
Out of the great respect they bear to **beauty**,
But leave their flocks, and, under your fair conduct,
Crave leave to view **these ladies** and **entreat**

68   *Chapter Five*

```
An hour of revels with 'em.
Wolsey:          Say, Lord Chamberlain,
They have done my poor house grace, for which I pay 'em
A thousand thanks, and pray 'em take their pleasures.
                        Choose ladies; King and Anne Bullen.
King: The fairest hand I ever touched! O beauty,
Till now I never knew thee!      Music. Dance. . . .
Wolsey:          . . . is the banquet ready
I'th' privy chamber?
Lovell:                          Yes, my lord.
Wolsey:                                  Your Grace,
I fear, with dancing is a little heated. (1.4.49–100)
```

Even the order of the shared elements is the same:

- trumpets and drums-(shot/chambers)-discharged
- ambassador-prince-receive(d)-him('em)-honorably(nobly)
- could(can)-speak-French-went to entertain (go, give 'em welcome)
- this heaven(ly)-beauty(ies)-troop of-these ladies-grace(d)-presence
- -no-English (language); view (behold)-ladies; as *spectatores formarum* (out of the great respect they bear to beauty)
- entreat-take-lady-music-dance; dancing-banquet-the chamber

The banquet in which Henry VIII, disguised as a shepherd, first courts Anne is historical, and many scholars assume Shakespeare's source was Holinshed (921–22). But, here again, we find that Holinshed was following Cavendish's *Life of Wolsey* (43–47). North had used Cavendish's passage for his own description of the international banquet and made sure to include this scene in the play. Again, we also find that the playwright veered from Cavendish to make it more like North's experiences, and many of the shared groupings are unique to the journal and play.[12]

One of the more interesting parallels is the playwright's allusion to those guests who could not speak the language of their beautiful hosts but wanted to be spectators "Out of the great respect they bear to beauty." This precise line is a peculiarly apt translation of North's *spectatores formarum*, also referring to men who could not speak the language of their alluring hostesses. North uses "*this heavenly*" to refer to the "*beauties*" of the duchess's "*troop of ladies*" who graced the men with their "*presence*," which is peculiarly close to the play's "noble *troop of* strangers" entering the "*presence*" of "*this heaven of beauty*." And, in fact, as first noticed by H. N. Hudson, the description

Table 5.1.

Isolated Correspondences	
North's Journal 16–19 May	*Henry VIII*
Trumpets and drums . . . shot **discharged**	**Drum and trumpet.** Chambers **discharged**
prince-ambassador [being welcomed]	**ambassadors-princes** [being welcomed]
received him very honor**ably**	**receive** 'em **nobly** [**honorably received him** (4.2.19)]
her **Grace**	Your **Grace**
as many of us as **could speak** Italian or **French** <u>went to entertain</u> **these ladies** and gentlewomen	<u>Go, give 'em welcome</u>; you **can speak** the **French** tongue
The rest . . . that <u>had **no** language</u> . . . <u>to</u> behold (as *spectatores formarum*) the glory of their surpassing **beauties**. **This heavenly** angelical **troop of ladies** . . . graced by their honorable **presence** [**to** behold **this heavenly** . . . **troop of ladies, beauty, this heavenly, graced-presence**]	noble **troop of** strangers Into our **presence**, where **this heaven of beauty** Shall shine at full upon them Because they speak **no** English But of the great respect they bear to **beauty** Crave leave **to view these ladies** . . . They have done my poor house **grace** [**troop of, to view these ladies, this heaven of beauty, presence, grace**]
no language . . . as *spectatores formarum*, **to** behold, **beauties, to** entertain **these ladies**	**no** English . . . <u>Out of the great respect they bear to</u> **beauty**, **to** view **these ladies**
they were presented with the **music** of the virginals, lute, and viol . . . the prince **entreated** our gentlemen that could **dance** <u>to **take** out a **lady**</u> or gentlewoman to **dance** withal [**entreat, take, lady, music, dance**]	**entreat** / An hour of revels with 'em pray 'em **take** their pleasures. <u>Choose</u> **ladies** . . . **Music. Dance.** [**entreat, take, lady, music, dance**]
The **dancing** ended, a great **banquet** was made for us, which ended we departed out of **the chamber** and there left the duchess with her ladies.	Wolsey: is the **banquet** ready . . . I**'th'** privy **chamber**? . . . Your Grace, I fear, with **dancing** is a little heated.

of the celestial loveliness of the women appears to have been inspired by a different section from Cavendish's manuscript: "They seemed to all men to be rather celestial angels descended from heaven than flesh and bone. Surely to my simple soul it was inestimable."[13] Once again, North conflated two descriptions of Cavendish for both his journal and the play.

North's journal includes elaborate descriptions of only two processions. One, already mentioned, was the parade of cardinals that resembled the stage direction for Wolsey's (and Campeius's) entrance. The other was a grand carnivalesque Palm Sunday parade that occurred in Asti, the same place where North was almost shot by a nervous scout. The description is notable for being one of the few sixteenth-century English accounts of the Italian carnival. During this great "rejoicing," North noted "such a number of friars, as **I never saw** together in all my life **before**, and above 2000 **people** I am sure" (7 April). Evidently, the outlandishly masked and costumed women made an impression on him: "The **women** went **strangely** apparelled, fitter in my judgment for maskers and players than for women" (7 April).

The town of Asti has been renowned for its carnival for centuries, and especially the "Maschere Astesane" or Astigani masks worn by the townspeople during the festivities. Even today, the people of Asti continue to reenact their ancient carnival. Typically, these pre-Lent celebrations begin on Shrove Sunday and end on Shrove Tuesday, the day before Ash Wednesday. In the U.S., the Mardi Gras celebration in New Orleans is perhaps the most famous relic of this Catholic tradition. Palm Sunday, the day that North witnessed the Asti procession, is another Easter-related holiday, celebrating Christ's triumphal entrance into Jerusalem on an ass. Italian towns at that time, as they still do today, often commemorated the day with a symbolic reenactment of his procession, with the crowds waving their palm fronds and throwing their cloaks into the streets in front of the procession. This is how, according to the Gospels, the people of Jerusalem welcomed Jesus.

So why did the residents of Asti add the theatrical costuming of carnival to their Palm Sunday procession? It seemed to North that the elaborate celebrations of the townspeople were fueled, at least in part, by their belief that the English embassy's arrival signaled an end to the Hapsburg-Valois war that was raging across the region and threatened the town. All around northern Italy, local leaders also permitted or perhaps even encouraged carnivalesque celebrations to commemorate new and important beginnings: births, baptisms, and weddings, and it seems in Asti, on 7 April 1555, the possibility of a new peace encouraged the Astigani to add their masked and costumed women of their renowned carnival revels to their Palm Sunday procession. North's entries for his journey from Avigliana to Asti show the devastation and fear the war caused among the locals as the opposing armies of Emperor Charles V and the French King Henry II fought over the towns of northwestern Italy. North's entourage took a long detour around French-controlled Turin as they could not be allowed within the gates with the Imperial enemies so close. He refers to "daily skirmishes" (7 April) in the region between the battling states and to passing by towns "decayed by the wars" (6 April) or "spoiled and burnt" (7 April).

Asti was also on the frontline of the conflict, "the frontier town of both parties" and "first town of the emperor's" (7 April). And while North did note that Asti did have defensive walls, he makes clear that they were not as substantial as those surrounding Milan or Ferrara: "The town of Asti is not very strong of itself, but it is very well guarded with men **of war**" (7 April). And it seemed to North that the overwrought and theatrical celebrations of the stressed and fearful townspeople were fueled, at least in part, by their belief that peace was now at hand. But it was the way they celebrated that seemed especially peculiar to North. The colorful, raucous, and womanly elements of carnival, mixed with Palm Sunday revelry, were almost an entirely continental phenomenon, and the young Englishman expressed wonder at them:

> About 4 a clock in the afternoon, there was a general procession in the town, in token of **rejoicing** (as it seemed) at our coming, supposing the lords' journey had been as well to have treated a peace betwixt the emperor and the French king as for any other matter besides. In this procession there were 13 crosses, and **such** a number of friars **as I never saw** together in all my life **before**, and above 2000 **people** I am sure. The **women** went **strangely** appareled, fitter in my judgment for maskers and players than for women. (7 April)

Although North does not give specifics of the "strangely appareled" women, we know from accounts of Italian carnival that the costumes of women would have likely portrayed "female grotesques" and often flaunted great bellies suggesting pregnancy. As a late winter or early spring celebration, carnival subsumed pagan festivities that commemorated fertility and the upcoming renewal of the Earth and was traditionally obsessed with voluptuous and pregnant bodies. As Ruth Ginsburg observes: "The grotesque body is an ever-pregnant body. Its pregnancy embodies the structural principles of carnival."[14] Likewise, Jan Kott notes that "The Saturnalian and carnival signs epitomize the perpetuity and continuity of life . . . The death that gives birth in a carnival farce is not a young woman, pregnant with a new death, but an old hag pregnant with a new fetus. The body, which is decaying, conceives."[15]

Later in the journal, in an entry on Cologne, North would echo his line "**as I never saw**" when again commenting on remarkable women: "the **beaut**ifulest creatures **that ever I saw and the goodliest women**" (6–7 August). North would then bring all this together in *Henry VIII* in the Third Gentleman's description of Anne's coronation, augmenting it with a peculiar combination of strange and vivid images of Palm Sunday cloak throwing, costumed women of carnival, throngs of jubilant people, and battering-rams threatening walls of cities:

> Among the <u>crowd</u> i'th'Abbey, where a finger
> Could not be wedged in more. I am stifled
> With the mere rankness of their **joy**. . . .
> The rich stream
> Of **lords** and ladies, having brought the Queen
> To a prepared place in the choir. . . .
> In a rich chair of state, opposing freely
> The **beauty** of her person to the **people**.
> Believe me, sir, she is **the goodliest woman**
> **That ever** lay by man; which when the **people**
> Had the full view of, <u>such a noise arose</u>
> As the shrouds make at sea in a stiff tempest,
> As loud, and to as many tunes. <u>Hats</u>, **cloaks**—
> <u>Doublets, I think—flew up; and had their faces</u>
> <u>Been loose, this day they had been lost</u>. Such **joy**
> **I never saw before. Great-bellied women,**
> **That had had not half a week to go**, like rams
> In <u>the old time **of war**</u>, would shake the press
> And make 'em reel before 'em. <u>No man living</u>
> <u>Could say "This is my wife" there</u>, **all were woven**
> **So strangely in one piece**.* (4.1.57–59, 62–81)

*woven / So strangely in one piece = dressed identically; wearing the same strange costume

Like many editors, McMullan, in the Arden *King Henry VIII*, notes that this striking description is the invention of the playwright: "This entire section (for which . . . there is no precedent in Holinshed) is remarkable for its sensuousness and the intensity of its description of popular energy channelled into royal occasion."[16] Moreover, like a number of scholars, he especially stresses that the scene overflows with images of carnival. McMullan describes it as "classic carnivalesque personification and grotesque exaggeration" and glosses "Great-bellied women" as "further carnivalesque imagery."[17] The suggestion of "loose" and detachable faces that can be thrown into the air is a not-so-subtle allusion to the masks of carnival. The fact that men could not pick out their own wives because "all were woven / So strangely in one piece" means the women were unrecognizable and indistinguishable because they all wore the same costume.[18]

Barbara Hodgdon emphasizes this surreal addition of the playwright, who tried to transform Anne's London coronation into an Italian carnival:

> The procession crosses the stage, its "sight of honor" giving way to the Third Gentleman's report of the noisy coronation spectators—among them "Great-bellied women / That had not half a week to go" who, "like rams / In the old time of war" (4.1.76–78), overpower the crowd, battering their way into royal space, making of themselves a spectacle that threatens to displace state ceremonial with carnival.[19]

Colin Jager also discusses the scene's "distinction between decorum and carnival."[20] And, while the throwing of cloaks and doublets onto the streets was not a typical feature of carnival, this was and remains a well-known part of Palm Sunday processions. So the Third Gentleman's descriptions once again seem peculiarly relevant to North's experiences in Italy. Indeed, consider the extraordinary specificity of the identical contexts shared by North's entries and *Henry VIII*. Both the journalist and the playwright turned to the same pages of Hall's *Union*, those discussing Anne's coronation (ccxv–ccxvi), for help with related descriptions. Both also describe a striking visual of a Palm Sunday-type procession overtaken by raucous crowds and costumed women of carnival. Even the image of city walls broken down and invaded by armies—"like [battering] rams / In the old time **of war** . . . / And make 'em reel before 'em"—fits with North's stay at war-weary Asti among the battered towns of Piedmont and his recording of the vulnerability of its walls.

The play and the journal once again share unique language:

North's Journal: They be **the beauti**fulest creatures **that ever I saw** and **the goodliest women**. (6–7 August)
Henry VIII: **The beauty** of her person to the people. / Believe me, sir, she is **the goodliest woman** / **That ever** lay by man (4.1.68–70)
North's Journal: re**joicing** . . . **such** . . . **I never saw** . . . **before** . . . **women** went **strangely** appareled (7 April)
Henry VIII: **Such joy** / **I never saw before**. Great-bellied **women**
 . . . were woven / So **strangely** . . . (4.1.75–77, 80–81)

EEBO and Google confirm these shared word-groupings are unique.[21]

Thus, this extraordinarily distinctive grouping of a Palm Sunday procession, the costumed women of carnival, and borrowings from Hall's description of Anne's coronation—a peculiar combination that we first find in

North's journal—is repeated in *Henry VIII* and often with unique verbal echoes from the relevant entries.

In Wolsey's final scene in *Henry VIII*, North closely follows Cavendish's manuscript and uses many of the cardinal's speeches found in that document. But at one point, North also adds a lesson from his own *Dial of Princes* involving the dangers faced by those at court who compete for power. First, Wolsey complains about two other ambitious court-climbers: Anne Boleyn and Thomas Cranmer:

> . . . that she should lie **i'th' bosom of**
> Our hard-ruled **king**. Again, there is sprung up
> An heretic, an arch one, Cranmer, one
> Hath **crawled into the favor of the King** (3.2.101–104)

Wolsey speaks of the "favor of the King" as a precarious perch, a truth that certainly would not have been lost on Tudor audiences that both Boleyn and Cranmer would eventually be executed—and the latter in the early reign of Mary.[22] Cardinal Wolsey soon realizes he himself had been similarly greedy for power, seeking preference from the king, and he partly blames that for his own downfall:

> I feel my heart new opened. Oh, how wretched
> Is that poor **man** that hangs on **princes' favors**!
> There is, betwixt that smile we would **aspire to**,
> That sweet aspect **of princes**, and their ruin,
> **More** pangs and **fears** than wars or women have. (3.2.367–71)

This passage on the poor *man* who does *aspire to* get into the favor of the ruler and then must live constantly in *fear* clearly derives from this passage in North's *Dial* (table 5.2).

The context for both passages in *Henry VIII* and *The Dial* is the same. Both passages serve as warnings for the poor *man* who does *aspire* to *creep* (or *crawl*) *into the prince's favor*, for they fail to realize that the *more* they are *favored* the more they have to *fear*. Both passages use the word *prince* in "*prince's/princes' favor(s)*" and "aspect/accepted of *princes*" in the same way: not to refer any specific prince but as a general term for rulers, whether kings, queens, emperors, or dukes. That is also how the word is used in North's title, *The Dial of Princes*. Both EEBO and Google confirm that the connection is unique and that North's translation is the inspiration.[23]

North's crafting of Wolsey's final scene in *Henry VIII* would influence his work on a later translation. In *The Moral Philosophy of Doni*, North evidently came across a situation that reminded him of Wolsey's circumstances,

Table 5.2.

North's *Dial of Princes*	*Henry VIII*
Now in the palaces of **princes**, it is a natural thing for <u>each **man** to desire to aspire and to creep into the prince's favor</u> . . . The **more** they are rich, noble, and of great power, that are <u>beloved and accepted **of princes**</u>: so much <u>the **more** ought they to be circumspect and to live in **fear**</u> and doubt of such disgraces and misfortunes that may happen to them —645	Hath <u>crawled **into the favor**</u> of the King . . . I feel my heart new opened. Oh, how wretched Is that <u>poor **man** that hangs on **princes' favors**</u>! There is, betwixt that smile we would **aspire to**, <u>That sweet aspect **of princes**</u>, and their ruin, **More** pangs and **fears** than wars or women have. —3.2.104, 367–71
Isolated Correspondences	
Creep **into the** prince's **favor**	crawled **into the favor** of the King
man, to aspire, prince's favor	**man**, aspire to, princes' favors
accepted **of princes**-more-**fear**	aspect **of princes-more-fears**

especially involving the counselor role he plays to Thomas Cromwell and the advice he gives him. Here, the translator veered from the original Italian of Anton Francesco Doni and shaped the passage so that it follows this Wolsey-Cromwell exchange in *Henry VIII*, in which the elder cardinal instructs the younger Cromwell to enter the service of the king:

> Wolsey: I feel my heart new opened. Oh, how wretched
> Is that poor man that hangs on **princes' favors**! . . .
> I am a poor fall'n man, unworthy now
> To be <u>**thy** lord and **master**</u>. Seek **the King**;
> That sun, I pray, may never set! I have told him
> What and how <u>**true thou art**</u>. He will advance thee;
> Some little **memory** of me will stir him—
> I know his noble nature—not to let
> Thy hopeful **service** perish too. Good Cromwell,
> Neglect him not . . .
> Cromwell: O my lord,
> Must I then, leave you? must I needs forgo
> So good, so noble, and <u>**so true a master**</u>? . . .
> **The King** shall have my **service**, but my prayers
> Forever and forever shall be yours. . . .

> Wolsey: . . . Say, I . . .
> Found thee a way, out of his wreck, to rise in,
> A sure and safe one, though **thy master** missed it.
> Mark but my fall, and that that ruin'd me.
> Cromwell, <u>**I charge thee**</u>, **fling away ambition** . . .
> **Corruption** wins not more than honesty. . . .
> **Serve the King** . . .
> There take an inventory of all I have,
> To the last **penny**; 'tis **the King's**. . . .
> Cromwell: Good sir, have **patience**. (3.2.367–459 passim)

Wolsey's advice to the young hopeful would have ominous overtones, for, as was and remains well known, Cromwell would also gain great power that ultimately resulted with his neck on the executioner's block. But Wolsey did not really say all this to Cromwell. As *The Life of Wolsey* confirms, the playwright was borrowing from a final exchange that the cardinal really had with William Kingston, the constable of the tower. Evidently, the playwright thought that Cromwell would make a more historically compelling listener. All this is conventional. Still, it is not often noted that some of Wolsey's comments that are reproduced in the play *exclusively* appear in Cavendish's manuscript (table 5.3)[24]—and not in any other later source (e.g., Hall, Stowe, Holinshed).

While Stowe (1580, 1592) and Holinshed (1587) do record the last line quoted in table 5.3, beginning with "But if I had served God . . .," only Cavendish's manuscript includes the earlier comment in which the cardinal emphasizes that he intends to leave all his worldly possessions to the king, down to the last penny. This confirms that Cavendish's Marian manuscript was not just the *seminal* source for this language but the *only possible* source.

Even more significantly, North recreates this same exchange with both quotations and paraphrases in *The Moral Philosophy of Doni*. When North began to translate a discussion in the main beast fable of *Doni* in which an Elder Ass plays the Wolseyan role to his younger brother, the Mule, he clearly recollected his work on *Henry VIII*. The Ass was mentoring the sibling on his decision to enter the service of the king and advising him to be ever loyal and not betray him. Of course, the Mule does not follow this advice and ends up executed. The similarities in the situations in this animal story to scene 3.2 in *Henry VIII* led North to deviate from his Italian original and adopt Wolsey's idiom from that scene, even quoting him at one point:

> Thou must also be <u>**true**</u> <u>**to thy master**</u>, and when **thou art** once retained in **service,** thou must not betray thy Lord for any gold or <u>**corruption**</u> <u>in the world.</u> For many times those that are in **favor with Princes**, and near about them, are sought unto to . . . subvert their whole state. For no respect **in the world**, whilest

thou art **in service** (nor after) see thou <u>**deceive him not of a mite**. **I do advise thee**</u> also to be **patient**. . . .

The Mule . . . as one whose judgment with **ambition** was **corrupted**, he took his heels, and on his **way** to the **Court** he **flingeth** to this Princely **King** and . . . even forthwith **he crept into his bosom and got into his favor** . . . (30v, 33–33v)

In this discussion in *Doni*, North reuses much of the language from 3.2 in *Henry VIII*, but there is one notable exception. With "**deceive him not of a mite**," North is actually quoting Wolsey's historical speech in *The Life of Wolsey*: "rather than I would, Master Kingston, embezzle, **or deceive him of a mite**, I would it were molt, and put in my mouth" (179). This is the same speech from Cavendish's manuscript that the playwright also used for Wolsey's final speech—except in *Henry VIII* that phrase is left out. And in *Doni*, there is simply no question that North is quoting Wolsey's speech. A search for either *deceive him of a mite* or *deceive him not of a mite* in the tens of millions of searchable Google Books or any of Google's roughly 130 trillion webpages results in only quotations from North's *Moral Philosophy of Doni*

Table 5.3.

Cavendish's *Life of Wolsey*	*Henry VIII*
Ah, good Lord! how much doth it grieve me that the King should think in me such deceit, wherein <u>I should deceive him of any one **penny** that **I**</u> have. Rather than I would, Master Kingston, embezzle, **or deceive him of a mite***, I would it were molt, and put in my mouth; . . . **I have** nothing, nor never had . . . but that I took it for **the King's** goods, having but the bare use of the same during my life,<u> and after my death to leave</u> it to **the King** . . . <u>will not keep one **penny** from **the King**</u> . . . I tarry <u>but the will and pleasure of **God**, to render unto him my simple soul</u> into his divine hands . . . **But if <u>I had served God</u> as diligently <u>as I have done the king, he would not have given me</u> over in my grey hairs.** —179–82	There take an inventory of <u>all **I have**, To the last **penny**</u>; 'tis **the King's**. My robe, And <u>my integrity to heaven, is all I dare now call mine own. O Cromwell,</u> Cromwell, **<u>Had I but served my God</u>** with half the zeal <u>I served my **king, he would not**</u> in mine age <u>Have left **me** naked to mine enemies</u>. —3.2.452–58

*mite = Flemish coin of little value

Table 5.4.

Isolated Correspondences	
North's *Moral Philosophy of Doni*	*Henry VIII/The Life of Wolsey*
true to **thy master**	so **true** a **master**; **thy master**
be **true** . . . and when **thou art**	What and how **true thou art**
This **Princely King** . . . he <u>crept</u> into his bosom and got <u>into his favor</u>	lie **i'th' bosom** of / Our hard-ruled **king** . . . Hath <u>crawled into the favor</u>
deceive him not **of a mite**	[do not] **deceive him of a mite***
favor with **Princes**	**Princes' favors**
ambition was **corrupted** . . . he **flingeth** to this princely **King**	**fling** away **ambition corruption** . . . serve the **King**.
I do advise **thee**	I charge **thee**
Court, service, patient	**Court, service,** patience

*from the Cardinal's final speech in Cavendish's *Life of Wolsey*

or Cavendish's *Life of Wolsey*.[25] The same is true for a Google or Google Books search of "*deceive him*" AROUND(10) "*of a mite*." EEBO also shows no other results.

Again, it is not Doni's original Italian work that is responsible for this language in the translation,[26] and North was necessarily influenced by Cavendish's own rendition of Wolsey's last scene. In each case, the context is the same: a Wolseyan-type counselor is advising someone younger who is entering the ***service*** of the ***king*** to avoid ***corruption***, to stay ***true*** to ***thy master***, that those in ***princes' favors*** should proceed with caution, and, to make sure, when dealing with the king, not ***to deceive him of a mite***.

Earlier, we saw how certain descriptions and elaborate stage directions in *Henry VIII* represent a conflation of events detailed in North's journal with the very same historical source passages (from either Cavendish or Hall) that North had used for those entries. Similarly, an exchange in North's *Doni* shows influence from *both* the play *Henry VIII* and the very source passage in *The Life of Wolsey* used for that scene. In every instance, each pair of the three works (history text, *Henry VIII*, North's work) shows exclusive connections that are absent in the third (and every other known work). For example, here, *Doni* and *The Life of Wolsey* both have *deceive him . . . of a mite*, which does not appear in *Henry VIII* (or in any other known work in the English language). Meanwhile, *Henry VIII* and *The Life of Wolsey* share elements from that speech not found in *Doni*, and, likewise, the play and North's translation share still other elements not found in *The Life of Wolsey*.

This confirms beyond doubt that North originally wrote this part of *Henry VIII*. In crafting this advice in *Doni*, he has mentally conflated both a similar play passage with its historical source passage from an unpublished text, something only the playwright could do. One cannot suppose that, decades later, Fletcher was actually the one who combined a passage from Cavendish with one from North's *Doni*, for how likely is it that Fletcher, working around 1613, would randomly choose two different texts, one handwritten in the 1550s and another printed in 1570, then manage to conflate the only two known passages in history to contain the phrase "deceive him (not) of a mite"?

Below is a list of the Northern passages that clearly link to *Henry VIII* (table 5.5).

Table 5.5.

North's Writings	Henry VIII
North's Journal 10–12 June	*Henry VIII* 2.4.1–20 (Shakespeare)
North's Journal 16–19 May	*Henry VIII* 1.4.50.s.d.–77.s.d. (Fletcher)
North's Journal 7 April, 28 April, 19 May, 12 June	*Henry VIII* 4.1.36.s.d.(1-25); 57–81 (Fletcher)
The Moral Philosophy of Doni 30v, 33–33v	*Henry VIII* 3.2.101–104 (Shakespeare), *Henry VIII* 3.2.366–459 (Fletcher)
The Dial of Princes 645	*Henry VIII* 3.2.367–71 (Fletcher)
The Dial of Princes 714	*Henry VIII* 2.4.86–152 (Shakespeare)

The remarkable fact is that it is not simply North's journal (and its sources) that appears to have influenced both Shakespeare and Fletcher. Both playwrights also seem to have had the ability to recall different passages from North's *Doni* and *The Dial*, while conflating them with North's source texts. The only reasonable explanation for these extensive literary connections is that both Shakespeare and Fletcher were reworking an early Catholic play by North on the falls of Wolsey and Katherine. It was the young translator whose travel experiences and related studies influenced *Henry VIII*, and it was North who would then frequently echo his own earlier passages.

NOTES

1. J. Christopher Warner links Thomas North with this group, which also included William Rastell, John Roper, and Stephen Heywood. See J. Christopher Warner, *The Making and Marketing of Tottel's Miscellany, 1557: Songs and Sonnets in the Summer of the Martyrs' Fires* (Burlington, VT: Ashgate, 2013), 21.

2. We examine this at greater length in our Epilogue, but Warner also discusses Jasper Heywood's Prologue and the allusion to Thomas North. See J. Christopher Warner, *The Making and Marketing of Tottel's Miscellany*, 21–23.

3. John Heywood, *The playe called the foure PP: A newe and a very mery enterlude of A palmer. A pardoner. A potycary. A pedler* (London: Wyllyam Myddylton, 1544).

4. Susan Frye, "Spectres of Female Sovereignty in Shakespeare's Plays," in *The Oxford Handbook of Shakespeare and Embodiment*, ed. Valerie Traub (Oxford: Oxford University Press, 2016), 112–30; 126.

5. Ruth Vanita, "Mariological Memory in *The Winter's Tale* and *Henry VIII*," *Studies in English Literature, 1500-1900* 40.2 (2000): 311–37; 329–31.

6. Gordon McMullan, Introduction to *King Henry VIII (All Is True)*, ed. Gordon McMullan (London: The Arden Shakespeare, 2000), 66.

7. Jay L. Halio, Introduction to *King Henry VIII or All Is True*, ed. Jay L. Halio (Oxford: Oxford University Press, 2000), 25.

8. Thomas Betteridge, "Writing Faithfully in a Post-Confessional World," in *Late Shakespeare: 1608–1613*, ed. Andrew J. Power and Rory Loughnane (Cambridge: Cambridge University Press, 2013), 225–42; 241.

9. Paul Vincent Budra, *A Mirror for Magistrates and the de casibus Tradition* (Toronto: University of Toronto Press, 2000), 7. See also Mike Pincombe, "A Place in the Shade: George Cavendish and *De Casibus* Tragedy," in *The Oxford Handbook of Tudor Literature, 1485–1603*, ed. Mike Pincombe and Cathy Shrank (Oxford: Oxford University Press, 2009), 372–88; 374.

10. J. Spedding, "Who Wrote Shakspere's *Henry VIII?*," *Gentleman's Magazine* 178 (1850): 115–23; 116–17. See also Brian Vickers, *Shakespeare, Co-Author: A Historical Study of Five Collaborative Plays* (Oxford: Oxford University Press, 2002), 489–90.

11. See, for example, the description of *Henry VIII* in the Random House advertisement for *"King John" and "Henry VIII,"* ed. David Bevington and David Scott Kastan (The New Bantam Shakespeare, 1988): randomhousebooks.com/books/164696/.

12. For example, if we focus on just one small group of shared elements—*this heaven(ly)*, *presence*, *speak*, *French*—and stretch the EEBO search out to 100 words, thereby casting a wide net for other possible matches, we get only *Henry VIII*. The precise search we used was *this heaven** NEAR.100 *presence* NEAR.100 *speak* NEAR.100 *French*. The asterisk with *heaven** ensures we will find all instances of either *heaven* or *heavenly*. This search would have resulted in North's journal were it in the database. Similarly, a search of Google and Google Books for *"this heaven"* AROUND(100) *presence* AROUND(100) *speak* AROUND(100) *French* and *"this heavenly"* AROUND(100) *presence* AROUND(100) *speak* AROUND(100) *French* yield only *Henry VIII* and quotations from North's journal, respectively.

13. H. N. Hudson, ed., *The Works of Shakespeare: The Text Carefully Restored According to the First Editions; with Introductions, Notes Original and Selected, and a Life of the Poet* (Boston: Estes and Lauriat, 1883), 4:243n5.

14. Ruth Ginsburg, "Pregnant Text: *Bakhtin's Ur-Chronotype: The Womb*," in *Bakhtin: Carnival and Other Subjects: Selected Papers from the Fifth International Bakhtin Conference, University of Manchester*, ed. David Shepherd, *Critical Studies* 3.2–4–4.1/2 (Amsterdam-Atlanta: Rodopi, 1993), 165–76; 168.

15. Jan Kott, *Theater of Essence* (Evanston, IL: Northwestern University Press, 1984), 101.

16. Gordon McMullan, Introduction to *King Henry VIII (All Is True)*, 369n57–81.

17. Gordon McMullan, Introduction to *King Henry VIII (All Is True)*, 371n73–75, 76.

18. North uses this same language elsewhere, again referring to many wearing the same outfit as *all* being *appareled* in *one* piece: "We ordain that **all** be **appareled** with **one** cloth, and hosed of **one** sort" (*The Dial* 103). Shakespeare does too: "and I will **apparel** them **all** in **one** livery" (*2 Henry VI* 4.2.71–72).

19. Barbara Hodgdon, *The End Crowns All: Closure and Contradiction in Shakespeare's History* (Princeton: Princeton University Press), 215.

20. Colin Jager, *Unquiet Things: Secularism in the Romantic Age* (Philadelphia: University of Pennsylvania Press, 2015), 49.

21. An EEBO search for the first grouping within twenty words—*beaut** NEAR.20 *goodliest women* NEAR.20 *that ever*—results only in *Henry VIII*, confirming it is unique. The search would also turn up North's journal were it in the database. Even a Google and Google Books search for "*the goodliest woman*" AROUND(10) "*that ever*" yields only the history play or quotations of the history play. Likewise, an EEBO search of *I never saw* FBY.50 *before* FBY.50 *women* FBY.50 *strangely* yields only *Henry VIII*.

22. North would have certainly been familiar with the fall of Cranmer as shortly after he returned home, in January of 1556, his master, Bishop Thirlby, was forced to supervise the degradation of Cranmer, in which the formal clothing of all his authority—the various vestments of deacon, priest, bishop, and archbishop—were all put upon him and then removed from him one by one. Cranmer had been a good friend to Thirlby, and Thirlby cried during the grand defrocking. Cranmer was then burned at the stake on 21 March 1556. North likely wrote the original version of *Henry VIII*, consisting of much of the first four acts, after this. Cranmer would actually become a major character in the post-Marian fifth act.

23. An EEBO search for *man* NEAR.20 *aspire* NEAR.20 *princes favor* yields only North's *Dial* and Wolsey's speech in *Henry VIII*. A Google search for *man* AROUND(20) *aspire* AROUND(20) "*princes favor*" also yields only *Henry VIII* or works quoting *Henry VIII*.

24. The quotation in table 5.3 is from *The Life and Death of Cardinal Wolsey. Written by George Cavendish, Illustrated with Portraits by Holbein* (Boston and New York: Houghton Mifflin, 1905).

25. A Google search of "*deceive him of a mite*" confirms that all are quotations from Cavendish's manuscript, whether the lines appear in editions of books on the life of Wolsey or are in works quoting that particular line. This can be double-checked by using the minus sign ("–") to subtract *Cavendish* and *Master Kingston* from the results. This quickly confirms that no other work contains that phrase. This is also true of *deceive him not of a mite*, which appears only in North's *Doni*.

26. Nearly all of *Doni*'s similarities to both *The Life of Wolsey* and the play are due to changes made by North. For example, Anton Francesco Doni originally wrote *non lo ingannar di cosa alcuna* (26), which means *do not lie to him about anything*. But North changed this to *deceive him not of a mite*—a Wolsey phrase, quoted by Cavendish, that occurs nowhere else in EEBO (*deceive* FBY *of a mite* yields only *Doni*) or anywhere else in Google. Likewise, North translates *i familiari de principi* (*the families of princes*) as *those that are in favor with princes*, echoing Wolsey's *princes' favors* in *Henry VIII*. And, again, *true to thy master, corruption, service*, and *I do advise thee* were all the result of additions or modifications by North. North has transformed *Doni*'s original paragraph into Wolseyan advice that he had written about previously.

Chapter Six

The Winter's Tale
An Homage to Queen Mary

Much of the charm of Shakespeare's *Winter's Tale* is in its miscellany of exotic, imaginative, and impossible elements. The play's settings are widely separated and remote: the kingdoms of Sicily and Bohemia, one ruled by Leontes, the other by Polixenes. Despite the distance between their realms, the kings have evidently grown up with each other and been inseparable friends since childhood. In fact, they repeatedly refer to each other as "brother," including six times in the first scene in which they appear together.

These distant settings serve as the backdrop for an eclectic mix of scenes that includes a pagan sheep-shearing feast with Leontes's daughter, Perdita, dressed as the goddess Flora, distributing flowers symbolic of time. This is soon followed by a dance of satyrs. The pastoral banquet also includes allusions to very peculiar mythological imagery: Dis's kidnapping of Proserpine in a wagon, Jupiter and Neptune changing into "the shapes of beasts," and Apollo dressed as a humble swain—all to seduce mortal women. Juno and Cythera also find mention during the sheep-shearing feast.

The last act replaces these unusually pagan visuals with striking Catholic ones, particularly evocative of the Virgin Mary. This includes a woman kneeling before and kissing a remarkably lifelike statue of "our gracious Lady" behind a curtained recess in a chapel, inspiring a miracle of resurrection. This image is foreshadowed by an allusion to praying for such a resurrection on the barren and frozen mountains. Some scholars have highlighted this scene as an example of the play's seemingly endless homage to Catholicism. Quoting Daryll Grantley:

> The "statue" of Hermione in the final scene is yet another reminder of the Virgin; positioned as it is within a recess (as suggested by the curtain in front), it would have brought to the minds of the original audiences the statue of the

Virgin. The "miracle" of the coming to life of the statue can possibly be seen to echo the legends of the miracles associated with the Virgin and frequently occurring as a result of prayers and offerings to her statue. . . . The Virgin's accessibility to sinners earned her the epithet *scala peccatorum* in the Middle Ages; this formed no part of the official Anglicanism prevalent at the date of *The Winter's Tale* . . .[1]

Other elements throughout the play also respectfully recall and at times celebrate Catholic traditions and festivities, leading many scholars to suspect the playwright's favoritism of or at least sympathy for the old religion.

Yet other researchers notice that when Autolycus sells his "trumpery"—his horn-ring and lawn, etc.—he does so as a con-man selling fake Catholic relics. As Autolycus notes, the throngs purchase his wares "as if my trinkets had been hallowed and brought a benediction to the buyer" (4.4.604–605). Richard Burt writes: "It is precisely because the rustics naively believe that Autolycus's 'popish' peddled wares have the sacramental efficacy of relics that he can cut purses."[2] John Pitcher, in the Arden III *Winter's Tale*, makes this same point,[3] as does David Kaula, who contends this is consistent with an anti-Catholic view.[4]

These seeming religious inconsistencies are intertwined with strange geographical errors: although Bohemia was a northeastern region located within the modern-day Czech Republic, Shakespeare notoriously gives it a coastline and a desert, when it has neither. Dis's kidnapping of Proserpine and the twin dangers of the man-eater on the coast (like Scylla) and a ship-destroying maelstrom just off-shore (like Charybdis) are all set in or near Bohemia when they are clearly Sicilian. Moreover, the Prince of Bohemia is somehow involved in a Mediterranean conflict with a noble and warlike Governor of Libya, a region that had never directly interacted with Bohemia and had been firmly in the hands of the Ottoman Empire for more than five decades when Shakespeare staged the play in 1610 or 1611. And just as Bohemia seems to be confused with a southern Mediterranean country, Sicily appears bizarrely Bohemian. Its court is surrounded by a "tuft of pines," and the Sicilian queen is somehow a daughter of the Emperor of Russia. Even the names of the kings suggest they are ruling the wrong lands. Pitcher writes: "The national symbol of real Bohemia was a lion, but in Shakespeare it is the King of Sicily who is called Leontes (*Leo*, Latin for 'lion'), while the King of Bohemia has a Greek name, Polixenes, thus associated with Sicily and the Mediterranean."[5] Indeed, as various scholars have noted, the Bohemian king's name is taken from the Sicilian Polixenes in North's *Plutarch's Lives*. The name of Polixenes' son, Florizel, derives from a knight in the Spanish romance *Amadis de Gaul*, once again linking the prince of Shakespeare's Bohemia to Mediterranean adventurism.

Of special interest to Shakespeareans is the peculiar allusion to Giulio Romano, the only Renaissance artist mentioned by name in the Shakespeare canon, and his supposed creation of the lifelike painted statue of Hermione. Some scholars have claimed that Giulio was not even a sculptor, adding another incongruity to the tragicomedy.[6] Others discuss the possibility of a trip by the playwright or one of his acquaintances to the province of Mantua, where they may have been exposed to the wonders of Romano's work on Castiglione's tomb in Santa Maria delle Grazie and the chapel's painted wax figures.[7] Still others link the play to Mantua's Palazzo Te, a pleasure palace filled with the frescoes of Romano, and especially its dining room, the Sala di Psyche, where the Gonzagas, the Dukes of Mantua, entertained visitors with great feasts.[8] Many of the images of *The Winter's Tale* seem to come from that particular room. Others have pointed out how perplexing the mystery is. As Leonard Barkan writes:

> The mention of Giulio Romano stands out as exceptional, not only in the *Winter's Tale* but in all of Shakespeare's oeuvre, where references to real-life people are rare and to contemporary Italian artists otherwise nonexistent. The passage raises many vexing questions: how did Shakespeare know of Giulio Romano and in what connection? could he have seen any of Giulio's works? why, if he knew anything at all about the artist, did he choose a man renowned for his painting and architecture to be the exemplary sculptor? Ingenious solutions have been proposed, including the appearance of paintings by Giulio Romano in England, parallels between Hermione's life and that of a subject of a Giulio portrait, or even a Shakespearean holiday in Mantua during the "lost" years of his young adulthood. Finally, no definitive solution may be possible . . .[9]

The play is also home to an allegorical figure of Time, whose Prologue transports the reader through sixteen years of narrated action. Prompted by Time's presence and by the play's interest in the fantastic and surreal, Ros King pointed out that "Everything about the story of *The Winter's Tale* from its geography to its statue is impossible."[10] The "impossible" has led editors to categorize the tragicomedy as a romance, a companion to other late plays of Shakespeare. Yet despite all this, most editors observe that English Tudor history also makes an appearance, noting that King Leontes' public trial of Queen Hermione for adultery closely resembles that of Henry VIII's public trial of Queen Katherine—with Katherine's and Hermione's impassioned claims of innocence sharing many elements.

Finally, many of the play's source texts seem strangely outdated for the early seventeenth century. Besides Chaucer, Boccaccio, Homer, Ovid, and the Bible, the playwright also seems to have borrowed from French and English texts published between 1544 and 1557. These include Pierre de Ronsard's poem *L'Alouette* (1556) and the French versions of the *Amadis de Gaul*, a series of Spanish romances that were translated into French by Nicholas d'Herberay, Jacques Gohorry, and others in the mid sixteenth century. Early Tudor English sources include *The Play of the Four P's* (1544), *Respublica* (1553), *The History of Quintus Curtius* (1553), *The Life of Wolsey* (1554–56), *A Memorial of Such Princes* (1554), and *The Dial of Princes* (1557).

But why, near the end of his career, did Shakespeare cram all these whimsical, fantastic, confusing, archaic, and seemingly unrelated elements into the same play? Remarkably, Thomas North's 1555 journal resolves these mysteries. For North's journal is itself a kind of *Winter's Tale*, combining the same exotic ingredients that adorn the play and evoking the same sense of the outlandish and darkly magical. When one reads North's journal alongside *The Winter's Tale*, all the play's loose ends are tied up, its errors rectified, and the purpose of every mysterious element made clear. In fact, the play is perfectly coherent; nothing is extraneous, and the underlying story that it relates is true. Specifically, *The Winter's Tale* is an historical allegory of events in the reign of Henry VIII and their aftermath, focusing on the divorce of Katherine and the return of her daughter, Queen Mary Tudor. These events are then combined with some of the most dramatic moments of North's trip to Italy.

AN HOMAGE TO THE LIFE OF QUEEN MARY

The mission behind North's 1555 trip to Rome was to unite formerly Protestant England with the pope. Mary's father, Henry VIII, had pushed England into Protestantism during his effort to divorce Mary's mother, Katherine of Aragon. Henry's charge was that she had consummated her earlier, brief marriage with the king's older brother, Arthur, Prince of Wales. Katherine and Arthur were young children when their respective royal fathers, Henry VII and Ferdinand II of Spain, contracted a marriage between the young heirs. The ceremony eventually took place when they were fifteen, on 14 November 1501, but Arthur died of a mysterious illness, perhaps "sweating sickness," five months later, 2 April 1502. The Kings of England and Spain decided the marriage had not been consummated and agreed to affiance Katherine with Arthur's younger brother. In 1527, eighteen years after Henry and Katherine were married, the king, who was still without a male heir, used the possibility of her having had sex with his brother as an excuse for the divorce.

The public trial of Katherine did not just end her marriage; it also delegitimized her daughter, Mary, leading to her demotion from princess to bastard and then banishment as a young girl to Hatfield. As Pope Clement VII refused to grant the divorce and eventually excommunicated Henry, the king's "great matter" also brought about the English reformation and the criminalization of many traditional Catholic practices, including miracle stories, religious festivities, and statues of the Virgin Mary.

In 1553, with the surprising death of Edward VI, the fifteen-year-old son of Henry VIII and his third wife, Jane Seymour, Mary's right to the throne was reestablished and she became queen, immediately reinstating Catholicism as the national religion and overthrowing laws that forbade its practices, traditions, images, and icons. Her coronation returned power to both Queen Mary and the Virgin Mary—and seemed to justify the faith of the frustrated early Tudor Catholics that Henry's turn toward Protestantism was simply a temporary error that would soon be rectified by Providence. Thus, Mary at her coronation adopted the motto *Veritas Temporis Filia*: "Truth is the daughter of Time." Mary also solidified her Catholic *bona fides* by marrying Philip II, son of the Holy Roman Emperor, Charles V—once again uniting England with Catholic Spain, the two Sicilies, and the Hapsburg dominions, including Bohemia.

These and other events throughout the life of Mary recreate the complicated and fantastic storyline for *The Winter's Tale*. Indeed, scholarly comparisons of King Leontes with King Henry VIII and Queen Hermione with Queen Katherine are common. It is not simply that the stories share the same peculiar details—even Leontes's accusation that Hermione had sex with his "brother" Polixenes matches Henry VIII's accusation that Katherine had sex with his brother—the playwright has even based many of Queen Hermione's speeches on the historical speeches of Katherine. The court scene, from the officer demanding silence and the command to read the charge to Hermione's passionate and moving monologue proclaiming her innocence, follows the trial of Katherine, comment by comment. Indeed, the seminal source for the queen's speeches was Cavendish's *Life of Wolsey*, the unpublished manuscript that North used as a template for both his own travel journal and his play on Henry VIII.

North adds numerous details to *The Winter's Tale* in order to secure the identities of Henry VIII, Katherine, Mary, Philip II, Sir Thomas More, the pope, and young Edward VI. Time's introduction to Act 4 paraphrases and echoes the allegorical description of Time in the celebration of Mary's coronation in *Respublica*. Perdita, like Mary, is the daughter of Time, rectifying error and returning truth to the country. The rural festivities of the sheep-shearing feast in 4.4, often compared to Whitsuntide celebrations, also promote Catholic traditions criminalized during the reformation. As Phebe Jensen writes:

> Whitsuntide celebrations, church ales, wakes, May games, and even bearbaitings and morris dances were, according to the reformers, vestiges of popish idolatry and superstition which encouraged religious backwardness . . .

In this context, *The Winter's Tale* can be seen to deploy festivity as part of a larger, anti-iconoclastic aesthetic agenda, one that aligns the play with a Catholic past and present.[11]

Likewise, the unveiling of the statue of the saintly mother, Hermione, is symbolic of the Marian return of Catholic icons to the English landscape—especially statues of the Virgin Mary—as well as a belief in Mary's miraculous powers. As Ruth Vanita points out:

> Hermione as statue appears in a "chapel" and she herself has lived in Paulina's "removed house" with other statues. Her preservation and revelation as a statue after sixteen years suggests the way many parishioners who bought images, vestments, and other church property auctioned under Henry and Edward VI, preserved and restored them to churches in Mary Tudor's reign.[12]

That is what *The Winter's Tale* is: an homage to the return of Queen Mary and rehabilitation of her mother, Katherine, centered on the story of the tragic divorce and ending with a celebration of the attendant decriminalization of Mariolatry, miracle tales, and other long-practiced features of Catholic devotion—and all of it adorned with the otherworldly visuals of North's continental journey.

REVERSING THE KINGDOMS

In order to appreciate the parallels between the play and the life of Queen Mary, it is important to understand that when Shakespeare adapted *The Winter's Tale* in *c.* 1610, he transposed the settings of Sicily and Bohemia, likely for political reasons. Scholars accept the geographical swap as well as Shakespeare's responsibility for it because, in Robert Greene's early version of the tale, *Pandosto* (1585, published in 1588), Sicily and Bohemia are reversed, and Greene's work had to have preceded Shakespeare's. In reality, as we intend to show, both Greene and Shakespeare were adapting the same North play, but the upshot in either case is the same: Shakespeare switched the kingdoms.

Jonathan Bate has suggested a likely reason for the substitution: in 1610, England still harbored hatred toward Philip II, who led the terrifying Spanish Armada attack on England in 1588 and had been King of Sicily and Spain until his death ten years later, when his son, Philip III, took over the titles. Conversely, in 1610, James I was on friendly terms with Rudolf II, the King of Bohemia. As Bate remarks:

> Fictional and fanciful as *The Winter's Tale* may be, the fact is that when the play was written the king of Sicilia was Philip III of Spain, and the king of Bohemia

was the emperor Rudolf II. There were strong links between the courts of James in London and Rudolf in Prague. . . .

Conversely . . . the residual English hostility to all things Spanish, dating back to the Armada and beyond, had not gone away. In these circumstances, it seems eminently plausible that on deciding to dramatize a story about the kings of Sicilia and Bohemia, and knowing that the play would at some point go into the court repertoire, Shakespeare thought it would be politic to make the monarch with Spanish, as opposed to Rudolfine, associations the one who is irrational, cruel, and blasphemous.

Bate goes on to clarify that he is "not proposing that Leontes is in any sense a representation of Philip [III] or Polixenes of Rudolf."[13] Indeed, they would appear to have nothing in common with their dramatic counterparts other than their royal titles. These two kings were not brothers but second cousins, and they did not grow up with each other. Rudolf II was twenty-six in 1578, the year Philip III was born in Madrid. As we shall see, it was their respective grandfathers, Ferdinand I and Charles V, whom North had in mind—a point made clear when we reverse the locations, which in turn mends the play's numerous geographical disjunctions.

Once we return the settings to their proper placement, the lion, the symbol of Bohemia, links with Leontes (Latin for *lion*); Russia, the Bohemian queen's homeland, is now nearby; and a tuft of pines surrounds Leontes' court. Meanwhile, all of the conspicuously Sicilian elements of Polixenes' kingdom—its seacoast and desert; its Mediterranean conflict with Libya; the Dionysian feast; the names Polixenes, Sinalus, and Florizel; and the legend of Proserpine and Dis—are now all rightly placed in and around Sicily.

Switching the kingdoms back also helps uncover another mythical analogy that gains clarity in the right setting. When Antigonus's "ship hath touched upon the deserts of" Sicily (not Bohemia), the Mariner warns, "this place is famous for the creatures / Of prey that keep upon't" (3.3.11–12). It is Sicily that is legendary for man-eating beasts, including Polyphemus (Cyclops) and Scylla. Later in the scene, the Clown gives a dual description of the horrific "sights, by sea and by land!" (3.3.81–82). And the Clown's back-and-forth accounts of the twin dreads facing those who sail near the coast of Sicily, with the turbulent sea threatening the Mariners and the fearsome man-eater (the bear) waiting on the coast, is, of course, a take-off on the same twofold horrors of Charybdis, the ship-destroying maelstrom, and Scylla, the man-eater, who endanger all who enter the Straits of Sicily. The playwright follows Odysseus's description in the famous scene of Homer's poem quite closely, recounting both events in the same order and matching numerous details. This includes screaming Mariners just off shore, first being pushed skyward, then sucked down to the bottom of the sea—interspersed with a gruesome depiction of a man on the coast being devoured alive, shrieking to the narrator for help as he is eaten. Later, the Third Gentleman would describe the fate of Antigonus as "Like an old tale" (5.2.62). He was certainly correct about that: the Clown's story, which we examine in Chapter 8, is a parody of Odysseus's.

Most importantly, the switch of kingdoms also helps define in sharper detail the real-life counterparts for the play's characters. Now the allegory is precise (see table 6.1).

Table 6.1.

The Winter's Tale Characters/Places	Historical Counterparts
Catholic Sicily	Catholic Sicily (Southern Hapsburg)
Protestant Bohemia	Protestant England
Leontes, King of Bohemia	Henry VIII (with a nod to Ferdinand, King of Bohemia)
Queen Hermione, the accused innocent	Queen Katherine, the accused innocent
Perdita, their banished daughter	Mary, their banished daughter
Mamillius, the young, unfortunate Prince	Edward VI, the young, unfortunate Prince
Polixenes, King of Sicily	Charles V, King of Sicily (with a nod to Arthur, Prince of Wales)
Florizel, Prince of Sicily	Philip II, Prince of Sicily
Sinalus, Governor of Libya and Mediterranean warrior	Turgut Re'is, Governor of Libya and Mediterranean warrior
Camillo, counselor "priest" of Leontes	Sir Thomas More
Oracle of Apollo, the foreign priest, and supreme and divine arbiter	The Pope, Clement VII
Cleomenes and Dion, messengers sent to the Oracle	Edward Carne and William Benet, diplomats sent to the Pope
Paulina	A Pauline symbol of the Catholic Church

The reasons behind North's choice of Bohemia and Sicily—with Bohemia as the reformation sister to England and Sicily as a synecdoche for Charles's (and then his son, Philip's) southern Catholic empire—become obvious with a reading of North's journal. Indeed, the subtitle of the journal could read "North's Journey through the Dominions of the Kings of Bohemia and Sicily" (see figure 6.1).

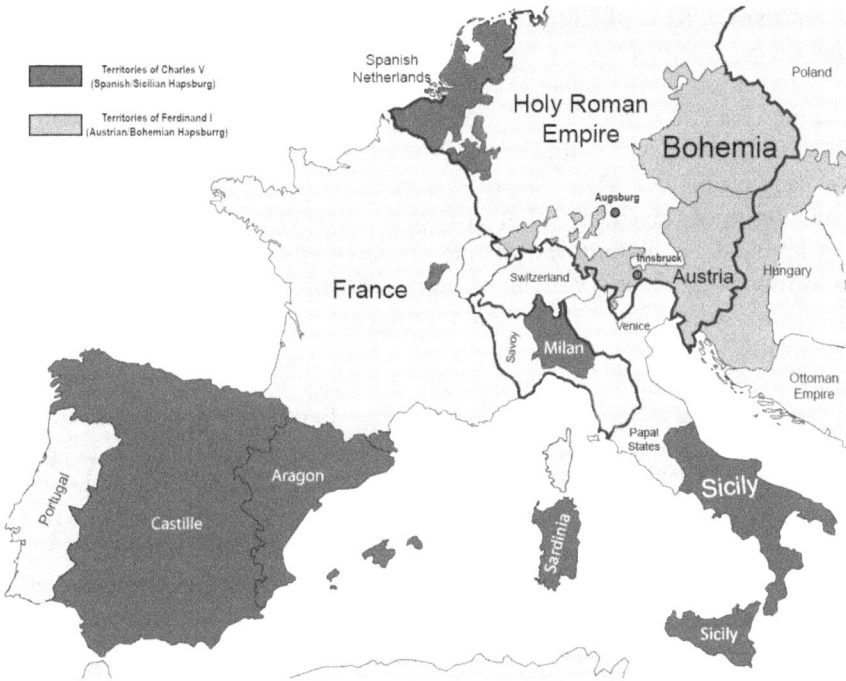

Figure 6.1. The approximate domains of the brother Kings of Bohemia and Sicily.

In 1555, the brothers Ferdinand I and Charles V controlled the northern and southern realms of the Hapsburg Empire. In terms of number of mentions, both kings were main characters in North's journal, with North referring to Ferdinand eight times and Charles V more than twenty, even stressing they were brothers. North would discuss their various political activities, relationships, and histories—and he especially noted these when he traveled into their kingdoms. Along the Brenner Pass, between Sterzing and Steinach, North records the place where the two brothers reunited in 1530, after eight years of being apart. Charles V had just been coronated in Rome and traveled with his huge train northward, where his brother met him at the edge of Austrian/Bohemian Hapsburg territory. As North wrote in his journal, "A Dutch mile beyond the town, **Ferdinando met with the emperor his brother when he came out of Spain**" (15–16 July). Ferdinand had built a large monument at the exact location of the meeting, and North echoes the story inscribed on its brass panel: "Imp[eratori] Caes[ari] Carolo V. P. F. Aug: ex Hispaniis Italiaque Susceptis Imperialibus Coronis advenienti & Ferdinando Hung[ariae] Bohemiaeque Regi . . . quod Fratres . . . convenerunt"[14] (i.e, **The emperor Charles . . . arriving out of Spain** and Italy with the imperial crown, **and**

Ferdinando, King of Hungary and Bohemia, coming from Pannonia . . . **the brothers . . . met**).

The reason North chose Ferdinand's Bohemia as one of the two major settings for *The Winter's Tale*—rather than, say, his Hungary or Austria—is its special connection with England's reformation, a point made by Cardinal Wolsey on his deathbed. As we saw in the previous chapter, North read a manuscript of Cavendish's *Life of Wolsey* to provide him with the historical background for his journey, and, in the cardinal's final speech, he offered a warning for Henry VIII about following in the dangerous footsteps of Bohemia, whose own Protestant reformation was closely associated with England's.

Both movements began through the teachings of reformer John Wycliffe, who was a professor at Oxford in the late fourteenth century, during the reign of Richard II and his queen, Anne of Bohemia. His teachings critical of the Roman Catholic church soon spread from England to Bohemia, likely through the queen and various scholarly visitors from her homeland. Numerous histories on the origins of Protestantism note that Wycliffe was the "'morning star of the Reformation' for Bohemia as well as for England."[15] Jan Hus became the main preacher of Wycliffe's doctrines in Bohemia until he was burned at the stake in 1415. The Bohemian reformation persisted with his followers, the Hussites, who in turn paved the way for Martin Luther in neighboring Germany.

The dying Wolsey was thinking of this shared history when he urged Sir William Kingston, constable of the tower, to relay the following warning to the king:

> I request his Grace, on God's name, that he have a vigilant eye to depress this new sort of Lutherans, that it do not increase through his negligence, in such a sort, as he be at length compelled to put harness upon his back to subdue them; as the king of Bohemia did, who had good game to see his commons infected with Wickliffe's heresies to spoil the spiritual men of his realm . . . (272)[16]

Wolsey continues discussing the violent history of Bohemia, brought about by the spread of "Wickliffe's heresies."

In Innsbruck, on 17 July, the day after he recorded the meeting of Charles and Ferdinand in the Brenner Pass, North writes: "We saw also all the pedigree of the house of Austria cast in brass, with many other pictures so lively and notably wrought that I am not able to describe them. Every picture cost 1000 Crowns." North stresses that Ferdinand was then building a monastery in Innsbruck where these statues would all eventually be placed. The young journalist was referring to the Hofkirche ("Court Church"), which today contains 28 bronze statues of the then King and Queen of Bohemia's ancestors overlooking the cenotaph of Ferdinand's grandfather, Maximilian I (1459–1519). The statues that awed North included kings, queens, dukes, duchesses, and, surprisingly, the English King Arthur, who, according to local legend, was an ancestor to Ferdinand's wife, Anna of Bohemia and Hungary (1503–1547).[17] (Ferdinand's wife should not be confused with the fourteenth-century Anne of Bohemia who was Richard II's wife.)

The next week, 23–24 July, North and the entourage reached Augsburg, Germany, where the young journalist notes that Ferdinand was also staying in the city. This was the same year that the King of Bohemia would negotiate the Peace of Augsburg, temporarily returning his own realm to Catholicism, at least officially. The Diet of the Holy Roman Empire had assembled there in February of that year, and the Peace of Augsburg was eventually promulgated on 25 September 1555, helping to prevent wars between Catholic and Lutheran regions and to establish the principle of *cuius regio, eius religio*: "whose realm, his religion." This meant that each ruler had the right to determine the faith of his own dominions, and so this would mark Ferdinand's official cessation and reversal of the Bohemian reformation.

In other words, not only does Protestantism in England and Bohemia have an identical origin, each dawning at about the same time and each through the teachings of Wycliffe; the two nations also experienced an ultimately temporary, mini counter-reformation in which both officially returned to Catholicism at the same time: in 1555.[18] Importantly, North was present at both places—in Rome for the official unification of England with Catholic Europe and in Augsburg during the year of Ferdinand's official unification of Bohemia with Catholic Europe. The parallels between the religious evolution of Bohemia and England—including uniting with southern Italy (i.e., Sicily) through the Hapsburg monarchy—were obvious. And so North used Bohemia as an allegorical substitute for England.

Sicily also fits perfectly into the Marian storyline of *The Winter's Tale*. The brother of Ferdinand, King of Bohemia, was the King of Sicily, Charles V (i.e., Polixenes). And Charles's son, of course, was the Prince of Sicily, Philip II (i.e., Florizel), who married Queen Mary (i.e., Perdita). Although in the play the kings are not technically brothers, they have grown up with each other and repeatedly refer to one another as such. In their first appearance on stage together, Polixenes immediately addresses Leontes as his "brother." Within thirteen lines, Leontes uses the same sobriquet for Polixenes, while begging him to extend his visit. They continue this throughout the scene: "our brother," "best brother," "my brother," "our brother's welcome." Again, in 5.1, when Leontes first sees Polixenes' son, he says: "Your father's image is so hit in you, / His very air, that I should call you brother, / as I did him" (5.1.127–29). Florizel makes the same point back to Leontes, noting that

Polixenes had commanded him to "Give you all the greetings that a king . . . / Can send his brother" (5.1.140–41). Leontes then thinks about the wrong he has done to Polixenes and calls out "O my brother!" (5.1.147). Again, in the final scene, Paulina refers to Polixenes as Leontes' "crowned brother" (5.3.5). A few lines later, Polixenes addresses Leontes as "Dear my brother" (5.3.53). And in the final passage of the play, Leontes asks the resurrected Hermione to "Look upon my brother. Both your pardons, / That e'er I put between your holy looks / My ill suspicion" (5.3.149–51). We do not need to search hard for the identities. The only time in history when the King of Sicily was the brother to the King of Bohemia was with Charles V and Ferdinand I—and this ended in 1554, when Charles abdicated the throne of Sicily to his son Philip for the sake of his marriage to Mary. Of course, within the storyline of *The Winter's Tale*, the playwright cannot make the kings actual brothers as this would make Perdita and Florizel first cousins, but even this provides an apt historical analogy as Philip II was indeed Queen Mary's first cousin once removed.

The historical and emotional meeting between the brother Kings of Sicily and Bohemia that occurred just on the edge of the Northern Hapsburg territory (which North records in his 15–16 July entry) also appears to find mention in *The Winter's Tale*:

> *Third Gentleman:* Did you see the meeting of the two kings?
> *Second Gentleman:* No.
> *Third Gentleman:* Then have you lost a sight which was to be seen, cannot be spoken of. There might you have beheld one joy crown another, so and in such manner that it seemed Sorrow wept to take leave of them, for their joy waded in tears. There was casting up of eyes, holding up of hands, with countenances of such distraction that they were to be known by garment, not by favor. (5.2.40–50)

The kingdoms of the Sicilies incorporated more than the island; they also included the southern part of Italy, and so, as Bate notes about *The Winter's Tale*, Sicily did indeed represent "the heart" of Hapsburg's Catholic empire: "Sicilia—or more exactly, the kingdom of the two Sicilies, one consisting of the island and the other of southern Italy (otherwise known as the kingdom of Naples)—was at the heart of the Mediterranean empire of Philip II of Spain." Thus, as Bohemia was symbolic of English-inspired Protestantism, Sicily was symbolic of Catholicism. As Bate writes:

> The other crucial difference was religious: Sicily was Catholic, whereas for two hundred years the Bohemians had been divided from Rome—the Hussite rising of 1419–20 was perhaps the first enduring religious reformation in Europe.

Anti-papal, anti-clerical and highly moralistic, the Bohemians were effectively Protestants before Protestantism was invented.[19]

Bate observes that the play thus "works on a north-south axis" with a climactic reunification through marriage of the princess and prince of a Protestant northern country and the "implicitly Catholic" Sicilian south.[20] And, of course, this is exactly what happens with England and Sicily in 1553–1555. Indeed, as Katherine was Spanish-Catholic and the aunt of Charles V, the divorce and subsequent bastardization of her daughter did cause friction between the nations that found temporary resolution with Mary's return to royalty and marriage to Philip II. The correspondence with the play is exact, and the Catholic unification of Bohemia with Sicily at the same time (1555), involving Charles V and his brother, both of whom were so relevant to North's trip to Rome, made them natural candidates as literary stand-ins for the English history story. Indeed, North's choice of his first published translation, *The Dial of Princes*, the text of which he may have picked up during his journey, stresses his focus on the Hapsburgs, Mary's marriage, and England's alliance with Spain and Sicily. The title-page of North's translation boldly declares that *The Dial* had been originally written (in Spanish) "by Don Antony of Guevara, Bishop of Guadix, preacher and chronicler to Charles the fifth," and his dedication to Mary addresses her as "Queen of England, Spain . . . both Sicilies . . . countess of Hapsburg."

Here, then, is the storyline that *The Winter's Tale* shares with the actual history or play of Henry VIII:

1. The king (Henry VIII, Leontes) accuses his queen (Katherine, Hermione) of sleeping with his "brother."
2. An honest priest-like counselor sides with the queen—and the king threatens him with execution (Sir Thomas More, Camillo).
3. The king puts the queen on trial over this issue. (This was an historical first: a monarch facing a court trial. Yet it did indeed happen to Katherine of Aragon—and to both her dramatic counterparts, Katherine in *Henry VIII*, Hermione in *The Winter's Tale*).
4. The queen at the trial offers an eloquent declaration of innocence, and Hermione's speech is a line-by-line paraphrase of the historical Katherine's speech (e.g., each queen emphasizes she is the daughter of foreign royalty, that she will not get a fair trial, that she will refuse to weep, that she has given the king children, that the king should search his conscience).
5. The queen refuses to accept the verdict of her husband but appeals to a foreign priest (the pope in *Henry VIII*, the Oracle of Apollo in *The Winter's Tale*).

6. The foreign priest represents God on Earth, and his verdicts are believed to be divinely inspired.
7. Messengers are sent to this foreign priest (as Carne and Benet journey to the pope, Cleomenes and Dion travel to the Oracle of Apollo).
8. The foreign priest sides with the queen.
9. The king disregards the verdict of the foreign priest, breaks with him, and declares her guilty anyway.
10. The queen gives birth to a daughter whose survival was in doubt but then is described as *lusty* and likely to live. (After Katherine had suffered miscarriages, premature births, and children who died in infancy, the court was relieved that baby Mary was "healthy and likely to live ... 'a right *lusty* princess.'"[21] Similarly, after Hermione's stressful and premature birth, Paulina describes baby Perdita as "*Lusty* and *like to live*" [2.2.27].)
11. As the result of the outcome of the queen's trial, the daughter's title of princess is rescinded. She is declared a bastard and banished from the court.
12. The queen prays for blessings to be poured from the heavens upon her daughter's head (*Henry VIII* 4.2.132–33, *Winter's Tale* 5.3.122–24).
13. There is a pastoral feast with beautiful women and royalty disguised as shepherds (*Henry VIII* 1.4, *Winter's Tale* 4.4).
14. The queen dies soon after being deposed, appearing in a ghostly vision in white robes; the vision then vanishes into the air (*Henry VIII* 4.2.82.s.d., *Winter's Tale* 3.3.16–36).
15. Surprisingly, the king's young prince dies (the young Edward VI in 1553, Mamillius in *Winter's Tale*), leaving the king with no remaining legal heirs, a fate thought by some to be divine punishment for his false accusation and abandonment of his queen.
16. The banished daughter, who has now grown up, regains her royal status and is betrothed to the Prince of Sicily (Perdita marries Florizel, Queen Mary marries Philip II).
17. This Prince of Sicily is a Mediterranean warrior involved in a conflict with the Governor of Libya (Sinalus, Turgut Re'is [a/k/a Dragut Rais]).
18. The Prince of Sicily emulates the heroic knights of the Spanish romance *Amadis of Gaul* (i.e., Florizel is a knight from *Amadis de Gaul*, and Philip II would appear as an *Amadis de Gaul* knight in entertainments).
19. During the heralding of the daughter's triumphant return, the princess is described as Truth, the daughter of Time, which always rectifies error. (Time's Prologue that introduces Perdita [4.1] is based on the description of Time in *Respublica* (1553), written for Mary's coronation.)
20. The repeated celebration of Catholicism throughout *The Winter's Tale*—including Catholic festivals, Mariolatry, supplication to a statue of a

woman in a recess in a chapel, and a miraculous resurrection—speaks to Mary's decriminalization of idolatry, festivals, and miracle stories in England.
21. Bonfires celebrate the princess's rise, the return of Catholicism to a formerly Protestant nation, and her nation's reuniting with Sicily and the southern Catholic nations (*Winter's Tale* 5.2.23–26, North's journal 16 June).
22. In commemoration of the reconciliation, the king has sent a man to measure the exact distance *over both land and sea* between their realms (*Winter's Tale* 5.1.143–45, North's journal, especially 21–25 August).

Among early Tudor plays, historical allegories, particularly involving Henry VIII and his divorce, were not uncommon, and North's *Winter's Tale*, preserved in Shakespeare's adaptation, is probably the most obvious.

HERMIONE AS KATHERINE AND MARY AS PERDITA

While few scholars have detected the full extent of the parallels between *The Winter's Tale* and the life of Queen Mary, many have discussed the most obvious ones. Gordon McMullan, in the Arden edition of *Henry VIII*, compares the corresponding passages, noting that "Katherine's defence of her marriage in the Blackfriars courtroom has strong resemblances to Hermione's resistance to Leontes' irrational jealousy."[22] Table 6.2 includes the parallels pointed out by McMullan and adds a few more.

Table 6.2.

First, the Officer demands silence while the charge is read in court, and the Queen is then introduced.	
Trial of Katherine in *Henry VIII*	Trial of Hermione in *The Winter's Tale*
Wolsey: Whilst <u>our commission from Rome is **read**</u>, Let **silence** be commanded. . . . Scribe: Say, "Katherine **Queen** of England, come **into the court**." Crier: Katherine **Queen** of England, come into the court. —2.4.1–2, 9–10	Officer: It is His Highness' pleasure that the **Queen** <u>Appear in person here **in court**. **Silence**</u>! [Enter] Hermione . . . [Paulina, and] Ladies. Leontes. **Read** the indictment. Officer: [reads] "Hermione, **Q**ueen to the worthy Leontes . . ." —3.2.9–13.s.d.

(continued)

Table 6.2. *(continued)*

Each Queen begins by claiming she will not get a fair trial and ends by appealing to a foreign judge who speaks the word of God.	
Katherine in *Henry VIII*	Hermione in *The Winter's Tale*
. . . having here No judge indifferent, nor no more assurance Of equal friendship and proceeding —2.4.14–16	. . . it shall scarce boot me To say 'not guilty.' Mine integrity, Being counted falsehood, shall, as I express it, Be so received. —3.2.25–28
I do refuse you for my judge; and here <u>Before **you all**, appeal **unto the** Pope</u>, To bring my whole cause 'fore His Holiness, And to be **judged** by him. —2.4.116–19	. . . if I shall be condemned Upon surmises, all proofs sleeping else But what your jealousies awake, I tell you 'Tis rigor and not law. **Your** Honors **all**, **I do** <u>refer me **to the** oracle</u>. Apollo be my **judge**! —3.2.111–16

Each Queen then addresses the King; each says she has been a true and humble wife who has given him children. The exchange in *The Winter's Tale* also includes language from *Henry VIII*.	
Katherine in *Henry VIII*	Hermione in *The Winter's Tale*
I have been to you a **true** and humble wife, At all times to your will conformable . . . . . . Sir, call to mind That I have been your wife, in this obedience Upward of twenty years, and <u>have been blessed With many children by you</u>. —2.4.21–22, 32–35	. . . <u>You, my lord, best know, Who least will seem to do so, my past life</u> Hath been as continent, as **chaste**, as **true** As I am now unhappy; which is more Than history can pattern, though devised And played to take spectators. <u>For behold me—</u> A **fellow** of the royal **bed**, which owe A moiety of the throne, **a** great **king's daughter**, <u>The mother to a hopeful prince</u>—here standing To prate and talk for life and honor 'fore Who please to come and hear. —3.2.32–39
So sweet a bedfellow —2.2.142	A **fellow** of the royal **bed** —3.2.30 To bless the **bed** of majesty again With a **sweet fellow** to't? —5.1.33–34

(continued)

Table 6.2. *(continued)*

I was a **chaste wife** . . . and **daughter to a king**. —4.2.171–73	The **daughter of a king**, our **wife** . . . as **chaste**, as **true** . . . —3.2.3, 34

Each Queen questions how she could have fallen from the King's grace and swears that, if she has done anything against her own honor, let everyone hold her in contempt and may she suffer stern justice.

Katherine in *Henry VIII*	Hermione in *The Winter's Tale*
. . . Alas, sir, In what have I offended you? <u>What cause</u> <u>Hath my behavior</u> given to your displeasure That thus you should proceed to put me off And take **your** good **grace** from me? . . . <u>If, in the course</u> <u>And process of this time, you can report,</u> <u>And prove it too, against mine **honor**</u> <u>aught—</u> . . . Against your sacred person—in God's name <u>Turn me away, and let the foul'st contempt</u> <u>Shut door upon me, and so give me up</u> <u>To the sharp'st kind of justice.</u> —2.4.16–20, 35–42	For **honor**, 'Tis a derivative from me to mine, And only that I stand for. **I appeal** **To your own conscience**, sir, before Polixenes Came to your court, how I was in **your grace**, How merited to be so; since he came, With <u>what encounter</u> so uncurrent I Have strained t'appear thus; <u>if one jot beyond</u> <u>The bound of **honor**, or in act or will</u> <u>That way inclining, hardened be the hearts</u> <u>Of all that hear me, and my near'st of kin</u> <u>Cry "Fie" upon my grave!</u> —3.2.43–54

Each play stresses multiple times that the Queen is the daughter of a King—and, indeed, that she is the daughter of a foreign monarch.

Katherine in *Henry VIII*	Hermione in *The Winter's Tale*
The daughter of a **king** —2.4.70	**The daughter of a king**, our **wife** . . . —3.2.3
I was a chaste **wife** . . . and **daughter to a king** —4.2.170, 172	a great **king's daughter** . . . —3.2.39
My father, King **of** Spain —2.4.46	The Emperor **of** Russia was **my father** —3.2.119

(continued)

Table 6.2. *(continued)*

Each Queen argues that all she did was out of **obedience** and she did **love** his **friend**(s)—as honor required.	
Katherine in *Henry VIII*	Hermione in *The Winter's Tale*
when was the hour I ever <u>contradicted your desire</u>, Or made it not mine too? Or which of **your friends** Have I not strove to **love**, although I knew He were mine enemy? What **friend** of mine That had to him derived your anger did I Continue in my liking, nay, gave notice He was from thence discharged? Sir, call to mind That I have been your wife, in this **obedience** —2.4.25–33	I loved him as in honor he required; With such a kind of **love** as might become A lady like me; with a **love** even such, So, and no other, as yourself commanded; Which not to have done I think had been in me Both dis**obedience** and ingratitude To you and toward **your friend**, whose **love** had spoke, Even since it could speak, from an infant, freely That it was yours. —3.2.63–71
Each Queen confirms she will **be patient**, as God or the heavens are looking on, and she will not **weep**. Instead, she will turn **tears** (or lack of **tears**) into **fire** (or that which **burns**). Both passages also refer to **dew**.	
Katherine in *Henry VIII*	Hermione in *The Winter's Tale*
Sir, I am about **to weep**; but, thinking that We are a queen, or long have dreamed so, certain The daughter of a king, my drops of **tears** I'll turn to <u>sparks of fire</u>. Wolsey: **Be patient** yet. Katherine: **I will** when you are humble; nay, before, <u>Or God</u> will punish me . . . For it is you Have blown <u>this coal</u> betwixt my lord and me— Which God's **dew** quench! —2.4.67–73, 76–78	I must **be patient** till <u>the heavens</u> look With an aspect more favorable. Good my lords, I am not prone **to weeping**, as our sex Commonly are the want of which vain **dew** Perchance shall dry your pities; but I have That honorable grief lodged here which <u>burns</u> Worse than **tears** drown . . . —2.1.107–13
Each Queen prays for blessings to be poured down upon the head of her daughter.	
Katherine in *Henry VIII*	Hermione in *The Winter's Tale*
The model of our chaste loves, his young **daughter**— The <u>dews of heaven fall thick</u> in blessings **on** her! —4.2.132–33	You gods, look down And <u>from your sacred vials pour your graces</u> **Upon** my **daughter's** head! —5.3.122–24

Other scholars have also noted some of these resemblances. As Michael Dobson observes: "The difference between the two cases is that whereas Hermione is on trial for adultery, Katharine is accused of incest, but the way in which the latter trial seems deliberately to recall the former invites us to parallel or conflate them . . ."[23] Dobson refers to Katherine's crime as "incest" because of the accusation that she had sex with both Henry VIII and his brother. As we have shown, the situation with Hermione is actually not that different, as both Leontes and Polixenes repeatedly refer to each other as "brother." More significantly, he is also correct that the playwright has deliberately modelled the speeches of the one on the other. But as North had written *Henry VIII* prior to *The Winter's Tale*, it is Hermione's that is following Katherine's. And we know this had to be the case anyway as Katherine's trial is factual and the playwright borrowed the trial scene of Henry VIII, including Katherine's speeches, nearly *verbatim*, from Cavendish. This includes taking those elements (e.g., being a true and humble wife who has given him children, loving the king's friends for his sake, being the daughter of a king) that also appear in Hermione's speeches in *The Winter's Tale* (see table 6.3).

McMullan makes the same point in his gloss of Katherine's speech in *Henry VIII* (2.4.11–55), noting that the queen seems to be following two different sources. Katherine speech, he states, "is effectively versified Holinshed" (i.e., Holinshed quoting Cavendish), adding that "Katherine's speech here (and her situation in general) bears close comparison with that of Hermione at *WT* 3.2, especially 21–53 . . ."[24] Yet how could Shakespeare, when writing *The Winter's Tale* in *c.* 1610, invent out of whole cloth a speech for Hermione that miraculously anticipates Katherine's *verbatim* reproduction of an historical speech in *Henry VIII* (1613)? Certainly, there is no doubt that the one scene seems "deliberately to recall" the other—but it is Hermione's trial and speech that recall the actual trial and speech of Katherine. Cavendish's quotations of Katherine obviously have precedence. And the playwright of *The Winter's Tale* had to have studied these quotations of the historical Katherine *prior to* the crafting of the speeches of Hermione in the trial scene and then deliberately borrowed from them. The only reason the playwright would do this is if Hermione were meant to represent Katherine. The late date of Shakespeare's adaptation of *Henry VIII* has obscured this obvious point.

Moreover, at times Hermione more closely follows the historical quotations of the real-life Katherine than does her counterpart in the history play. For example, at precisely the same moment in their trial speeches—right after the queens each stress that they have shared the king's bed and given him children and just before each admits her willingness to accept any punishment if guilt can be proved—the historical Katherine says, **"I put it to your**

Table 6.3.

Cavendish's *Life of Wolsey*	*Henry VIII*
Sir, quoth she, **I beseech you do me justice and right**, and take some **pity upon me for I am a poor woman and a stranger, born out of your dominion**, having here no **indifferent** counsel, and less **assurance of friendship: alas Sir, what have I offended you** . . .	**Sir, I desire you do me right and justice**, And to bestow your **pity on me**; for I am a most **poor woman, and a stranger, Born out of your dominions**, having here No judge **indifferent**, nor no more assurance Of equal **friendship** and proceeding. Alas, sir, In **what have I offended you**? . . .
I take God to be my judge, **I have been to you a true and an humble wife**, ever **conformable to your will** . . .	Heaven witness, **I have been to you a true and humble wife,** At all times **to your will conformable**
I have **loved** for your sake all men whom ye loved, whether **I** had cause or no cause; or whether they were my **friends or enemies.**	Or which of your **friends** Have I not strove to **love**, although I knew He were mine **enemy**?
The King your Father was in his time of such **an excellent wit**, that he was accompted among all men for his wisdom a second Solomon. And **the King of Spain, my father, Ferdinand, was reckoned** to be **one** of the **wisest princes that reigned** in Spain, **many years before** his days. —129	**The King your father was** reputed for A prince most prudent, of **an excellent** And unmatched **wit** and judgment. **Ferdinand My father, King of Spain, was reckoned one** **The wisest prince that** there had **reigned** by **many** A **year before**. —2.4.11–17, 20–22, 27–29, 43–48

conscience" (129), while Hermione says, "**I appeal to your own conscience**" (3.2.45–46). This is a distinctive line that does not appear in Holinshed, Hall, Stowe, or *Henry VIII* but only in Cavendish's rendition of the trial scene and Hermione's trial speech. This again confirms that the writing of her monologue—indeed, the construction of all the characters in *The Winter's Tale* and their speeches—required careful research and a concern for historical accuracy on the part of the playwright. The care with which the playwright studied Katherine's speeches and her trial strongly suggests that he intended the scene to represent the historical one. Why would Shakespeare research actual events so intently to create a fairytale filled with impossibilities?

Cavendish's description of Katherine's trial is not the only historically significant early Tudor work that is relevant to *The Winter's Tale*. The choric speech of Time in the Prologue to Act 4 derives from the Prologue on Time in *Respublica*, an allegorical play attributed to Nicholas Udall and performed at the coronation of Queen Mary. Both playwrights used the speech on Time for precisely the same purpose: to celebrate the return of Mary/Perdita, whose arrival signaled the repeal of the old, oppressive anti-Catholic laws. Mary/Perdita represents Truth, the daughter of Time—*veritas temporis filia*—and she will rectify the error of the reformation. In an essay on Shakespeare's use of the motto *veritas temporis filia*, Soji Iwasaki identifies Perdita as the representation of Truth in *The Winter's Tale* and notes the relevance of the Prologue on time in *Respublica*:

> Contrary uses of the same motto were made at Mary Tudor's coronation in 1553; Mary, coming back from exile, was seen as Truth rescued by Time after a period of Catholic sufferings. It is known that Mary herself chose the Latin motto "Veritas Temporis Filia" for her personal device, for the legend on her crest, on the State seal of her reign, and on her coins. And for Christmas 1553, an anonymous interlude *Respublica* was performed at Mary's court to celebrate, as the original full title says, "the most prosperous Reigne of our moste gracious Soveraigne, Quene Marye the first." In the interlude, acted by a company of children in London, the late enthroning of the monarchy of Catholic faith is viewed as the redemption of the hidden Truth by her father Time: "tyme trieth all and tyme bringeth truth to lyght / . . . veritee the daughter of sage old Father Tyme / Shewith all as yt ys bee yt virtue or cryme."[25]

As shown in table 6.4, it is clear that the playwright used this passage on Time for Time's own speech in *The Winter's Tale*, again implying that Perdita, daughter of Hermione, is Mary, daughter of Katherine, and that the play is celebrating the counter-reformation.

Both the Prologue to *Respublica* and the Prologue to Act 4 of *The Winter's Tale* begin by noting that *Time tries all*: in *Respublica*, "*time tries all* . . . be it virtue or crime"; in *The Winter's Tale*, "I . . . *try all*, both . . . / good and bad." In both, this is soon followed by a *Time-crime* couplet. EEBO confirms the match is unique.[26] Both Prologues end by addressing the audience in the second person with the *if-you-now* line. And, most significantly, both Prologues stress that Time rectifies mistakes: it turns *wrong* into *right* (*Respublica*) or *unfolds error* (*The Winter's Tale*)—and so will now end the oppressive acts of the reformation. It will "reforme th'abuses" (*Respublica*) and "o'erthrow law" (*The Winter's Tale*).[27]

In 5.1, a servant describes Perdita as one whose powers and charms are such that she could change the faith of all her subjects and "quench the zeal" of "professors" of other religions:

> This is a creature,
> Would she begin a sect, might quench the zeal
> Of all professors else, make proselytes
> Of who she but bid follow. (5.1.106–109)

Table 6.4.

Prologue to *Respublica*: Mary is Truth, the Daughter of Time	*The Winter's Tale*, the Speech of Time: Perdita is Truth, the Daughter of Time
Time tries all, and Time brings truth to light, that <u>wrong</u> may not ever still reign in place of right (ll. 27-28) Verity, the **daughter** of sage old father **Time**, shows all as it is, <u>be it virtue or crime</u>. (ll. 33-34) With whom anon is linked tranquility and peace to common weal's **joy** and perpetual increase (ll. 37-38) so for **good** England sake this present **hour** and day, In hope of her restoring from her late decay (ll. 45-46) . . . thank God and Rejoice That he hath sent **Mary** our Sovereign and Queen (ll. 48-49) <u>to reform th'abuses</u> which hitherto hath been. And that ills which long time have **reigned** <u>uncorrect</u>. shall now forever be redressed with effect. She is our most wise and worthy Nemesis, Of whom are play meaneth, t'amend that is amiss; Which to bring to pass, that she may have time and space, Let us, both young and old, to God commend her **grace**. **Now, if you** so please, I will go and hither send, That shall make **you** laugh well, **if you** abide th'end. (ll. 50–58)	**Time**: I, that please some, **try all**, both **joy** and terror Of **good** <u>and bad</u>, that makes and unfolds <u>error</u>, Now take upon me, in the name of **Time**, To use my wings. Impute it not a **crime** To me or my swift passage that I slide O'er sixteen years and leave the growth **untried** Of that wide gap, since it is in my power To <u>o'erthrow law</u> and in one self-born **hour** To plant and o'erwhelm custom. . . . To th' freshest things now **reigning** . . . I now name to you; and with speed so pace To speak of **Perdita**, now grown in **grace** Equal with wond'ring. What of her ensues I list not prophecy; but let **Time's** news Be known when 'tis brought forth. A shepherd's **daughter**, And what to her adheres, which follows after, Is th' argument of **Time**. Of this allow, **If** ever **you** have spent time worse ere **now**; If never, yet that **Time** himself doth say He wishes earnestly **you** never may. —4.1.1–9, 13, 23–32
[**Time-try all, time-crime, daughter, good, joy, grace, hour, reigned, if-you-now**]	[**Time-try all, Time-crime, daughter, good, joy, grace, hour, reigning, if-you-now**]
Isolated Correspondences	
Time tries all . . . Time Shows all as it is, <u>be it virtue or **crime**</u>	**Time**: I . . . **try all**, both **joy** and terror Of <u>good and bad</u>
Verity, the daughter of sage old Father **Time**, shows all as it is, <u>be it virtue or **crime**</u>	Now take upon me, in the name of **Time**, To use my wings. Impute it not a **crime**

(continued)

Table 6.4. *(continued)*

That <u>wrong</u> may not ever still reign in place of right . . . to reform th'abuses	that makes and unfolds <u>error</u> . . . To overthrow law . . . o'erwhelm custom
That he hath sent **Mary** our Sovereign and Queen . . . to God commend her **grace**	To speak of **Perdita**, now grown in **grace**
Now, **if you** so please	**If** ever **you** have spent time worse ere **now**

This is plainly religious language: *sect, zeal, professors, proselytes, follow* are all terms describing a princess with the power and desire to affect the spiritual transformation of a nation.

In 5.2, the playwright once more emphasizes Perdita as Truth, the daughter of Time—and does so with a news report of Perdita's return that follows a similar exchange in *Respublica* about news of the return of Verity (Mary). In both cases, it is made clear that the news of the return will bring glorious change to the land (see table 6.5).

Table 6.5.

Respublica on news of the return of Verity (Mary)	*The Winter's Tale* on news of the return of Perdita (Mary)
Adulation: O Noble **Lady** Respublica, well you be. Respublica: All shall be now, such **news** I have to me brought Adulation: I **hear** it told for **truth**. Policy, all will be nought. Respublica: **hearest** thou any joyful **news** abroad, or not? Adulation: yea, I have certain **news** which are both brim and hot, there is new stirred up a **lady** called **Verity** Respublica: Then am I all safe, and sure of prosperity . . . Avarice: Of which **Verity** was't, trow you, that they spake it? Adulation: Of the general **Verity**, <u>**Old Time's daughter**</u>. —*Respublica* 241–42	Here comes a gentleman that haply knows more.—The **news**, Rugero? Second Gentleman: Nothing but bonfires. The oracle is fulfilled; the King's **daughter** is found. Such a deal of wonder is broken out within this hour that ballad makers cannot be able to express it. Enter another Gentleman. Here comes the **Lady** Paulina's steward. He can <u>deliver</u> you more.—How goes it now, sir? This **news** which is called **true** is so like an **old** tale, that the **verity** of it is in strong suspicion. Has the King found his heir? Third Gentleman: Most **true**, if ever <u>**truth** were pregnant by circumstance</u>. That which **you hear** you'll swear you see, there is such unity in the proofs. —5.2.21–33
[**news, hear, verity, old, truth, lady, daughter**]	[**news, hear, verity, old, truth, lady, daughter**]

Again, in this exchange as well, scholars have observed the association of Perdita with Truth, the daughter of Time. Marion Wells remarks:

> The redemption of lost truth, in the person of Perdita, happens offstage and is reported by the courtiers in terms reminiscent of the original debate between Paulina and Leontes as to the "truth" of her parentage: "This news which is called true is so like an old tale that the verity of it is in strong suspicion" (5.2.27–29). The "news which is called true", is the lost daughter, whose true name is revealed only now, when the "argument of Time" has worked its magic. She is the lost truth (veritas) of the *veritas filia temporis* motto, abandoned when Leontes sets his face against the truth of Hermione's maternity.[28]

It would seem the reason the playwright is here paraphrasing a counter-reformation allegory— especially its celebration of Queen Mary and her promise to allow Catholics to return to their faith—is that *The Winter's Tale*, in its original form, was also a counter-reformation allegory and was making the same point. After all, when Time notes that "it is in my power / To o'erthrow law and in one self-born hour / To plant and o'erwhelm custom," the allusion, as we know from *Respublica*, is to the oppressive laws and Protestant customs of the reformation. This is also the theme of the last two acts of *The Winter's Tale*, with its celebration of Catholic festivities, miracle stories, and the return of a statue of a woman kept hidden in a chapel. Many, if not all, of these resemblances to descriptions of Mary during her coronation (as well as other blatantly Catholic features) are fossils of North's Marian version of the play.

PHILIP II: FLORIZEL, KING OF SICILY

As *The Winter's Tale* began as an allegory, North would have had to choose all the names of characters himself. For example, according to Geoffrey Bullough, the playwright borrowed Florizel's name from a heroic knight in *Amadis de Gaul*, in which "two statues are substituted for living persons." Bullough also notes: "No English translation is known before 1693, but the hero's name is Florisel; he becomes a shepherd to woo his mistress; there is a good deal of pastoral talk and atmosphere; and she accompanies him on his travels."[29]

Gracing Philip's character with the name of a protagonist in *Amadis de Gaul* is a perfect fit. As noted by Teofilo F. Ruiz, *Amadis* was one of the Sicilian prince's "favorite books," and Philip even liked performing as the knights of the Spanish romance:

> Philip II's love for the Amadis of Gaul with its fantastic plot(s) helps explain his youthful enthusiasm for the running of the ring . . ., an old medieval test of equestrian skills. . . . These performances served as a prelude to the great and

rightly celebrated festivals and tournament hosted by Mary of Hungary at her palace at Binche (Bins), where portions of the *Amadis of Gaul* were performed, with Philip as one of the main knightly protagonists in the reenactment.[30]

At the time of his betrothal to Mary, Philip was embroiled in a war against the Ottomans in the Mediterranean and particularly against his Turkish counterpart, Turgut Re'is. Referred to by Francesco Balbi as "uncrowned King of the Mediterranean," Turgut was a fierce and respected North African ruler and Naval Commander of Greek descent. The Italian war (1551–59) that pitted the brothers Hapsburg against the French-Ottoman alliance began in earnest with Turgut's 1551 siege and then conquest of Tripoli. Spain had first conquered the Libyan outpost more than forty years earlier, in 1510. Then, twenty years later, Charles V entrusted it to the Knights of Malta, a military order from the island just south of Sicily. Mercenaries from both Sicily and Calabria, located on the southern tip of Italy on the other side of the Sicilian strait, joined with the Knights in defense of the city, but they were all captured and killed by Turgut during his successful siege. Libya then became an important outpost for Turgut's raids on Italian port cities. From Tripoli, Turgut led the Ottoman fleet in attacks on Licata in Sicily and then Calabria, in 1555.

Philip II was the Catholic hope for the Mediterranean; even when he ended the conflict with France in 1559, this former Prince of Sicily was still intent on recapturing Libya from Turgut. In 1559, he sent a fleet to accomplish the task but was overwhelmed at the battle of nearby Djerba in May of 1560. This date is important as it is the *terminus ad quem* for any rational claim that a Sicilian ruler may have been involved in a conflict with Libya.

North, of course, was well aware of these tensions. In his journal, he refers to an attack by Turgut. In the entry for Augsburg (23–24 July), North even mentions that Ferdinand did "desire aid of the Germans against the Turks, who were already entered into Calabria." "The Turk" who had captured Calabria was Turgut.

Florizel, like Philip II, also appears to have been involved in a conflict with a fierce Mediterranean warrior and Governor of Libya—referred to as "the warlike Sinalus" in the play. When he has to make up a story about Perdita's background for the sake of Leontes, Florizel claims he met her while he was in Libya and that she is Sinalus's daughter. This reconciliation of formerly hostile countries—Libya and Sicily—through the marriage of the children of their respective rulers foreshadows the ending of *The Winter's Tale*, in which Bohemia and Sicily are reconciled through the marriage of princess and prince. Importantly, linking the warlike Sinalus with Turgut once again exposes Florizel as Philip II.

The playwright adds other details supporting this identification. Florizel speculates on being "crowned the most imperial monarch" (4.4.372), which is a fitting description of Philip II after his marriage to Mary. Indeed, as Thomas James Dandelet observes, "Philip II was first and foremost an imperial monarch."[31] Leontes also says to Florizel, "You have a *holy* father" (5.1.170). Philip II's father, Charles V, was the Holy Roman Emperor.

CAMILLO AS SIR THOMAS MORE

Just as various scholars have noticed the resemblances between Katherine and Hermione—and Leontes and Henry VIII—still others have stressed similarities between Sir Thomas More and Camillo.[32] The representation seems fairly clear, as Camillo, like More, represents the honest, anti-divorce counselor who is willing to face execution rather than lie about his belief in the queen's innocence. As Leslie O'Dell writes:

> Can we find Sir Thomas More-like characters in Shakespeare's plays? I have always wondered about Camillo, the advisor of the jealous and paranoid Leontes in *The Winter's Tale* . . . A few of the correspondences line up strikingly: Camillo is the trusted confidant of a king who puts his queen on public trial for adultery. Camillo must choose between his loyalty to his monarch and his personal honor. More made just such a choice, in favor of private belief over loyal service, and King Henry executed not one but two wives for adultery.[33]

More had followed in Wolsey's footsteps, succeeding the Cardinal as Lord Chancellor in 1529. Wolsey, like More after him, had also hoped to stop Henry VIII from breaking with Rome and marrying Anne Boleyn. It is likely that the playwright added some elements of Wolsey to the characterization of Camillo too; thus Leontes' trusty advisor becomes a conflation of Henry VIII's pro-Catholic advisors. Again, we find many pointed comments helping to secure identification—as when Leontes describes Camillo as both counselor and priest:

> I have trusted thee, Camillo,
> With all the nearest things to my heart, as well
> My chamber councils, wherein, **priest**like, thou
> Hast cleansed my bosom. (1.2.234–37)

The lines stress Camillo's dual role as political advisor and Catholic religious authority—a priest who can absolve sin in his role as confessor. The lines also seem to target More and Wolsey, both priest-like figures. In *Henry VIII*, Wolsey is referred to multiple times as "priest" (2.2.20, 3.2.253, 277).

The excessive stressing of Camillo's honesty would, of course, point at Thomas More, who was willing to face the axe rather than sacrifice one jot of his legendary honesty. North appears to have gotten the name Camillo from Camillo Stanga, "a very honest gentleman," whom he met just outside of Mantua. In the journal, the honest Camillo appears in a sequence of entries (23–25 April) and remarkable experiences also plainly linked to *The Winter's Tale*.

HENRY VIII AS LEONTES

As the playwright deliberately crafted the passages on Hermione and Perdita after ones related to Katherine and Mary, he did the same with Leontes and Henry VIII. Indeed, as shown in Table 6.6, each king, suffering similar at-

Table 6.6

The King in *Henry VIII*	The King in *The Winter's Tale*
Go thy ways, Kate: **That man** i' **the world** who shall report he has **A better wife**, let him in nought be trusted, For speaking false in that: thou art, alone, If thy rare qualities, **sweet** gentleness, Thy meekness **saint-like**, **wife**-like government, Obeying in commanding, and thy parts Sovereign and pious else, could **speak** thee out, The queen of earthly queens: she's noble born; And, like her true nobility, she has Carried herself towards me. —2.4.130–40	Cleomenes: Sir, you have done enough, and have performed A **saint-like** sorrow. . . . Leontes: Whilst I remember Her and her virtues, I cannot forget My blemishes in them, and so still think of The wrong I did myself; which was so much That heirless it hath made my kingdom and Destroyed the **sweet'st** companion that e'er **man** Bred his hopes out of. . . . Paulina: Too true, my lord. **If** one by one you wedded **all the world**, Or from the all that are took something good To make a perfect woman, she you killed Would be unparalleled. Leontes: Thou **speak'st** truth. No more such wives, therefore, **no wife**. One worse, And **better** used, would make her **sainted** spirit Again possess her corpse —5.1.1–2, 6–12, 55–58
[man i' the world, speak, saint-like wife-like, sweet, better]	[man, all the world, saint-like, sainted, wife, speak, sweet'st, better]

tacks of conscience, praises his queen in precisely the same manner, stressing that she is *sweet, saint-like*, without equal, and that no *man* in *the world* had a better *wife*.

In the midst of these same passages, Leontes notes that if he were to marry again, the ghost of Hermione "would incense me / To murder her I married" (5.1.61–62). Again, this would seem a pointed allusion to Henry VIII, who does marry Anne Boleyn and then has her executed.

Both Leontes and Henry VIII also believe that their fail of issue is the result of God's judgment due to wrongs they have committed—and that it has left their kingdoms without an heir and in danger. Notice the similarity of language, as laid out in table 6.7.

Table 6.7.

King in *Henry VIII*	Leontes in *The Winter's Tale*
Hence I took a thought This was a judgment on me that **my kingdom**, Well worthy the best **heir** o'th' world, should not Be gladded in't by me. Then follows that I weighed the **danger** which my realms stood in By this my **issue's fail**, and that gave to me Many a groaning throe. —2.4.191–97	I cannot forget My blemishes in them, and so still think of The wrong I did myself; which was so much That **heirless** it hath made **my kingdom** . . . Dion: . . . You pity not the state nor the remembrance Of his most sovereign name, consider little What **dangers** by His Highness' **fail of issue**, May drop upon his **kingdom** and devour Incertain lookers-on. —5.1.7–10, 25–29
[my kingdom, issue's fail, heir, danger]	[my kingdom, fail of issue, heir, dangers]

As suggested by the correspondences outlined above, *The Winter's Tale* is an allegory on the life of Queen Mary, beginning with Henry VIII's trial of her mother, Katherine, and ending with Mary's triumphant return to power and marriage to the former Prince of Sicily, Philip II. Indeed, reading North's early play without understanding it as a *drama à clef* and thinking of it as just a fairytale with no deeper political purpose is like reading *Animal Farm* and believing the same thing. Indeed, it is worse. George Orwell provided a rather generalized and blurred picture of the Russian revolution in his animal fable. The allusions in *The Winter's Tale* include far more peculiar details, even to the extent of reproducing historical speeches, sometimes including a line-by-line paraphrase. Once one knows the story that the tragicomedy is retelling—along with the details of North's trip to Italy—everything makes sense.

Here, we have focused on the historical features of *The Winter's Tale*. But it is also the case that the most surreal and novel aspects of the play—those involving the painted statues of Giulio Romano, the obvious reverence for the Virgin Mary, and the miraculous resurrection—also derive from North's trip to Rome, especially his visit to Mantua.

NOTES

1. Darryll Grantley, "*The Winter's Tale* and Early Religious Drama," *Comparative Drama* 20.1 (1986): 17–37; 34.
2. Richard Burt, *Licensed by Authority: Ben Jonson and the Discourses of Censorship* (Ithaca: Cornell University Press, 1993), 95.
3. John Pitcher, Introduction to *The Winter's Tale*, ed. John Pitcher (London: Arden Shakespeare, 2014), 373–74.
4. David Kaula, "Autolycus's Trumpery," *Studies in English Literature, 1500–1900* 16 (1976): 287–303.
5. John Pitcher, Introduction to *The Winter's Tale*, 100.
6. See, for example, Bette Talvacchia, "The Rare Italian Master and the Posture of Hermione in *The Winter's Tale*," *Literary Interpretation Theory* 3.3 (1992): 163–74.
7. See, for example, Rita Severi, "Art in Shakespeare: Giulio Romano and Giovan Paolo Lomazzo," in *Art in Shakespeare and Other Essays* (Bologna: Pàtron Editore, 2018), 11–56.
8. See, for example, B. J. Sokol, *Art and Illusion in "The Winter's Tale"* (Manchester: Manchester University Press, 1994), 109–12.
9. Leonard Barkan, "'Living Sculptures': Ovid, Michelangelo, and *The Winter's Tale*," *ELH* 48.4 (1981): 639–67; 655.
10. Ros King, *"The Winter's Tale": A Guide to the Text and the Play in Performance* (Basingstroke: Palgrave-Macmillan, 2009), 85.
11. Phebe Jensen, "Singing Psalms to Horn-Pipes: Festivity, Iconoclasm, and Catholicism in *The Winter's Tale*," *Shakespeare Quarterly* 55.3 (2004): 279–306; 281.
12. Ruth Vanita, "Mariological Memory in *The Winter's Tale* and *Henry VIII*," *Studies in English Literature, 1500-1900* 40.2 (2000): 311–37; 320.
13. Jonathan Bate, "Shakespeare's Islands," in *Shakespeare and the Mediterranean: The Selected Proceedings of the International Shakespeare Association World Congress, Valencia, 2001*, ed. Tom Clayton, Susan Brock, and Vicente Forés (Newark: University of Delaware Press, 2004), 300.
14. Maximilien Misson, *A New Voyage to Italy. With Curious Observations on Several Other Countries; As Germany; Switzerland; Savoy; Geneva; Flanders; and*

Holland. Together, With Useful Instructions for those who shall Travel thither. In Four Volumes. Vol. Part 1. (London: R. Bonwicke, Ja. Tonson, W. Freeman, Tim. Godwin, J. Walthoe, M. Wotton, S. Manship, B. Tooke, J. Nicholson, R. Parker, and R. Smith, 1714), 173.

15. See, for example, *Library of Universal History, Volume VI: Mediæval History—Continued*, ed. Israel Smith Clare (New York and Chicago: Union Book Company, 1906), 1989.

16. *The Life of Cardinal Wolsey. By George Cavendish, His Gentleman Usher*, ed. John Holmes (London: Rivingtons, 1852). Quotations from Cavendish's manuscript in this chapter follow this edition.

17. This is obviously an example of convenient mythmaking involving the legendary Arthur. Indeed, Ferdinand's grandfather, Maximillian I, had paid the German artist Peter Vischer the Elder to cast the statue of King Arthur in 1513, eight years before Ferdinand's marriage to Anna. See Martin Biddle, "The Painting of the Round Table," in *King Arthur's Round Table: An Archaeological Investigation*, ed. Martin Biddle (Woodbridge: The Boydell Press, 2000), 425–73; 467.

18. After the Peace of Augsburg, Ferdinand immediately started placing Catholics in powerful positions in Bohemia. But by that time, too many Bohemians had already become Protestant, and neither Mary's nor Ferdinand's efforts were successful. See Mark A. Lamport, ed., *Encyclopedia of Martin Luther and the Reformation, Volume 2* (London: Rowman and Littlefield, 2017), 186.

19. Jonathan Bate, "Shakespeare's Islands," 289–307; 300.

20. Jonathan Bate, Introduction to *The Winter's Tale*, ed. Jonathan Bate and Eric Rasmussen (Basingstroke: Macmillan Publishers, 2009), 7, 9.

21. Beatrice Saunders, *Henry the Eighth* (London: Redman, 1963), 56.

22. Gordon McMullan, Introduction to *King Henry VIII (All Is True)*, ed. Gordon McMullan (London: The Arden Shakespeare, 2000), 125.

23. Michael Dobson, as quoted in Gordon McMullan, Introduction to *King Henry VIII (All Is True)*, 129. See Michael Dobson and Nicola J. Watson, *England's Elizabeth: An Afterlife in Fame and Fantasy* (Oxford: Oxford University Press, 2002).

24. Gordon McMullan, ed., *King Henry VIII (All Is True)*, 301.

25. Soji Iwasaki, "*Veritas Filia Temporis* and Shakespeare," *English Literary Renaissance* 3.2 (1973): 249–63; 251.

26. An EEBO search for *time* FBY *try all* FBY.50 *time* FBY.50 *crime* yields only *The Winter's Tale*.

27. Quotations from *Respublica* are from the Prologue to *Respublica, A.D. 1553: A Play on the Social Condition of England at the Accession of Queen Mary*," ed. Leonard A. Magnus (London: Kegan Paul, Trench, Trubner, 1905). Spelling and punctuation have been modernized.

28. Marion Wells, "Mistress Taleporter and the Triumph of Time, Slander and Old Wives' Tales in *The Winter's Tale*," *Shakespeare Survey 58* (2005): 247–59; 257.

29. Geoffrey Bullough, *Narrative and Dramatic Sources of Shakespeare, Vol. 8, Romances: "Cymbeline," "The Winter's Tale," "The Tempest"* (London: Routledge & Kegan Paul/New York: Columbia University Press, 1976), 133.

30. Teofilo F. Ruiz, *A King Travels: Festive Traditions in Late Medieval and Early Modern Spain: An Introduction* (Princeton: Princeton University Press, 2012), 22–23.

31. Thomas James Dandelet, *The Renaissance of Empire in Early Modern Europe* (New York: Cambridge University Press, 2014), 146.

32. Thomas Merriam, "Did Shakespeare Model Camillo in *The Winter's Tale* on Sir Thomas More?" *Moreana* 19.75/76 (1982): 91–101; Peter Milward "The Morean Counsellor in Shakespeare's Last Plays," *Moreana* 27.103 (1990): 25–32.

33. Leslie O'Dell, *Shakespearean Scholarship: A Guide for Actors and Students* (Westport, CT: Greenwood Press, 2002), 100.

Chapter Seven

The Winter's Tale and Mantua

THE STATUES OF GIULIO ROMANO

In the last weeks of April 1555, North traveled from Milan to Mantua with two memorable stopovers: the first in Cremona, where the lords attended a wedding between an Italian count and "the sister of Signior **Camillo** Stanga, a **very honest** gentleman" (23 April) and the second at the chapel of Santa Maria delle Grazie (Saint Mary of Grace) at nearby Curtatone. Once in Mantua, North enjoyed a banquet with Duke Gonzaga, his extended family, and the beautiful entourage of the duchess at the Palazzo Te. All three of these visits—Cremona, the chapel, and the banquet at Mantua—occurred between 23 and 25 April, and they inspired some of the best-known elements of *The Winter's Tale* and, especially, many of the uncanny images of the last two acts.

In Act 5 of *The Winter's Tale*, the Third Gentleman reports the existence of the eerily lifelike painted statue of Hermione, which is then unveiled and comes to life in the last scene. The Third Gentleman states that the statue was created by the Mantuan artist Giulio Romano:

> The Princess hearing of her mother's statue, which is in the keeping of Paulina—a piece many years in doing and now newly performed by that rare Italian master, Julio Romano, who, had he himself eternity and could put breath into his work, would beguile Nature of her custom, so perfectly he is her ape; he so near to Hermione hath done Hermione that they say one would speak to her and stand in hope of answer . . . (5.2.95–103)

Scholars have struggled to explain how Shakespeare could have known about Giulio Romano's work. Some have argued that the description required that

Shakespeare (or one of his acquaintances) had taken a trip to Mantua, with some also suggesting a side trip to nearby Curtatone, to the chapel of Santa Maria delle Grazie (Saint Mary of Grace). The chapel features the tomb of Baldassare Castiglione and his wife, Hippolita: Giulio had designed its red marble monument, making sure to emphasize Castiglione's fixation on resurrection. On top of the mausoleum, as Peter Fane-Saunders notes, "Romano has located a statue of the resurrected Christ who steps forth from the grave, displaying his wounds, to proclaim his victory over death . . . The idea of spiritual ascent and rebirth was close to Castiglione's heart . . ."[1] Giulio's paintings of various resurrection scenes also decorate the ceiling of the chapel, which in turn is relevant to Hermione's own miraculous resurrection. Along the length of one wall of the chapel and just above the heads of visitors runs a series of raised wooden recesses—like tiny balconies—that present colorful wax and papier-maché sculptures of tortured Catholics, whom the Virgin Mary, it was alleged, had miraculously saved from death. Just above that row, the recesses include painted sculptures of Italian noblewomen, their hands in a prayer pose, not unlike the Virgin Mary herself (see figure 7.1).

Figure 7.1. The painted wax and papier-maché figures of tortured Catholics saved by the Virgin Mary, Santa Maria delle Grazie.

In an important article on the allusion to Giulio Romano in *The Winter's Tale*, the Italian scholar Rita Severi discusses Hermione's statue and the apparent relevance of this Curtatone chapel:

> The statue of Hermione, in its lonely niche, hidden by a curtain, is to be seen as a monument in honor and memory of the dead queen. It's a funerary, polychromatic statue . . . Statues like this one had been popular for some time in Italy, in the naturalistic *tableaux* that adorned the Sacri Monti. Even in Mantua, at the time of Giulio Romano, not far from its center, it was possible to see polychromatic statues reproduced in wax, other different materials, and papier-maché. In the Gonzaga church of Santa Maria delle Grazie in Curtatone the walls above the chapels and the space above the portal support what is called "un'impalcata," a series of wooden niches that contain impressive life-size effigies, elaborately dressed, . . . each an ex-voto, to remind onlookers of the many faithful who received God's grace. . . . These ex-voto exhibited in a way to astonish the visitor, like so many figures from the museum of Madame Tussaud, transform the church into a spectacular, theatrical place. . . .[2]

Severi notes the suggestion that Shakespeare may have seen Giulio's works first-hand:

> Although there's no documentation whatsoever, Arthur Lytton Sells wrote favorably of the probability that William Shakespeare could have travelled to Italy in the years 1592–94, the so-called "lost years" in the Bard's biography, when London was infested by the plague. During that hypothetical voyage Shakespeare could have admired the particular talent and absolute greatness of the artist directly in Mantua.[3]

Severi also addresses the possibility that another English traveler had been there and visited this chapel near Mantua, reporting that Thomas Hoby, who was to translate Castiglione's *Il Cortegiano* in 1561, "was in Mantua in 1549 and again in 1554 and might have gone to 'le Grazie' to pay him homage." But in a footnote, she adds, "Hoby visits the outskirts of Mantua and mentions the lakes and marshes, but says nothing about the Sanctuary of the Beata Vergine Maria delle Grazie."[4]

Severi describes the polychrome statues in the gallery of the chapel as set up "to astonish the visitor" and "transform the church into a spectacular, theatrical place. . . ."[5] That was similar to North's appraisal of the gallery in the chapel, "where is the greatest offering in those parts of Italy" (25 April). And this in turn is echoed by Leontes, who describes the gallery in the chapel with the polychrome statue of Giulio Romano: it was "not without much content in many singularities" (5.2.9–12).

Here is the description in North's journal:

> We passed also through a town named Redondesco and by **Our Lady** of Mantua, **her chapel** [Santa Maria **delle Grazie**], **where is the greatest offering in those parts of Italy**. There they show **pictures** [i.e., statues] of men, which she [Mary] **preserved** (as they say) that were stricken into the brains and hearts

and in at the backs with swords and daggers and where is also **such wonderful works of wax as I never saw the like** before. (25 April)

In the margin, North writes "miracles" with a vertical line demarcating this section. His reference to the chapel as "Our Lady" underscores his awareness of the chapel's focus on the Virgin. Note also that North describes not only the tortured men on the walls whom Mary had saved from death but other lifelike works of wax as well. It is possible that some of these were Giulio Romano's works and were taken during the Sack of Mantua in 1630.

In her 2018 book, *Art in Shakespeare and Other Essays*, Severi includes a discussion of North's travel journal, *The Winter's Tale*, and Giulio Romano's artwork, stating that she has not read any other account of the interior of Santa Maria delle Grazie from the era.[6] Yet for his entry on the afternoon of 25 April, one day after leaving the ***very honest Camillo*** in Cremona (reminiscent of the extremely *honest Camillo* in *The Winter's Tale*), North not only provides such a description; he even expresses awe at its lifelike wax statues.

Other evidence confirms that this particular church dedicated to Mary was indeed the inspiration for the climax of the play. The final scene, as already noted, takes place in a chapel and repeatedly alludes to the Virgin Mary. As Jill Delsigne observes:

> Hermione's animate statue recalls not only biblical and hermetic animations, but also the Catholic legends of weeping, bleeding, and moving statues (particularly of the Virgin Mary) . . . the Catholic traces remain in the setting unapologetically: a shrine in a "chapel" to the "sainted spirit" of a queen whose resurrection depends upon the "faith" of the living.[7]

Similarly, David N. Beauregard points out the obviously purposeful connection between the Hermione statue and the Virgin Mary: "two distinctive Roman Catholic gestures find expression: the shepherd makes the sign of the cross, and Perdita kneels before the statue of her mother and implores its blessing, just as one would kneel before a statue of the Virgin Mary."[8] Alice Dailey makes a similar point about the Mariolatry of this last scene: "Paulina's explanation and the manner in which Hermione's statue is housed and displayed suggest, as Darryll Grantley has argued, that Hermione is intended to figure the Virgin Mary, whose statues would have been venerated by the Catholic faithful."[9] And Grantley points out correspondences between Hermione and the Virgin Mary that appear throughout the play:

> [Hermione's] role in the story also has correspondences with the life of the Virgin Mary: she too is the bearer of a child in adverse circumstances, through the medium of whom redemption is brought about. Even the accusations of adultery bring to mind Mary's plight in all the extant Cycles in which her account of the

Annunciation is doubted by Joseph, who berates her for her alleged unfaithfulness until he is enlightened through a vision. It is likely that the mere presence of the pregnant Hermione on stage would have recalled to Shakespeare's contemporaries the images, which had commonly appeared in both drama and the visual arts, of the most famous pregnant woman of all.[10]

Given the topicality of Queen Mary's legalization of statues of the Virgin Mary in England, it is understandable why North would focus on these statue-filled chapels, especially ones dedicated to "Our Lady" and the supposed miracles she could enact. This is what Queen Mary wanted to bring back to England, and those Catholics who had hid their statues of the Virgin during the reformation would now be able to bring them out from behind the curtains once again. North also made sure to describe the figures of tortured saints that appeared on the wall of Santa Maria delle Grazie. One is being stretched with his arms over his head as though he were on the rack; another appears in a well that looks like a pot. North refers to now missing statues of men stabbed in the backs and heads with daggers. Each was supposedly preserved by Mary's supernatural interventions.

The playwright also mixes similar images of tortured saints with the play's demonstrably Catholic and miraculous dramaturgy. As Vanita observes:

> Leontes repeatedly accuses Paulina of witchcraft, an accusation commonly leveled against recusants. Accepting her status as rebel, Paulina demands to know what wheels, racks, fires, flaying, or boiling in leads or oils Leontes has for her. This list of what she calls "old or newer torture" (III.ii.177) recalls not only the tortures inflicted on heretics on both sides of the divide, but also the saints' stories. Saints were often depicted in paintings and statues with the instruments of their torture.[11]

Again, these lines are peculiarly relevant to Santa Maria delle Grazie or, as North calls her, "Our Lady." Phebe Jensen also makes an important point about Hermione and "Our Lady": "The final scene is saturated with Marian iconography, as Vanita has shown; the queen is several times referred to as 'Lady,' and although she is never 'Our Lady,' the worship of her statue provides the unspoken possessive, as does Perdita's fear that her actions will be held 'superstition . . .'"[12]

Jensen's argument is strong, but she misses an important comment that would strengthen the connection between Hermione and the Virgin Mary. Paulina, at one point, does indeed call the queen "**our gracious Lady**" (2.2.21), a frequent sobriquet for the Catholic matriarch. Joan of Arc uses the same words in *1 Henry VI*: "Heaven and **Our Lady gracious** hath it pleased / To shine on my contemptible estate" (1.2.74–75), and here the allusion to the Virgin Mary is unmistakable. Leontes also refers to her "**sainted** spirit"

(5.1.57). North's own use of "**Our Lady**" for **Santa** Maria delle **Grazie (Saint** Mary of **Grace)** fits perfectly with the language of the play: *sainted*, *Our Gracious Lady*.

Severi describes the figures of the tortured saints as being there "to remind onlookers of the many faithful who received God's grace."[13] North refers to Mary's interventions on their behalf as having "**preserved**" them (25 April). This is the term that Hermione uses twice to refer to both her daughter's and her own miraculous defiance of death, which she also associates with **graces** granted by God. The exchange also juxtaposes *Our* and *Lady*:

> Paulina: . . . Turn, good **lady**;
> **Our** Perdita is found.
> Hermione: You gods, look down
> And from your sacred vials **pour your graces**
> **Upon** my daughter's head!—Tell me, mine own.
> Where hast thou been **preserved**? Where lived? How found
> Thy father's court? For thou shalt hear that I,
> Knowing by Paulina that the oracle
> Gave hope thou wast in being, **have preserved**
> Myself to see the issue. (5.3.121–29)

North uses the term "**pictures**" for the lifelike painted statues. So too does the Clown in *The Winter's Tale*: "our kindred, are going to see the **Queen's picture**" (5.2.174–75). North also describes the wax figures as "**wonder**ful" and writes "**I never saw the like**" (25 April). Paulina describes Hermione's statue in similar terms:

> So her dead **likeness**, I do well believe,
> <u>Excels whatever yet you looked upon</u> . . .
> I like your silence; it the more shows off
> Your **wonder**. (5.3.15–16, 21–22)

From the church, North and the train traveled to Mantua, where the chapel of San Barbara housed Giulio Romano's tomb. The epitaph reads, in part:

Videbat Jupiter corpora sculpta pictaque Spirare, aedes mortalium aequarier coelo Julii virtute Romani.

[Jupiter **saw sculpted and painted statues breathe** and earthly buildings made equal to those in heaven by the skill of Julio Romano.]

In the nineteenth century, Karl Elze pointed out how similar this was to the Shakespearean description that Giulio Romano "could put **breath** into work."

Horace Howard Furness quotes him in the Variorum edition of *The Winter's Tale*: "'And more than this, his praise of Giulio wonderfully agrees with the second epitaph, in which truth to nature and to life is likewise praised as being Julio's chief excellence" (if he could put breath into his work,—*videbat Jupiter corpora spirare*).' Elze asks, "Is this chance?"[14]

Indeed, the dramatist continues to place emphasis on the fact that the statue appears to breathe—especially when discussing the skill of the sculptor:

> Leontes: . . . What was he that did make it? See, my lord,
> Would you not deem it **breathed**? . . .
> Polixenes: Masterly done. . . .
> Leontes: . . . Still, methinks,
> There is an air comes from her. What fine chisel
> Could ever yet cut **breath**? . . . (5.3.63–65, 77–79)

Elze's "Is this chance?" was rhetorical, concluding that this was convincing evidence that Shakespeare had traveled to Mantua and experienced the artistry of Giulio.

Thus, in the climax of *The Winter's Tale*, we have a lifelike painted *picture* (i.e., statue) of Giulio Romano in a chapel with a gallery of striking offerings, juxtaposed with allusions to *Our Lady*, the Sainted Virgin Mary, and tormented Catholics miraculously *preserved*. Clearly, as some scholars have already considered, the inspiration for this derives from that chapel decorated by Giulio Romano in Italy at Curtatone. And Thomas North is the only known Englishman, perhaps the only known person from this era, to have visited there and described its interior. He even focused on the very elements—the lifelike painted statues and images of tortured Catholics—that moved the dramatist. If, indeed, as many have suggested, Shakespeare got the idea of the lifelike statue of Giulio Romano from a visitor to Mantua—and particularly a visitor to Santa Maria delle Grazie—then surely we must turn our attention to North, who is the only available candidate of the Shakespeare era who can be documented as a visitor to this chapel.

Just prior to the Third Gentleman's description of Giulio Romano's abilities, the character talks about the queen's death: "*I* would fain *say, bleed tears, for I* am sure my *heart wept blood*" (5.2.89–91). As shown in table 7.1, this echoes the language of North's *Dial of Princes*.

EEBO confirms the rarity of these connections.[15] In other words, just before he appears to paraphrase Giulio Romano's epitaph and sets up the climactic scene that appears to reproduce another striking visual from North's trip to Italy, the Third Gentleman makes a comment that contains a mixture of Northern verbal quirks.

Table 7.1.

North's *Dial of Princes*	*The Winter's Tale*
it is necessary that the **heart weep blood**. —36 What wilt thou that **I say** more unto thee? They **wept** for that they died, and I weep daily **tears of blood from my heart for** that I live. —760	I would fain **say**, **bleed tears**, **for I** am sure my **heart wept blood**. —5.2.89–91

PRAYING FOR A RESURRECTION BEFORE THE VIRGIN MARY

Santa Maria delle Grazie is not the only chapel described in North's journal. Indeed, in what is certainly the saddest entry, on 31 March, North describes a woman praying for the resurrection of a dead child "before the image of **Our Lady**" in a chapel in the town of St. André in the rugged and frozen Alps:

> I, coming into a church, about four a clock at afternoon, spied a young child lying dead upon a board before the image of **Our Lady, and** an old woman sitting, watching and **praying** by it, having also a tallow candle burning and a great many of peas and beans in a little tray, the which she had offered unto **Our Lady**. I asked her in French what she meant to do. And she made me answer again that the child was born dead and that she **looked for life of it**, or at the least to burst out a **bleeding** in some place of the body. And thus they do for the space of 15 days together until it stink. If it be so that it **bleed**, although it receive not **life**, it is christened; if not, then it is cast into the river.

North originally wrote in the margin for this entry: "A vain superstition about a child born dead." But he crosses the entire comment out because he does not like his use of the word *vain*, which would dismiss the superstition as *worthless* or *futile*. Beneath it, he substitutes "A ***fond*** **superstition** about a dead born child." This change from *vain* to *fond* adds a connotation about affection, now describing the belief as a *foolishly tender* one. In *Henry VIII*, Queen Katherine, the real-life model for Hermione, also places these words together as she testifies to her constant love and faithfulness to the king:

> Have I with all my full affections
> Still met the King, loved him next heav'n, obeyed him,
> Been, out of **fondness superstitious** to him (3.1.129–31)

North's journal passage comes in the midst of a series of entries describing the group's hazardous journey through the stormy Alps, with the roaring river, engorged by snow-melt, and the perpetual winter blizzard. The day prior, 30 March, he wrote that Saint-Jean-de-Maurienne "standeth very **barrenly** upon the river of Arc, the which falling from the **mountains** is so swift and maketh so great a noise that it is able to make a man deaf . . ." The rugged journey is broken up only by scenes of famine, death, and the occasional lonely chapels. On 1 April, North and his train slowly trudged "over a great mountain" amid others of "inestimable height" with "great rain and snow" and "the snow falling continually and thick." The rough conditions continued the day after: "By the way I did see a poor man lie almost drowned in the snow, making round balls of snow and eating of them for very hunger" (2 April). At the top of this mountain was "La Chapelle de Trancizes [Transis] (to wit, the chapel of the dead) . . . this chapel lieth full of dead men's skulls that have died upon that mountain for extreme cold and other misfortunes, and there seemeth to be more than **1000** persons" (2 April). Leaving the chapel, he again stresses the blizzards and perpetual winter:

> We had no other ground to go on but only snow that was but 2 foot broad and hardened with the continual frost that is there almost always . . . The very same day that we passed over this mountain, there were 4 persons drowned by going a little out of the way; we were in the more hazard by reason of the great wind that blew and the abundance of snow that fell so fast from the elements that one of us could not see another, being but a small way asunder, and such was all the way on the plain of the hill. (2 April)

Evidently, the severity of the trip to these Alpine chapels seemed to consecrate the journey and increase the chances that one's prayers would be heard:

> Upon the north side of Susa is a mountain called Rochemelone, by estimation 10 leagues high, upon the top whereof standeth a chapel of Our Lady of Niges [Notre Dame des Nieges/Our Lady of the Snows], the which was built by a Jew that made his vow: he would build a chapel upon the top of the highest mountain in Europe . . . the Duke of Bourbon went thither before he went to the sacking of Rome, to offer up his harness there to **Our Lady** of Niges. It was so high that he made 2 days journey to the very top of it. (2 April)

The relevant images of North's trip are a woman, her dead child beside her, praying "before the image of **Our Lady**" for fifteen days, as "she looked for the life of it"; North's allusion to her supplication as a ***fond superstition***; the perpetual winter and blizzards; the chapels and towns that sit ***barrenly*** in the ***mountains***; the starving man eating snow for "the very hunger"; the ***thousand*** skulls in the chapel of the dead; and the idea that the prayers at the top of these mountains are more likely answered. All of this imagery is repeated by Paulina, the symbol of the Catholic church:

> Paulina: I say she's **dead**. I'll swear't. If word nor oath
> Prevail not, go and see. <u>If you can bring</u>
> <u>Tincture or luster in her lip, her eye,</u>
> <u>Heat outwardly or breath within</u>, I'll serve you
> As I would do the gods. But, O thou tyrant!
> Do not repent these things, for they are heavier
> Than all thy woes can stir. Therefore betake thee
> To nothing but despair. <u>A **thousand** knees</u>
> <u>Ten thousand years together, naked, fasting,</u>
> <u>Upon a **barren mountain,** and still winter</u>
> <u>In storm perpetual,</u> could not move the gods
> To look that way thou wert. (3.2.203–14)

Everything is there: the group praying on the "**barren mountain**, and still winter / In storm perpetual"—which can only refer to a chapel in the Alps in this continental play—the hunger or fasting, the *thousand* who have made the rigorous trek, then take to their knees, praying continuously for 10,000 years—a wild exaggeration of the St. André woman who prayed continuously for fifteen days—and all for the resurrection of a departed loved one. Paulina even describes looking for the signs of life in the recently dead—as the St. André woman looked for the life of the child: "<u>If you can bring / Tincture or luster in her lip, her eye, / Heat outwardly or breath within</u>." Paulina's comment clearly foreshadows the climactic chapel scene in the play in which Perdita kneels and prays before a statue of a symbol of Mary, resulting in a resurrection:

> Perdita: And give me leave,
> And **do not say 'tis superstition, that**
> **I kneel and then implore her blessing. Lady,**
> **Dear Queen**, that ended when I but began,
> Give me **that hand of yours to kiss**. . . .
> Leontes: . . . See, my lord,
> Would you not deem it **breathed**? and that those veins
> Did verily bear **blood**?
> Polixenes: Masterly done.
> The very **life** seems warm upon her **lip**.
> Leontes: The fixture of her **eye** has motion in't . . .
> Paulina: . . . If you can behold it,
> I'll make the statue move indeed, descend
> And take you by the hand. But then you'll think—
> Which I protest against—I am assisted

By wicked powers.
Leontes: What you can make her do
I am content to look on, what to speak
I am content to hear; for 'tis as easy
To make her speak as move.
Paulina: It is required
You **do awake your faith**. Then all stand still.
On; those that think it is **unlawful business**
I am about, let them depart.
Leontes: Proceed.
No foot shall stir.
Paulina: Music, awake her; strike!
  'Tis time. Descend. Be stone no more. Approach.
Strike all that look upon with marvel. Come,
I'll fill your grave up. Stir, nay, come away,
Bequeath to death your numbness, for from him
Dear life redeems you.—You perceive she stirs.
          [*Hermione comes down.*]
Start not. Her actions shall be holy as
You hear my spell is lawful. . . .
Leontes: O, she's warm!
If this be magic, let it be an art
Lawful as eating. (5.3.42–46, 87–111)

All the lines in bold repeatedly confirm that this combination of miracle story and veneration of the Virgin Mary—all taking place in a chapel—are a brazen celebration of counter-reformation ideals and the legalization of beliefs and prayers before statues of the Virgin Mary. Prior to Marian rule, Protestants regarded such supplication to her image or stories of her supernatural capacities as "superstition." Indeed, North himself calls it that in the margin. The authorities also considered it the invocation of "wicked powers" and "unlawful business," but now, with Paulina's plea to "awake your faith," these Catholic traditions will once again be declared "lawful as eating." The conspicuous relevance of this scene to Catholicism and reformation acts is frequently noted. Vanita, who has unearthed so much of the religious relevance of the resurrection scene, explains:

> The word "superstition" had been highly charged for over half a century. It was the word invariably used to connote Catholic attachment to images, relics, and cults, whether cults of the saints or the cult of the dead, all condemned as idolatrous. Leontes follows Perdita's lead and wishes to kiss the statue. Traditional devotional practices of kneeling to statues and kissing them had been expressly forbidden from Henry's time onward, although many people continued surreptitiously to perform these actions. All images to which people were in the

habit of kneeling, lighting candles, and otherwise performing devotion such as kissing and asking blessing, were ordered to be destroyed because their presence encouraged superstition. Statues reported to come alive and perform miracles were the targets of special mockery.[16]

This criminalization of Virgin Mary statues and stories of her alleged miracles was a consequential aspect of the reformation that Perdita's counterpart, Mary, was now seeking to reverse—an effort punctuated by North's embassy to Rome. Vanita observes that Protestants also argued that the alleged visions of the Virgin Mary were the result of "demonic powers": "In this way, Catholicism was connected with witchcraft and condemned for its pagan links, hence Paulina's repeatedly expressed fears that she will be accused of 'wicked powers.' Even when reassured by Leontes, she asks those to leave who think her magic unlawful."[17]

Perhaps most obviously, "awake your faith" is a call to the citizens of England to return to their faith in the old religion, a faith in miracle stories and the Virgin Mary and the virtue of Queen Katherine and the legitimacy of her daughter, Mary. Vanita notes: "The words also reverberate with double meaning—it is a sleeping or buried faith that would require awaking." And, importantly, Vanita stresses, this "last scene, protected by the veneer of its pagan setting, would resonate with the miracle plays, based on saints' lives, of a half-century earlier . . ."[18] Jensen likewise writes: "In Act 5, when both Leontes and Perdita must 'awake [their] faith' (5.3.95) in ritual transformation and the power of visual created images, the play recuperates epistemologies of Catholic worship branded as idolatrous in post-Reformation England."[19]

The repeated plea for the legalization of these practices and the final acquiescence to make them "lawful as eating" are a vigorous nod to the decriminalization of Catholicism and all its traditions under Mary. This was foreshadowed by Time in the Prologue to Act 4, which celebrates Perdita's return and her "power / To o'erthrow law" (4.1.7–8) and "make proselytes / Of who she but bid follow" (5.1.108–109). In other words, it celebrates the return of a banished princess who is changing the religion of a nation. Again, the reason *The Winter's Tale* seems so much like a counter-reformation allegory is that, in its original form, it was a counter-reformation allegory.

But why would Shakespeare, near the end of his career, write such a play after a fifty-year English tradition of Protestantism, a play that might unsettle an early Jacobean audience? If we exclude the comparatively minor feat of supernaturalism at the end of *Arden of Faversham*, Shakespeare appears to show no such reverence for Catholic miracles prior to *The Winter's Tale* and even appears to mock them in such undeniably Protestant works as *1 Henry VI* with its attack on Joan of Arc. This question has so flummoxed scholars, particularly with regard to Hermione's coming back to life, that many do not even believe Shakespeare meant to suggest that a resurrection actually occurred. They instead contend that Hermione never died, that Paulina lied about her death in 3.2, that the queen simply hid in Paulina's chapel for sixteen years, and that the final scene was just the dénouement of an extended, melodramatic hoax. And they argue this despite Hermione's reappearance to Antigonus in a ghostly vision. Editor John Pitcher provides an excellent point-counterpoint discussion of this very problem:

> Whatever it is, this offstage dream spectre is as real and necessary as any ghost in Shakespeare, and it proves, almost certainly we say, that Hermione is dead.
> Yet despite this, at the end of the play, a marvellous statue of the queen comes to life in Paulina's chapel (5.3.99–103). Common sense tells us that this is impossible. A woman can't literally die, reappear as a spirit and then be alive again. This is even more implausible than a statue becoming a living person. Surely we know the truth. Hermione, aided by Paulina, went into hiding in 3.2 . . . But if Hermione isn't dead, where did that creature in white come from, directing Antigonus, naming Perdita, and foretelling his death?[20]

How does Pitcher end up explaining this? He offers an ingenious solution that is similar to the way quantum physicists try to explain wave-particle duality and Schrödinger's Cat. Romance is filled with contradictions, so "Hermione, in romance, is and isn't dead."[21] Naturally, those who have studied Shakespeare's time would have to wonder who would ever believe that a woman praying on her knees in a chapel before a statue of a Mary-like figure could actually lead to the resurrection of a loved one. But those who have read North's journal know this answer: that poor Catholic woman of St. André did indeed believe exactly this, which is why she prayed for fifteen days before the Virgin Mary for just such a resurrection, and this is why North made it the climax of his play.

GIULIO ROMANO AND THE
PASTORAL FEAST OF THE LESSER GODS

In Mantua, North and the train met Duke Guglielmo Gonzaga, then seventeen years old, and his family, including the young duke's mother, Duchess Margaret Paleologa Gonzaga; the duke's sister, Isabella Gonzaga; the duke's aunt, Eleanora Gonzaga, Duchess of Urbino; and a "lady called Hippolita, one of the fairest ladies in the world" (25 April), presumably a relative.[22] The duke's father, Federico II Gonzaga (1500–1540), had commissioned Giulio Romano to design, build, and decorate the pleasure palace, the Palazzo Te, where they entertained visitors. Giulio had also adorned their traditional, sprawling residence, Palazzo Ducale, with his artwork.

Once they were situated at the old Palace, North and the ambassadors officially delivered the queen's letters to the Gonzagas at the Palazzo Te, where they enjoyed a banquet in the palace's famous dining room, where the duke wined and dined his noble visitors. Giulio Romano had painted a pastoral wedding feast of Cupid and Psyche around the walls of the room, with some relevant mythological scenes depicted in the arcing lunettes that touched the ceiling. The story of their courtship and the travails of Psyche appear in Lucius Apuleius's second-century Roman novel, *Metamorphoses* or *The Golden Ass*. Giulio's frescoes were also clearly the inspiration for the pastoral feast in *The Winter's Tale* (4.4).

The bucolic scene, though late in the North-Shakespeare play, introduces the young lovers Florizel and Perdita, who are destined to be engaged with the blessings of their royal fathers in the final scene. But this countryside sheep-shearing feast, with maidens and shepherds and the disguised king, clearly evokes images of their future wedding. As Florizel says to Perdita:

> . . . darken not
> The mirth o'th' feast. . . .
> Lift up your countenance as it were the day
> Of celebration of that nuptial which
> We two have sworn shall come. (4.4.41–42, 49–51)

At the opening of the scene, Florizel also notes that Perdita is dressed as the goddess Flora despite the fact that she is meant to shear sheep:

> These your unusual weeds to each part of you
> Do give a life; no shepherdess, but Flora
> Peering in April's front. This your sheepshearing
> Is as a meeting of the petty gods,
> And you the queen on't. (4.4.1–5)

Flora is one of the goddesses of time and the seasons, also known as the "Horae." Perdita humbly agrees: "and me, poor lowly maid, / Most goddess-like pranked up" (4.4.9–10). Later in the scene, she even behaves like Flora, handing guests flowers that symbolize the passing of time. To the elderly, she gives evergreens—"For you there's rosemary and rue; these keep / Seeming and savor all the winter long" (4.4.74–75). Polixenes responds, ". . . well you fit our ages / With flowers of winter" (4.4.77–78). Then she hands flowers to those of middle-age: "These are flowers / Of middle summer, and I think they are given / To men of middle age. You're very welcome" (4.4.106–108). For the youth, Perdita notes: "I would I had some flow'rs o'th' spring that might /

Become your time of day" (4.4.113–14). As she hands out flowers, she refers to various mythological figures: Proserpina with Dis, Juno, and Cytherea. Perdita tells Florizel she wants certain flowers: "To make you garlands of, and my sweet friend, / To strew him o'er and o'er!" (4.4.128–29) and imagines them with these garlands embracing and lying near a river: "like a bank for Love to lie and play on, . . . / quick and in mine arms" (4.4.130, 132).

Florizel, a prince, also explains away Perdita's concern that her station is too low for him, noting gods, taking the forms of beasts, have often loved mortal women. In the midst of this mythological imagery, the guests of the pseudo-wedding feast are then entertained by the dance of the twelve satyrs.

These are the picturesque details in 4.4 of *The Winter's Tale*, and, astonishingly, despite the multiplicity of images and the specificity of their elaborations, Giulio Romano had painted them all onto the walls of the Sala di Psyche in Palazzo Te, where the Gonzagas entertained North and the ambassadors. They were the focus of his frescoes.

Figure 7.2 shows the west wall of the room, depicting the pastoral feast that celebrates the wedding of Psyche to Cupid. This is the focus of the room and meant to represent the type of banquets that the Gonzagas would host within its walls. This is also what the feast of *The Winter's Tale* is supposed to look like. The end of the south wall shows the recently betrothed lying on a chaise longue, near the bank of a river. The pair are intertwined, and a winged lesser god is placing garlands on their heads.

Figure 7.3 provides a close-up of the center of the west wall. Sabine Poeschel describes the figures as two "charming horae" who "spread flowers,"[23] and it is the goddess Flora who is the Hora known for distributing flowers

Figure 7.2. Giulio Romano's *Banchetto rustico* on the west wall of Sala di Psyche in Palazzo Te, depicting the pastoral wedding feast with Flora and her attendants (Giulio Romano, 1526–28).

Figure 7.3. Detail of Flora and the satyrs, the focus of the west wall of Sala di Psyche, Palazzo Te (Giulio Romano, 1526–28).

symbolic of the passing seasons. Two satyrs watch them, and the walls around the Sala di Psyche contain depictions of numerous other satyrs.

The fresco closely resembles what Perdita should look like as she hands out flowers as "Flora Peering in April's front"—and the satyrs around Giulio Romano's Flora would serve as the model for the play's "dance of the satyrs."[24] Even the name of the west-wall fresco—*Banchetto rustico*—may have had influence: the word *rustic* appears in only three plays of the Shakespeare canon, including twice in *The Winter's Tale*—both times in this same pastoral scene (4.4.84, 718).

As Perdita discusses those flowers that symbolize youth, she says:

     . . . O Proserpina,
For the flow'rs now that, frighted, thou let'st fall
From Dis's wagon! (4.4.116–18)

On the west wall, directly above the depiction of Flora distributing flowers, are three lunettes, all relating to the Proserpina sub-plot. The lunette on the left, visible in figure 7.2, shows Proserpina with Dis (i.e., Pluto). Dis is holding his arm around her, and Proserpina is holding a jar of her own beauty. One of Psyche's ordeals was that she had to visit Hell and request the jar from Proserpina.

A stucco bas relief depicting the exact scene described in *The Winter's Tale* of Proserpine and Dis in the wagon appears in another room of the Palazzo Te, the Sala delle Aquile.

Perdita then also refers to both Juno and Cytherea:

> ... O **Proserpina**,
> For the flow'rs now that, frighted, thou let'st fall
> From **Dis's** wagon! Daffodils,
> That come before the swallow dares, and take
> The winds of March with beauty; violets dim,
> But sweeter than the lids of **Juno's** eyes
> Or **Cytherea's** breath; pale primroses,
> That die unmarried ... (4.4.116–23)

In one of the lunettes on the east wall, Psyche entreats Juno.

Cytherea, or Cythera, another name for Venus, appears in three scenes in the room, including the north wall, bathing with Mars. She also appears in the lunette just above this wall picture. The fresco depicts the second impossible task that Venus (Cythera) ordered for Psyche: she must retrieve wool from violent sheep. Hence, the playwright twice describes Perdita's duty as a sheep-shearer. While it should seem rather peculiar to mix Giulio Romano, the goddess Flora, Cythera, Proserpine, Dis, and sheep-shearing all at a bucolic wedding feast, both the Gonzaga banquet room and *The Winter's Tale* do just that.

Cythera is an alternative title for Venus because that is the name of the island where the goddess was born. This would have had special relevance to North. As Poeschel wrote about Gonzaga's new palace: "Thus the Palazzo Te, which is surrounded by water, is transformed into the kingdom of **Venus on the isle of Cythera**, where Federico Gonzaga takes on the part of Jupiter and his guests assist at the banquet as the Olympic Gods."[25] Recall Florizel's description of the rustic banquet with "Flora / Peering in April's front. This your sheep-shearing / Is as a meeting of the petty gods" (4.4.2–4), which is perhaps an even more accurate description of the frescoes of the banquet room than Poeschel's.

Finally, Florizel notes that his falcon brought them both together when he flew off onto her father's property. Perdita responds, "Now Jove afford you cause!" (4.4.16), thus crediting Jupiter (Jove) with the raptor's matchmaking. In the next few lines, Perdita expresses fear that Florizel's father might find them together—a prince with a shepherd's lass! Florizel counters that such disparate couplings are not uncommon and that even gods have seduced mortal women by taking animal form:

> ... The gods themselves,
> Humbling their deities to love, have taken
> The shapes of **beasts** upon them. **Jupiter**
> Became **a bull**, and bellowed; the green **Neptune**
> A ram, and bleated; and **the fire-robed god**,
> Golden **Apollo**, a poor humble swain,
> As I seem now. (4.4.25–31)

The east wall of the dining room is occupied by two large frescoes of such bestial liaisons. In one, Pasiphae, who has been made by Neptune to fall in love with a bull, is stepping into a cow suit in order to entice her future mate. In the other (see figure 7.4), Jupiter as half-serpent embraces Olympia as her husband, Philip of Macedon, tries to look on. Jupiter's eagle is complicit in

Figure 7.4. Fresco on the east wall of Sala di Psyche, Palazzo Te, of Jupiter as half-serpent embracing Olympia while her husband, Philip of Macedon, tries to look on (Giulio Romano, 1526–28).

their adultery, blinding the husband with a lightning bolt so he cannot witness their coupling.

Likewise, Florizel's falcon helped bring him to Perdita, who in turn credits Jupiter for the raptor's help with the affair and expresses dread at the thought of his father looking on:

> Perdita: . . . Even now I tremble
> To think your father by some accident
> Should pass this way as you did. Oh, the Fates!
> How would he look to see his work, so noble,
> Vilely bound up? (4.4.18–22)

Florizel immediately follows these allusions with his discussion of women having sex with Jupiter and Neptune as beasts. Also, as with the scene of Proserpine and Dis in the wagon, Jupiter's kidnapping of Europa as a bull appears in one of the four *stucco* scenes in the Sala delle Aquile of the Palazzo Te.

Florizel's final allusion describes "the fire-robed god, / Golden Apollo," who dressed as "a poor humble swain" in an effort to court mortal women. Pitcher notes that the allusion refers to Apollo's stint as a shepherd when he was banished from heaven.[26] Again, these references have peculiar relevance to Giulio Romano's frescoes of the Sala di Psyche.

In a different room of the Palazzo Te, on the ceiling of the Stanza del Sole (Room of the Sun), Apollo appears in a fiery red cape, driving his chariot of the sun. However, in Sala di Psyche, the fresco of the south wall (figure 7.5) shows golden-haired Apollo (sitting on the left) in his earthier role as a shepherd, enjoying the company of mortal women. He is naked except for a blue garment draped over his right shoulder and arm. And he has traded his celestial chariot for a staff. As Flora spreading flowers is perhaps the most prominent image of the west wall, the depiction of Apollo, now acting the part of the "humble swain," is a focus of the south wall.

If we look at the full picture of the south wall, we find an elephant and camel—and, indeed, a full train of beasts of burden and porters hauling sacks to the feast from the coast. The man at the table to Apollo's left has one of the large sacks of Mediterranean ingredients on his shoulder. In other words, the spice trade will furnish the goods for the rustic banquet.

This is also true with the rustic banquet in *The Winter's Tale*. The Clown is the one sent to purchase all the necessary goods, and his list comprises all foreign ingredients emblematic of the spice trade, and he is buying them by the sack-full:

> Let me see; what am I to buy for our sheepshearing feast? Three pound of **sugar**, five pound of **currants**, **rice**—what will this sister of mine do with rice?

Figure 7.5. South wall of Sala di Psyche, Palazzo Te, depicting the golden-haired Apollo, dressed as a shepherd, cavorting with mortal women (Giulio Romano, 1526–28).

But my father hath made her mistress of the feast, and she lays it on . . . I must have **saffron** to color the warden pies; **mace**; **dates**?—none, that's out of my note; **nutmegs**, seven; a race or two of **ginger**, but that I may beg; four pound of **prunes**, and as many of **raisins o'th' sun** . . . I must go **buy spices** for our sheep-shearing (4.3.36–40, 45–48, 114–15).

It is remarkable to note that this fabulous imagery of 4.4 in *The Winter's Tale* maps directly onto the Sala di Psyche of Palazzo Te in a nearly one-to-one correspondence. The attention of visitors is naturally drawn to the elaborate depictions of the banquet of the petty gods that take up the south and west walls. Gonzaga's guests were meant to feel they were a part of this Mediterranean feast, with Apollo as shepherd, Flora dressed like Spring, and satyrs all around. To whet the appetite, the frescoes show the importation of the sacks of the tastiest ingredients within the extensive reach of the spice trade. This, in and of itself, is a remarkably precise description of the Sicilian, seaside banquet of Perdita and Florizel, who are dressed as Flora and Apollo, who are entertained by a dance of satyrs, and whose feast is furnished with sacks of spices and such: currants, rice, mace, dates, nutmegs, saffron, ginger, prunes, and raisins. Appearing on the other walls and lunettes in Gonzaga's banquet room are Proserpine and Dis, Juno, Cythera, and the legends of Jupiter and Neptune-inspired bestiality. This too finds mention in this same scene in what would appear to be one of the most extensive and detailed examples of ekphrasis in the canon. And all this occurs within a conspicuously Mantuan play that famously praises the artistic prowess of Giulio Romano.

Perhaps even more remarkably, North enjoyed this pagan banquet of the Gonzagas on the evening after a visit to a chapel dedicated to the Virgin Mary and adorned with images of resurrection. Santa Maria delle Grazie was also decorated by Giulio, and the young journalist praises the depictions of its lifelike painted statues and Mary's miracles of preservation. And this occurs right after a wedding involving a *very honest Camillo*. Astonishingly, this unique combination of Catholic Mariolotry, pagan mythology, and Renaissance artistry describes all the high points of the three-day leg of North's journey from 23 to 25 April. And these are also the most conspicuous and widely discussed features of the last two acts of *The Winter's Tale*.

There also may be some added significance to the fact that *The Winter's Tale*, as with the art of Giulio Romano, conflates allusions to classical gods fathering extraordinary children with the story of the Virgin Mary. The point: maidens impregnated by gods is a classical Roman motif. It is all part of a gorgeous, operatic Mediterranean mythology, and one can draw a straight line from the idea of Roman gods impregnating mortal women to produce worldly kings to a Christian God doing precisely the same thing.

One of the main purposes of young North's play was to ask the audience—including the cynics like himself—for a gracious suspension of disbelief. He wanted to make the miracle stories seem romantic, beautiful, and uplifting, a product of hope and an inspiration of art, not a threatening attack on the Protestant God. Consider again the woman of St. André, kneeling and praying before the statue of the Virgin Mary for the dead child. Despite the sympathy she evokes, North still describes it as a *fond superstition*. When he recreates this image in *The Winter's Tale*, with the sad Perdita kneeling before the statue of Hermione, she implores the audience to avoid this same reaction:

Perdita: **And give me leave,**
And do not say 'tis superstition, that
I kneel and then implore her blessing. (5.3.42–44)

North's travels to Rome and his unforgettable experiences with the Renaissance art of the Cinquecento gave him an optimistic view of Italy's politics and culture. By associating the legends of Jupiter, Apollo, and Neptune with the Catholic mythology of Mary, he hoped to make the latter seem less like the hallucinations of a sinister cult and more of a voluptuous and dramatic art form that should be revered. After all, most Tudor scholars had embraced the myths of Classical Rome and used their motifs in their writings, so why not the Catholic ones, which so closely resemble and descend from them?

North wanted to stress that, despite their flagrant impossibilities, these Roman miracle stories, both pagan and Catholic, had the potential of remaining a glorious foundation for a thriving and enlightened aristocracy.

In brief, we believe that Jensen's remarkably perceptive description of *The Winter's Tale* as a play that "defends the old religion on aesthetic grounds"[27] is *exactly* correct. And this appreciation of the beauty of Catholicism came from North's late April experiences with the extraordinary art of Giulio Romano's Mantua, which mixed images of miracles of resurrection, lifelike painted statues, supplication to the Virgin Mary, and a pagan feast of the lesser gods.

NOTES

1. Peter Fane-Saunders, *Pliny the Elder and the Emergence of Renaissance Architecture* (Cambridge: Cambridge University Press, 2016), 300.

2. Rita Severi, "Art in Shakespeare: Giulio Romano and Giovan Paolo Lomazzo," in *Art in Shakespeare and Other Essays* (Bologna: Pàtron Editore, 2018), 11–56; 35. Severi's essay was originally a lecture read at the British Institute, Florence, on 29 June 2013. In quoting the essay, we rely on its 2018 publication.

3. Rita Severi, *Art in Shakespeare*, 20.

4. Rita Severi, *Art in Shakespeare*, 36–37, 37n97.

5. Rita Severi, *Art in Shakespeare*, 35.

6. Knowing her interest in Santa Maria delle Grazie and its relationship to *The Winter's Tale*, we sent Severi an email about the travel journal and its description of the interior of Santa Maria delle Grazie. She responded that she was aware of the journal and has amended her earlier essay. In her 2018 book, she references the 1555 journal and describes its entries on Mantua at length. Working from *Miscellaneous State Papers*, she speaks of the journalist as "anonymous," a possible secretary to Bishop Thirlby. See Rita Severi, *Art in Shakespeare*, 57–104; 77–80.

7. Jill Delsigne, "Hermetic Miracles in *The Winter's Tale*," in *Magical Transformations on the Early Modern English Stage*, ed. Lisa Hopkins and Helen Ostovich (New York: Routledge, 2016): 91–110; 92.

8. David N. Beauregard, "Shakespeare against the Skeptics: Nature and Grace in *The Winter's Tale*," in *Shakespeare's Last Plays: Essays in Literature and Politics*, ed. Stephen W. Smith and Travis Curtright (Lanham, MD: Lexington Books, 2002), 53–72; 55.

9. Alice Dailey, "Easter Scenes from an Unholy Tomb: Christian Parody in *The Widow's Tears*," in *Marian Moments in Early Modern British Drama*, ed. Regina Buccola and Lisa Hopkins (New York: Routledge, 2007), 127–40; 134.

10. Darryll Grantley, "*The Winter's Tale* and Early Religious Drama," *Comparative Drama* 20.1 (1986): 17–37; 33.

11. Ruth Vanita, "Mariological Memory in *The Winter's Tale* and *Henry VIII*," *Studies in English Literature, 1500–1900* 40.2 (2000): 311–37; 317.

12. Phebe Jensen, "Singing Psalms to Horn-Pipes: Festivity, Iconoclasm, and Catholicism in *The Winter's Tale*," *Shakespeare Quarterly* 55.3 (2004): 279–306; 303.

13. Rita Severi, *Art in Shakespeare*, 35.

14. Quoted in *A New Variorum Edition of Shakespeare, Vol. XI: "The Winter's Tale,"* ed. Horace Howard Furness (Philadelphia: J. B. Lippincott, 1898), 286n99.

15. An EEBO search for all forms and spellings of the phrase *heart weep blood* yields only two results that were published prior to 1610, the year Shakespeare wrote *The Winter's Tale*, and one of them is North's *Dial of Princes*. Likewise, the first works that result in an EEBO search for *I* FBY *say* NEAR *wept* NEAR *blood* NEAR *tears* are North's *Dial of Princes* and Shakespeare's *Winter's Tale*.

16. Ruth Vanita, "Mariological Memory in *The Winter's Tale* and *Henry VIII*," 321.

17. Ruth Vanita, "Mariological Memory in *The Winter's Tale* and *Henry VIII*," 322.

18. Ruth Vanita, "Mariological Memory in *The Winter's Tale* and *Henry VIII*," 322.

19. Phebe Jensen, "Singing Psalms to Horn-Pipes," 282.

20. John Pitcher, Introduction to *The Winter's Tale*, ed. John Pitcher (London: Arden Shakespeare, 2014), 5.

21. John Pitcher, Introduction to *The Winter's Tale*, 6.

22. The identity of this beauty is unknown, but she is likely either the thirty-year-old Hippolita della Rovere, the daughter of Eleanora Gonzaga, Duchess of Urbino, or the twenty-year-old Hippolita Gonzaga, daughter of Ferrante Gonzaga. She was the widow of Fabrizio Colonna and was then married to Antonio Carafa, Duke of Mondragone.

23. Sabine Poeschel, "Raphael's Nudes Painted by Giulio's Hand," in *The Translation of Raphael's Roman Style*, ed. Henk Th. van Veen (Leuven: Peeters, 2007), 35–48; 42.

24. Only one other Shakespeare play even uses the word "satyr" (*Hamlet* 1.2.140), and no other work refers to Flora or the Horae. While scholars have observed that Ben Jonson uses satyrs in his *Masque of Oberon*, which was performed on 1 January 1611, the conventional date of Shakespeare's composition (1610–11) has left scholars questioning who may have borrowed from whom. But satyrs were frequently a part of entertainments in the early Tudor era. They appeared in an entertainment before Edward VI in 1553, and Queen Elizabeth enjoyed a dance of satyrs in 1565. Our answer is that Jonson was following Shakespeare, who was adapting North. See Suzanne Westfall, "The Boy Who Would Be King: Court Revels of King Edward VI, 1547–1553," *Comparative Drama* 35.3 (2001): 271–90; 284 and W. Y. Durand, "A Comedy on Marriage and Some Early Anti-Masques, March 5, 1565," *The Journal of English and Germanic Philology* 6.3 (1907): 412–18; 415.

25. Sabine Poeschel, "Raphael's Nudes Painted by Giulio's Hand," 35–48; 41.

26. John Pitcher, ed., *The Winter's Tale*, 261n29–30.

27. Phebe Jensen, "Singing Psalms to Horn-Pipes," 282.

Chapter Eight

Further Thoughts on *The Winter's Tale*

THE BANISHED ANTIGONUS

The name of Antigonus, the banished nobleman who must travel to Sicily with Perdita, derives from North's *Dial of Princes*.[1] Specifically, two successive letters in *The Dial* tell two related stories of "the Monster of Sicily, and of the banishment of Antigonus from Rome" (730). The latter was an old, noble Roman who would be exiled to Palermo, on the coast of Sicily, for minor trespasses of petty laws; his wife and daughter, also transgressors, suffer exile with him.

While Antigonus was in Palermo, an unearthly monster entered the city on a chariot, drawn by two lions and two bears. The gods, it was believed, had sent the Cyclops-like creature—"he had but one Eye, which was in the midst of his fore-head" (728)—to punish the Sicilians of Palermo for the thievery of their pirates. The terrified townspeople prayed for mercy—and many pregnant women were so stressed that they delivered prematurely. The monster then went to a high hill, "in the sight of the City, the Lions with terrible voices roaring, the Bears with no less fearful cries raging" (728), and the monster was able to cast flames down onto the town's palace where the pirates were residing. Then the skies started to darken and a violent storm arose that levelled houses and killed 10,000 people. Not long after—"For commonly one mischance commeth not alone" (730)—an earthquake destroyed Antigonus's house, resulting in his daughter's death.

The wretched Antigonus wrote Emperor Marcus Aurelius complaining about the injustice of his banishment. The emperor responded with letters of sympathy about the cruelty of the judgment against him, lamenting that "Judges are so greedy to tear men's flesh, as if they were Bears & man's flesh were nointed with honey" (381).

139

These elements of the story of Antigonus are reflected in the Antigonus subplot of *The Winter's Tale*. That subplot also includes fear and stress leading to a premature delivery; the furious judgment against Antigonus and baby Perdita; the banishment to the coast of Sicily; a focus on the ominous darkening of the skies; the fear that this was punishment by angry gods; the loud and riotous storm that killed all the Mariners; and the raging and roaring of the bear, which eats Antigonus alive.

Some of these similarities are pointed. The story in *The Dial* stresses how much the skies had darkened and the day had dimmed: "there appeared in the Element a marvelous dark cloud, which seemed to darken the whole earth" (728) and that the people saw the threat as divine punishment and so started to offer sacrifices to "appease their wraths" (728). In *The Winter's Tale*, Antigonus also notes the unnaturally dark skies: "The day frowns more and more . . . I never saw / The heavens so dim by day" (3.3.53–55). The Mariner with him is the first to notice the threatening element and sees it as divine punishment. "We have landed in ill time: the skies look grimly / And threaten present blusters. In my conscience / The heavens with that we have in hand are angry / And frown upon 's" (3.3.3–6).

The Mariner also mentions that, beside the storm, the land is legendary for fierce beasts: "'Tis like to be loud weather. / Besides, this place is famous for the creatures / Of prey that keep upon't" (3.3.10–12). As the dual calamities ensue, the playwright focuses on the cacophony of the scene—a dreadful mix of noises that clearly derives from the story of Antigonus in *The Dial*: the doleful cries of the people, the raging and roaring of the bear, and the fury of the storm. Other similarities include Antigonus's introduction as a nobleman and his banishment to Sicily (table 8.1).

EEBO confirms that just the shared juxtaposition of the noble Antigonus and the roaring bears is unique.[2] Thus, in both North's *Winter's Tale* and *The Dial*, a nobleman named Antigonus is banished to Sicily with a doomed young girl, and both encounter roaring bears and deadly, dark storms that kill dozens of Mariners.

In *The Winter's Tale*, the Mariner's warning about the creatures that are widely known to prey on the coast of Sicily also hints at the monsters who attacked Odysseus as he travelled through the straits of Sicily—Scylla and Charybdis—and stayed in a nearby coastal cave on Sicily—Polyphemus (Cyclops). Indeed, the Clown's dual descriptions of the man-eater attacking Antigonus on the coast while his ship, just offshore, is tossed upward and downward, is clearly a literary parody of the analogous description in Homer. Table 8.2 provides a translation of the tale of Scylla and Charybdis,[3] which was clearly the inspiration for the Clown's interlacing horror stories of the ship-destroying maelstrom off the coast of Sicily and Antigonus's demise in the jaws of a man-eater.

Table 8.1.

Antigonus's Story in *The Dial of Princes*	Antigonus's Story in *The Winter's Tale*
And all the people . . . with <u>doleful **clamors** and **cries**</u>, making their importunate prayers. the Lions with terrible <u>voices **roaring**, the Bears</u> with no less <u>fearful **cries** raging</u> . . . there appeared in the <u>Element a marvelous dark cloud, which seemed to darken the whole earth</u>, and therewith it began to **thunder** and lightning so terrible . . . At the same time when this woeful chance happened in **the Isle**, there dwelled a Roman in the same City called **Antigonus, a man of a noble** blood, and well stricken in age, who with his wife and daughter were banished two years before from Rome. . . . The Censors . . . banished him unto **the Isle of Sicily** . . . **Antigonus** was not only deprived of his Honor, goods, and country, but also by an Earth-quake, his house fell down to the ground, and slew his dearly beloved daughter. —728–30	**Antigonus**: Thou art perfect then, our ship hath touched upon The deserts of Bohemia [i.e., **Sicily**]? **Mariner**: Ay, my lord, and **fear** We have landed in ill time: <u>the skies look grimly</u> And threaten present blusters. In my conscience, The heavens with that we have in hand are angry And frown upon 's. Besides, <u>this place is famous for the creatures</u> Of prey that keep upon't. **Antigonus**: . . .The storm begins . . . The day frowns more and more. Thou'rt like to have A lullaby too rough. <u>I never saw The heavens so dim by day</u>. A savage **clamor**! Clown: I would you did but see how it chafes, how it **rages** . . . Oh, the most <u>piteous **cry** of the poor souls</u>! . . . how he **cried** to me for help and said his name was **Antigonus, a nobleman**. But to make an end of the ship: to see how the sea flapdragoned it! But first, how the poor souls **roared** and the sea mocked them, and how the poor gentleman **roared** and **the bear** mocked him, both **roaring** louder than the sea or weather. —3.3.1–7, 11–12, 48, 53–55, 86–88, 93–99
Isolated Correspondences	
Element . . . dark	heavens so dim
called **Antigonus, a man of a noble** blood	his name was **Antigonus, a nobleman**
roaring, the Bears	**the bear** mocked him, both **roaring**
clamors, doleful-**cries**, **raging**	**clamor**, piteous **cry**, **rages**
the Isle of **Sicily**	The deserts **of** Bohemia [i.e., **Sicily**]

Table 8.2.

Translation of the tale of Scylla and Charybdis from the *Odyssey*	The Clown's Story of the Maelstrom and Man-eater in *The Winter's Tale*
I saw spray, and huge breakers, and heard their thunder	. . . see how it chafes, how it rages, how it takes up the shore!
So we sailed on through the narrow straits, **crying** aloud for fear	Oh, the most **piteous cry** of the poor souls!
Whenever she spewed it out again, it bubbled and seethed in turmoil like a cauldron on a vast fire, and high overhead the spray. . . When she **swallowed** the seas, her inner vortex could be seen	. . . now the ship boring the moon with her mainmast, and anon **swallowed** with yeast and froth, as you'd thrust a cork into a hogshead.
My crew turned pale as we gazed at her, fearing destruction, but even as we did so Scylla seized six of my strongest and ablest men from the deck. As I looked along the swift ship towards my friends **I saw their arms and legs dangling above me. In anguish they cried my name aloud one last time** . . . There at <u>the entrance to her cave she devoured them, as they shrieked and reached out their hands to me</u> in their last dreadful throes.	And then for the land-service, **to see how the bear tore out his shoulder-bone; how he cried to me for help** . . . and how the poor gentleman roared and the <u>bear mocked him, both roaring louder than the sea or weather</u>. —3.3.86–99

This also parallels the Antigonus of *The Dial*, who is also on Sicily during attacks by a conspicuously Homeric monster, the one-eyed creature, that kills all the sailors. One difference is that in *The Dial*, the pirates were burned to death when their palace "was ***consumed with fire***" (728), but even this seems to be echoed in the play: the first punishment that the king orders Antigonus to inflict upon Perdita is to "take it hence / And see it instantly ***consumed with fire***" (2.3.133–34).

Finally, the description of stress-induced premature delivery in *The Winter's Tale*, similar to that which occurs in Antigonus's Sicily, is clearly Northern, echoing three of his descriptions of births (table 8.3).

In *The Dial*, the cause of the premature births is "fear and terror"; in the play, it is "frights and griefs." And notice that the seven-word line the playwright uses about the childbirth matches, nearly *verbatim*, another line from another page in *The Dial*—also about a stress-induced premature birth:

Table 8.3.

North's Translations	*The Winter's Tale*
The <u>fear and terror</u> hereof was so **great** . . . that some Women with child were with **great** danger **delivered** . . . —*The Dial* 728 <u>she</u> **long before her time** was **delivered** —*The Dial* 206 she brought forth **a goodly Babe** —*Doni* 87v	Emilia: on her <u>frights and griefs</u> Which never tender lady hath borne **greater** <u>She</u> is something **before her time delivered**. Paulina: A boy? Emilia: A daughter, and **a goodly babe** —2.2.23–26

The Dial: <u>she</u> **long before her time** was **delivered** (206)
The Winter's Tale: <u>She</u> is something **before her time delivered** (2.2.27)

EEBO confirms the rarity of these links, including the near exclusivity of **a goodly babe**.[4]

That the playwright repeatedly borrowed from North's *Dial*, first published in 1557, should seem strange. The text is an example of counsel literature for princes—originally written by a Spanish bishop. It has nothing whatever to do with events of *The Winter's Tale* or the divorce of Katherine, the history of Henry VIII, or the life of Queen Mary. Why would Shakespeare start perusing it for information for his work on *The Winter's Tale*—or, for that matter, *Henry VIII*?

He didn't. *North* wrote the *original* versions of the plays not long after his trip to Rome. He was also translating *The Dial* at this time, so a number of elements of his translation ended up in the plays—as did the striking visuals of his Italian journey.

THE HONEST CAMILLO

As has been noted, North stresses that the marriage he attended on 23 April was between an Italian count, Despesiano Porzenno, and "the sister of Signior **Camillo** Stanga, a **very honest** gentleman." He even emphasizes in the margin that the bride was Camillo's sister.

Camillo is the only person in the journal whom North describes as *honest*—indeed *very honest*—and this naturally brings to mind Leontes' trusty servant, Camillo, in *The Winter's Tale*. He too is known as a paragon of honesty. In one online character study, the heading descriptions include "Camillo, the truth-telling servant," "Camillo as trustworthy," and "Camillo's unfailing honesty."⁵ An EEBO search for *Camillo* NEAR *honest* (or *honesty*) yields only seven examples in the database, and all seven can be traced back to *The Winter's Tale*. Five specifically appear in *The Winter's Tale*, and the other two appear in John Fletcher's *A Wife for a Month*, in which one of the "three honest court lords" has the name Camillo. Fletcher, co-author of *Henry VIII*, who was working with Shakespeare's company when Shakespeare reproduced the play, almost certainly found inspiration for the name from *The Winter's Tale*.

Camillo's virtuous candor is on display early in *The Winter's Tale*, where he vouches for the queen's fidelity, even against the king's threatening protests. Leontes even accuses him of lying, leading to a discussion on honesty. Camillo counters that while he himself "may be negligent, foolish and fearful" (1.2.149) at times, as all men are, he always maintains honesty. The servant is a kind of anti-Iago, using sincerity and frankness in an effort to ameliorate jealousy—rather than deceit to enflame it. Later, Hermione says, "All I know of it / Is that **Camillo** was an **honest** man" (3.2.73–74). Leontes, upon discovering that his servant had been right all along, says, "recall the good Camillo, / Whom I proclaim a man of truth, of mercy" (3.2.156–57). In the final act, when Florizel believes Camillo has betrayed him, he still notes that Camillo's "**honesty** till now / Endured all weathers" (5.1.193–94). In the last speech of the play, Leontes rewards Paulina with Camillo as an "honorable husband /... whose worth and **honesty** / Is richly noted and here justified / By us, a pair of Kings" (5.3.145–48).

North left the *very honest* Camillo in Cremona on 24 April and noted in a brief entry that he traveled to Canneto sull'Oglio in the duchy of Mantua, where "the **lords lay at the duke's charges**." In *The Dial*, North would use similarly rare expressions for the charging of expenses ("lay it to his charge"), including in metaphors for a punitive debt owed by a wrongdoer. This same expression used in the same type of metaphor occurs in the context of the honest Camillo in *The Winter's Tale* (see table 8.4).

Table 8.4.

North's Journal and *The Dial of Princes*	*The Winter's Tale*
Signior **Camillo** Stanga, a very **honest** gentleman. . . . From Cremona to Canneto . . . in this town the **Lords lay at the** Duke's **charges**. —23–24 April yet he shall have a just judge that will in another place **lay it to his charge**. —*The Dial* 398	Florizel: **Camillo** hath betrayed me; Whose honour and whose **honesty** till now Endured all weathers. Lord: **Lay it so to his charge** —5.1.192–94

This correspondence—with both works juxtaposing *Camillo-honest(y)-lord-lay-charge(s)*—is, of course, unique.

AUTOLYCUS, HEYWOOD'S PEDLAR, AND NORTH'S HORN-RING IN LAWN

As noted by William Elton, the character of Autolycus and especially the song about his goods derive from John Heywood's Pedlar and his song in the Catholic play *The Play of the Four P's* (1544).[6] John Heywood had also written a pro-Catholic allegorical drama, *The Play of the Weather* (published in 1533), on Henry VIII's marriage question, and an allegorical poem, *The Spider and the Fly* (1556), which depicts the new Queen Mary as England's savior, who will free the land from Protestants' dangerous webs. As J. Christopher Warner points out, Heywood's *The Four P's* "affirm[s] religious loyalties to Rome."[7] Table 8.5 makes it clear that Heywood's Pedlar[8] served as inspiration for Autolycus.

Many scholars have observed that Autolycus and other such pedlars were emblematic of Catholic-styled fraudsters, a fact that might seem at odds with its celebration of the old religion in most other scenes. But this criticism of Autolycus fits in with the brand of Catholicism promoted by Heywood, who, though opposed to Protestantism, still was critical of those who would use the Romish church for their own personal gain. John S. Farmer makes the same point about both Heywood's *The Play of the Four P's* and *The Pardoner and the Friar*, noting that, while each provides an "unsparing satire of the abuses of the Roman Communion," the dramatist was still indeed "a devout Catholic, a friend of Catholics, and wedded to papal authority in the Church as against the kingly claim thereto."[9] His criticisms were meant to improve the Catholic church and warn true Catholics against the practices of charlatans.

Recall that North, at Lincoln's Inn, was part of a group of Catholic playwrights that included the extant members of Sir Thomas More's circle and Heywood family members. In 1560, Jasper, John's son, would become the first to praise North's abilities as a tragic writer. This connection may explain why both *The Winter's Tale* and North's journal flaunt this same Heywood-inspired outlook; although awed by the Italian hospitality and papal ceremonies and supportive of England's reconciliation with Rome, North still repeatedly expresses this same cynicism of Catholic swindlers in his entries. For example, on 26 May in Perugia, the journalist could not conceal his disbelief at the display of a horn-ring in lawn that was supposedly the first ring worn by the Virgin Mary:

> Here we saw a special **relic**, forsooth, of Our Lady's ring, the first (they stick not to say) that ever she did wear, which is not shown, I tell you, without great

Table 8.5.

Heywood's Pedlar Song in *The Four P's*	Autolycus in *The Winter's Tale*
Pedlar: What! dost thou not know that every **pedlar** In all kind of **trifles** must be a **meddler**? Specially in women's triflings; Those use we chiefly above all things, Which things to see, if ye be disposed, Behold what ware here is disclosed! This gear showeth itself in such beauty, That each man thinketh it saith, "**Come, buy me!**" . . . **Gloves**, **pins**, combs, **glasses** unspotted, **Pomades**, **hooks**, and laces knotted; **Brooches**, rings, and all manner of beads; Laces, round and flat, **for** women's **heads**; Needles, **thread**, thimble, shears, and all such knacks Where lovers be, no such things **lacks**: Sipers **[Cyprus]**, swathbands, **ribbons**, and sleeve laces, Girdles, **knives**, purses, and pincases. . . . Forsooth, women have many lets, And they be masked in many nets: As frontlets, fillets, partlets, and **bracelets** . . . —35–36	as I am littered under Mercury, was likewise a snapper-up of unconsidered **trifles**. —4.3.24–26 **Lawn*** as white as driven snow, **Cyprus** black as e'er was crow, **Gloves** as sweet as damask roses . . . **Pins** and poking-sticks of steel, What maids lack from head to heel, **Come buy of me, come. Come buy, come buy.** Buy, lads, or else your lasses cry. **Come buy.** Will you buy any tape, Or lace for your cape, My dainty duck, my dear-a? Any silk, any **thread**, Any toys **for your head**, Of the new'st and fin'st, fin'st wear-a? Come to the **peddler**; Money's a **meddler** That doth utter all men's ware-a. Ha, ha, what a fool Honesty is! And Trust, his sworn brother, a very simple gentleman! I have sold all my trumpery; not a counterfeit stone, not a **ribbon**, **glass**, **pomander**, **brooch**, table **book**, ballad, **knife**, tape, **glove**, shoe tie, **bracelet**, horn ring, to keep my pack from fasting. They throng who should buy first . . . —4.4.218–20, 226–28, 315–23, 598–604
Isolated Correspondences	
What! dost thou not know that every **pedlar** In all kind of trifles must be a **meddler**?	Come to the **peddler** Money's a **meddler**
That each man thinketh it saith, "**Come, buy me!**"	**Come buy of me, come. Come buy, come buy.** Buy, lads, or else your lasses cry / **Come buy** . . .

(*continued*)

Table 8.5. *(continued)*

Heywood's Pedlar Song in *The Four P's*	Autolycus in *The Winter's Tale*
for women's heads Needles, thread	Any silk, any thread, Any toys for your head
Gloves, pins, combs, glasses unspotted Pomades, hooks, and laces knotted Brooches Sipers [Cyprus], swathbands, ribbons, and sleeve laces Girdles, knives . . . bracelets	Cyprus . . ., gloves . . ., pins . . ., ribbon, glass, pomander, brooch, table book, ballad, knife, tape, glove, shoe tie, bracelet

*Lawn = a high-quality linen

ceremony. **This ring is a great ring, all of black horn**, and hangeth in a pyx within a tabernacle, being clad with 2 or 3 fold of **lawn**. That is seen in mystery, as all of her **relics** be. When it is shown to anybody, there is wonderful much blessing, kissing, kneeling, and knocking . . .

In the margin, North wrote: "A foolish superstitious ceremony devised upon a supposed ring of Our Lady," and his colloquialisms—*forsooth* and *stick not to say*—underscore his disbelief.

Richard Burt is one of the scholars who have linked Autolycus's swindling to the display of fake popish relics: "It is precisely because the rustics naively believe that Autolycus's 'popish' peddled wares have the sacramental efficacy of relics that he can cut purses."[10] But notice that while most of the relics offered by Autolycus come from Heywood's Pedlar, the *horn-ring* and *lawn* that he mentions appear to be an invention of the playwright. In fact, the OED cites *The Winter's Tale* as the first instance of the use of *horn-ring*, and EEBO shows no examples prior to 1610, the conventional date of the play. It is North's experience in Italy with the Catholic tricksters displaying a hornring in lawn that likely explains their appearance among Autolycus's wares.

THE WINTER'S TALE, THE PLÉIADE, AND FRENCH AUTHORS

Geoffrey Bullough has noted that Florizel's name and other elements of *The Winter's Tale* derive from the Odyssean adventures of *Amadis de Gaul*.[11] The following are the relevant French volumes related to *Amadis de Gaul* upon which *The Winter's Tale* playwright relied:

Book IX: *Amadis de Grecia*, Nicholas d'Herberay (1546, 1548)
Book X: *Florisel de Niquea*, Giles Boileau, Claude Colet, and Jacques Gohorry (1551–52)
Book XI: *Rogel de Grecia*, Jacques Gohorry (1554)

Interestingly, *Amadis* is not the only Spanish work that Nicholas d'Herberay translated into French. He also published a French translation of Guevara's Spanish *Dial of Princes*, and it is Herberay's version that North used for his English translation of *The Dial*. In other words, North's interest in Herberay's *Amadis* is consistent with his published work from that time.

Gohorry also happened to be on a French ambassadorial mission to Rome from 1554 to 1556, so he would have been in Rome, in the pope's circle, at the same time as North. The three translators of Book X of *Amadis* were closely connected with the Pléiade, a group of ambitious young French poets headed by Pierre de Ronsard.[12] Ronsard had read the *Amadis* translations and used them for inspiration, and the three books of *Amadis* used for *The Winter's Tale*—and Book XII as well—all "contain preliminary verses" of the Pléiade.[13] Moreover, in an ode to Gohorry in his 1552 translation of *Florisel de Niquea*, Joachim du Bellay, another member of the poetic brigade, complimented Ronsard's verses.[14]

As shown in table 8.6, these links among Herberay, Gohorry, and Ronsard are interesting as Autolycus's song of the lark derives from—and at times appears to be a direct translation of—Ronsard's *L'Alouette*, which appeared in *Nouvelle Continuation des Amours* (1556). Autolycus's "tirra-lirra" refers to the supposed sound that larks make—or, to be more precise, the sound that larks make according to Ronsard.[15]

Ronsard's ode to the lark expresses the same theme, and, once translated, it does so in the same language as Autolycus's song. Both make the point that, in the spring, the return of the lark, who chants tirra-lirra, also signals the return of love and thieving hands:

> **When daffodils begin to peer,**
> With **heigh, the doxy over the dale!**
> **Why, then comes in the sweet o'the year;**
> For **the red blood reigns** in the winter's pale.
> The white sheet bleaching on the hedge,
> **With heigh, the sweet birds, oh, how they sing!**
> **Doth set my pugging tooth on edge,**
> **For a quart of ale is a dish for a king.**
> **The lark, that tirra-lirra chants,**
> With heigh, **the thrush**[16] **and the jay**
> **Are summer songs** for me and my aunts,
> While we lie tumbling in the hay. (4.3.1–12)

Table 8.7 shows the isolated correspondences.

Thus, the writers that seemed to have inspired various elements of *The Winter's Tale* include a peculiar combination of early Tudor writers connected to Lincoln's Inn (Heywood, Ferrers[17]) and French authors who were

Table 8.6.

Ronsard's L'Alouette 1556	English Translation
Hé, Dieu, que je porte d'envie	Heigh! God, do I envy
Aux felicitez de ta vie,	The happiness of your life,
Alouette, qui de l'amour	O lark, who of love
Caquettes dés le poinct du jour . . .	Does sing from the break of day. . .
Tu dis en l'air de si doux sons	You sing in the air with such sweet sounds
Composez de ta tirelire,	Composed of your tirra-lirra
Qu'il n'est amant qui ne desire	That he is not a lover who does not wish
Comme toy devenir oyseau,	To become such a bird as you
Pour desgoiser un chant si beau . . .	And chant so lovely a song . . .
Le Rossignol à haute voix	The nightingale in loud voice,
Caché dessous quelque verdure	Hidden beneath greenery,
Se plaint d'eux, et leur dit injure.	Complains of them, and the injuries they've done to him
Si fait bien l'Arondelle aussi	The swallow also does the same
Quand elle chante son cossi.	When she chants her song.
Ne laissez pas pourtant de dire	But don't stop singing,
Mieux que devant la tirelire,	Better than before, your tirra-lirra,
Et faites crever par despit	And have them die of spite,
Ces menteurs de ce qu'ils ont dit.	These liars, for what they've said.
Ne laissez pour cela de vivre	Never stop living
Joyeusement, et de poursuivre	Joyously and pursuing
A chaque retour du Printemps	With each return of Spring
Vos accoustumez passetemps	To your usual pastime
Ainsi jamais la main pillarde	So may the plundering hand
D'une pastourelle mignarde	of a pretty shepherdess [doxy]
Parmi les sillons espiant	peering over the furrows [dales]
Vostre nouveau nid pepiant,	spying your new nest
Quand vous chantez ne le desrobe	as you chant, never steal [the eggs]
Ou dans son sein ou dans sa robe.	[putting them] in her bosom or in her dress.
Vivez oiseaux et vous haussez	Live, birds! And rise
Tousjours en l'air, et annoncez	Always in the air, and announce
De vostre chant et de vostre aile	with your singing and flying
Que le Printemps se renouvelle.	That Spring is in renewal.

Table 8.7.

Isolated Correspondences	
Ronsard's *L'Alouette*	*The Winter's Tale*
Hé	Heigh
Alouette	lark
chant	chants
Tu dis en l'air de si doux sons Comme toy devenir oyseau	the **sweet birds**, oh, how they **sing**!
pastourelle mignarde Parmi les sillons espiant (shepherdess/ doxy peering over dales or furrows)	**to peer,** With, **heigh, the doxy over the dale!**
la main pillarde (thieving hand)	pugging tooth (thieving itch)
Le Rossignol . . . (nightingale) l'Arondelle aussi (sparrow) Quand elle chante son cossi	The throstle cock and the jay Are summer **songs**
Alouette. . . Tu dis en l'air de si doux sons Composez de ta **tirelire** . . . Pour desgoiser un **chant** si beau [**Alouette, tire-lire, chant**]	The **lark**, that **tirra-lirra chants** [**lark, tirra-lirra, chants**]

in vogue on the continent in the 1550s (Herberay, Gohorry, and Ronsard). North's association with both groups is well documented: after his journey, North would spend much of the next two years translating Herberay's French version of *The Dial*—and during this time he was master of revels at Lincoln's Inn. It seems less likely that Shakespeare, some 55 years later, would suddenly take an interest in various early Tudor works and old untranslated French texts—all dating from 1544 to 1557.

Finally, it appears that Greene borrowed from the same books of *Amadis* as did Shakespeare. After pointing out independent borrowings in both, Sir Henry Thomas asked:

> Shakespeare must have known something about the relationship of Greene's *Dorastus and Fawnia* [i.e., *Pandosto*] to *Amadis de Grecia*. Did he learn the name of Dorastus' prototype from better informed friends, or had he himself read *Amadis de Grecia*, which he might have done in the French version?[18]

So here we find the peculiar circumstance where it appears that Greene and Shakespeare independently borrowed from the same archaic French source.

In fact, it was North who was translating Herberay again, working from his *Amadis*, and Greene and Shakespeare were both borrowing from North's play.

NORTH'S ISLE OF DELPHOS ERROR

While the pastoral feast represents the only time in the play that many mythological entities are mentioned, allusions to Apollo are frequent in *The Winter's Tale*. That is due to the subplot centering on the messengers sent to the Oracle of Apollo on the Isle of Delphos to inquire whether the queen did indeed have an affair. This too has conspicuous relevance to Mantua. Manto, the city's namesake and the mother of Ocnus, the founder of Mantua, was a prophetess who lived in Delphi. Apollo sent her to Asia near Ionian Colophon in present-day Turkey, where she established the Oracle of Apollo in nearby Claros. Virgil names her as the mother of Mantuan founder Ocnus, while other accounts suggest she was also the mother of Mopsus, likely fathered by Apollo. This again revisits the theme of gods impregnating women, and Mopsus is likely the inspiration for the name of Mopsa, the Clown's girlfriend, whose appearance in the play is confined to Perdita's sheep-shearing feast (4.4). In other words, *The Winter's Tale*, despite its supposed settings in Bohemia, Sicily, and the Isle of Delphos, is perhaps most of all a Mantuan play. The subplot of the Oracle of Apollo, the rustic feast of the lesser gods, the chapel with the lifelike painted statue by Giulio Romano all point back to this northern Italian city.

Moreover, as Terence Spencer and others have pointed out, Shakespeare's Isle of Delphos was a mistake. While Apollo had allegedly been born on an island off Greece with the similar sounding name *Delos*, the Oracle of Apollo actually resided in *Delphi*, on the slope of Mount Parnassus in central Greece. As Spenser observes, many have mentioned the error: "Delphi is, of course, on the Greek mainland. Shakespeare's apparent geographical ignorance troubled some of the eighteenth-century editors. Warburton wanted to emend 'isle' to 'soil' in III.i.2. Johnson characteristically commented: 'Shakespeare is little careful of geography. . . .'"[19]

We can now trace this error back to North, who was misled by Guevara during his translation of *The Dial of Princes*: "he sent many and very rich gifts into **the Isle of Delphos, where the Oracle of Apollo was** . . ." (171). Other passages in *The Dial* on the Oracle of Apollo confirm that North's translation was the origin of the Isle of Delphos error (see table 8.8).

It is important to remember that this is a unique geographical error—and so it is rather simple to trace it back to its origins. Indeed, some may object that

Table 8.8.

North's *Dial of Princes*	*The Winter's Tale*
he himself with great reverence took the **sacred** vessels of the **Temples**, and the gods which were therein (especially the goddess Juno) and **brought them all** to Rome. . . . Another notable thing chanced in Rome, which was that the Romans sent two Tribunes, the which were called Caulius and Sergius, **into the Isle of Delphos** with great presents to offer unto the god **Apollo**. For as Titus Livius says, Rome yearly sent a present unto the god **Apollo**, and **Apollo** gave unto the Romans **counsel**. And as the Tribunes went out of the way, they fell into the hands of pirates and **rovers** on the sea —53 In **the Isle of Delphos**, where the **oracle of the god Apollo** was, there was a sumptuous **Temple** —523	. . . I have dispatched in post To **sacred Delphos**, to **Apollo's temple**, Cleomenes and Dion, whom you know Of stuffed sufficiency. Now from the **oracle** They will **bring all**, whose spiritual **counsel** had Shall stop or spur me. —2.1.183–86 Leontes: Next to thyself and my young **rover** . . . —1.2.176 Fertile the **isle**, the **temple much surpassing** The common praise it bears. 3.1.2–3
\multicolumn{2}{c}{Isolated Correspondences}	

sacred-**temples**	**sacred**-**temple**
Apollo, **isle of Delphos**	**Apollo**, **Delphos** . . . **isle**
brought them **all**, sent two tribunes . . . Caulius and Sergius . . . **counsel**	**bring all**, dispatched in post . . . Cleomenes and Dion . . . **counsel**
rovers	**rover**
sumptuous **temple**	**temple** much surpassing

Shakespeare had to get his "Isle of Delphos" error from Greene, but when we look at *Pandosto*[20] it is clear that Greene also got his "Isle of Delphos" mistake from North (see table 8.9). This is not because Greene had memorized passages from North's *Dial* but because Greene was also following North's *Winter's Tale*.

As shown, it is North's *Dial* that is the seminal source for the mistake of placing the Oracle of Apollo on a non-existent "Isle of Delphos" in both Greene's *Pandosto* and Shakespeare's *Winter's Tale*. Indeed, both Greene

Further Thoughts on The Winter's Tale   153

Table 8.9.

North's *Dial of Princes*	Greene's *Pandosto*
If perchance Princes would say it is good to carry **Priests** to the wars to offer **sacrifices to the gods**: To this I answer that the **Temples** are built to pray and the Fields ordained for to fight . . . and by the way he passed by **the temple of Apollo**, in **the isle of Delphos**: and as there he made a prayer unto **the god Apollo**, very long, to the end he would reveal unto him whether he should return victorious from Asia, or not? **The Oracle answered.** ". . . for our **divine** service . . ." —407 The first was that he sent many and very rich **gifts into the Isle of Delphos**, where the Oracle of Apollo was, to the end to present them with him, and to pray him that it would please him for to preserve his son. The other thing that he did was, that immediately he wrote a **letter** to the great Philosopher Aristotle, **wherein he said these words**. —171–72	that it would please his majesty to send six of his noble men whom he best trusted, **to the Isle of Delphos, there to enquire of the Oracle of Apollo**, whether she had committed adultery with Egistus, or conspired to poison him with Franion: and if **the god Apollo**, who by his **divine** essence knew all secrets, gave **answer** that she was guilty, she were content to suffer any torment, were it never so terrible. . . . he therefore agreed, that with as much speed as might be there should be certain Ambassadors dispatched to **the Isle of Delphos** . . . where they were no sooner set on land, but with great devotion they went to **the Temple of Apollo**, and there offering **sacrifice to the god**, and **gifts to the Priest**, as the custom was, they humbly craved an **answer** of their demand: they had not long kneeled at the Altar, but **Apollo** with a loud voice said: "Bohemians, what you find behind the Altar take and depart." They forthwith obeying **the Oracle** found a scroll of parchment, **wherein was written these words** in **letters** of Gold. —C1v–C2
Isolated Correspondences	
sacrifices to the gods the temple of Apollo the Isle of Delphos gifts into the the god Apollo wherein he said these words Priests, divine, letter	sacrifice to the god the temple of Apollo the Isle of Delphos gifts to the the god Apollo wherein was written these words Priest, divine, letter

and Shakespeare, working more than 25 years apart, appear to have borrowed the language and circumstances of the error as found in *The Dial*, with Greene using some elements and Shakespeare echoing others. As this scenario is highly unlikely, the most reasonable explanation—as with their independent borrowings from *Amadis*—is that both writers were following the same North play. And it was North who was echoing his own prior passages on the "Isle of Delphos."

Note also that North and Greene also coincide on the wording of the introduction of the Oracle's judgment: "**wherein** was written / he said **these words**," and the pronouncement that follows in *Pandosto* also appears in *The Winter's Tale* with little change. But, again, Shakespeare is not copying Greene; rather, Greene and Shakespeare have both borrowed from North, which explains why the lines and phrases are Northern (see table 8.10).

Table 8.10.

The Oracle's Judgment in Greene's *Pandosto*	The Oracle's Judgment in *The Winter's Tale*
Suspicion is no proof: Jealousy is an unequal judge: Bellaria **is chaste**: Egistus **blameless**: Franion **a true subject**: Pandosto treacherous: his **Babe** an **innocent, and the King shall live without an heir: if that which is lost be not found.** —C2	"Hermione is chaste, Polixenes **blameless**, Camillo **a true subject**, Leontes a jealous tyrant, his **innocent babe** truly begotten, **and the King shall live without an heir if that which is lost be not found.**" —3.2.132–36

North's Translations	Greene/Shakespeare Oracle
it was but suspicion and no proof [re: possibly adulterous wife] —*Doni* 79v	**Suspicion is no proof** [re: possibly adulterous wife]
innocent babe —*The Dial* 204, 268, 469–70	**innocent babe**
A true subject —*Doni* 54v	**a true subject**
that which in many I have **lost**, in Marcus Aurelius alone I have **found.** —*The Dial* 491	if **that which** is **lost** be not **found.**

In an EEBO search for the first result (*suspicion* FBY.5 *no proof*), the first two results are North's *Doni* (1570) and Greene's *Pandosto* (1588). And both comments appear in an identical context, with a husband consumed by jealousy over a possibly adulterous wife. Did Greene borrow this phrasing from North's *Doni*, as he borrowed the geographical error of the Oracle of Apollo from North's *Dial*? No, the reason these passages are so plainly

Northern is that Greene and Shakespeare were both working from the same Northern play.

PLUTARCH'S LIVES AND GREENE'S PANDOSTO

We know from his writings that North was an inveterate reviser. His manuscript journal contains numerous deletions, corrections, and additions, many done following further research after his return from Rome. In 1568, he corrected and augmented *The Dial of Princes*, adding a fourth book, *The Favoured Courtier*. In 1603, he revised his *Plutarch's Lives*, adding chapters from his final translation, *Nepos' Lives*. Indeed, the margins of North's personal copy of the second edition of his *Moral Philosophy of Doni* (1582) are filled with emendations, deletions, and substituted words and phrases in his own hand.[21]

Revisions were not unusual for the time. Ben Jonson is known to have revised his work repeatedly. For the only collection of his works (1616), he changed the names of the major characters in *Every Man In His Humor* (1598). Shakespeare also revised, not always with great care. One of his more famous revisions was the change of Sir John Oldcastle's name to Sir John Falstaff. In the late 1570s or early 1580s, North likewise reworked his *Winter's Tale*, changing the original names of several characters. We are not sure why he returned to this decades-old play at that particular time, but it is possible that the original names were random, with no suggestive meaning—or perhaps he had originally adopted the early Tudor practice of using allegorical names like Jealousy, Truth, Patience, etc., which would have become old-fashioned by the 1570s. Whatever his reason, he replaced the names of six of the characters with an historically suitable set of names that he found in his most recent translation: *Plutarch's Lives* (1579/80). Specifically, he took Polixenes, Dion, and Sinalus from the chapter on "The Life of Dion"—all from pages 1038–1040—and borrowed Leonidas (Leontes), Archidamus, and Cleomenes from "The Life of Agis and Cleomenes," especially focusing on page 857.

Leonidas, "Son of the Lion," offered an appropriate name for Leontes, King of Bohemia, whose symbol was the lion. In *Plutarch's Lives*, King Leonidas had married a foreigner and ordered the murder of a rival king and that king's brother, Archidamus. The latter discovered the plot and managed to flee to Sicily. Similarly, in *The Winter's Tale*, King Leontes had married a foreigner and ordered the murder of King Polixenes and presumably his lord, Archidamus. The plot is discovered, and they manage to escape back to Sicily. In *Plutarch's Lives*, Cleomenes is the son of Leonidas, and his name appears in the title of the chapter. He is also discussed in the relevant passage on Leonides and Archidamus. In *The Winter's Tale*, Cleomenes is the name for Leontes' trusted messenger.

The name of the other messenger, Dion, also derives from the title character of a later chapter. According to North's "Life of Dion," before the Greek king traveled across the Mediterranean to liberate Syracuse in Sicily, Dion took advice from the Soothsayer Miltas and made a sacrifice in the Temple of Apollo (1038–1039). Thus, in *The Winter's Tale*, Dion becomes the name of the Mediterranean messenger who, along with Cleomenes, visits the Oracle at the Temple of Apollo in Greece.

In the same Plutarchan chapter—indeed, on the very same pages—North also recounts a story of the Sicilian Prince Polyxenus, the son of Dionysius, who had married his father's sister, infuriating the king and causing Polyxenus to flee in secret. This story would have reminded North of his own Sicilian (not Bohemian) monarch in *The Winter's Tale*, who also fled in secret in order to escape a king whom he had enraged for an alleged, quasi-incestuous dalliance. Thus, in *Plutarch's Lives*, both Polyxenus and Archidamus are connected to Sicily, and both must flee for their lives after angering a king— like their namesakes in the play.

We also find that during this revision of *The Winter's Tale*, North adds a brief story about Florizel (or perhaps augments an earlier one) that further connects the play to this particular section of the chapter. Specifically, on these same pages—1039–1040—North describes how a storm blew Dion's ships across the Mediterranean to *Libya*, then "there rose a little **South wind**" and "making their prayers unto the gods they **crossed** the sea, and sailed from the coast of **Libya**" (1040) to Minoa, a Sicilian port-city then controlled by a noble North African captain and governor, Sinalus Carthaginian. Fortunately for the Greek Dion, Sinalus was an old friend.

Here we find the origin of the name of the North African warrior-lord from Libya in *The Winter's Tale*.[22] Desiring to give Perdita nobility, Florizel falsely claims to Leontes that she is the daughter of Sinalus, ruler of Libya, where, for some unknown reason, Florizel had stopped before he traveled to the kingdom of Leontes. As noted, the fact that Florizel is in conflict with a Governor of Libya reflects the historical circumstances of his counterpart, Philip II, Prince (then King) of Sicily, who in the 1550s was at war with the Governor of Libya, Turgut Re'is. As with Sinalus, Turgut had indeed taken over and controlled parts of Sicily—and, as mentioned, North had recorded the 1555 attack of Turgut on Calabria in his journal (while discussing Ferdinand, King of Bohemia) (3 July).

The false identity that Florizel gives Perdita, making her the daughter of an enemy, also corresponds to their current situation. And Florizel's alleged reconciliation of Sicily and Libya through engagement to the Libyan princess foreshadows the ending of the tragicomedy in which marriage to the Bohemian princess would signal the reconciliation of Bohemia and Sicily (and England's uniting with Sicily and Catholic Europe).

Florizel seems to bring up Perdita's invented background apropos of nothing, responding specifically to Leontes' concern about the dangers of the sea:

> Leontes: ... And hath he too
> Exposed this paragon to th' fearful usage—
> At least ungentle—of the dreadful Neptune,
> To greet a man not worth her pains, much less
> Th'adventure of her person? ...
> Florizel: She came from **Libya**.
> Leontes: Where the **warlike Sinalus**,
> That noble honored lord, is feared and loved?
> Florizel: Most royal sir, from thence, from him, whose daughter
> His tears proclaimed his, parting with her. Thence,
> A prosperous **south wind** friendly, we have **crossed** (5.1.152–61)

An EEBO search for *south wind* NEAR.100 *Libya* NEAR.100 *cross* yields only *The Winter's Tale* and the relevant passage in North's chapter on Dion—and both passages are referring to the feared North African ruler, Sinalus. This borrowing is well known, and the conventional claim that this page in North's *Plutarch's Lives* was the source for this description is indisputable.

But why does Florizel's story include no explanation for why he was in Libya? Because Shakespeare took it out. Notice that Leontes' expression of concern for the perils of sea voyage—with the threat "of the dreadful Neptune"—would seem to set up Florizel to relate a harrowing tale of a sea storm. Yet Florizel does not mention one even though at this precise moment in the supposed source tale, *Pandosto*, Greene does describe in detail a sea storm experienced by Florizel's counterpart, Dorastus. And, remarkably, Greene's description also derives from *Plutarch's Lives*. In fact, it derives from the beginning of this very same passage on pages 1039–1040.

As shown in table 8.11, Dorastus' storm in Greene's *Pandosto* is based on the description of the very same tempest that blew Dion from Sicily to the coast of Libya just before he encountered Sinalus.

This connection is secure. Many of the lines that Greene borrowed from North are unique, and the descriptions even follow the same order. First, both ships start out with fortunate weather, that is, with *so pleasant* (*lucky*) *a gale of wind* for *the space of* a *day* (or *days*). We need go no further. An EEBO search for just the first correspondence—*so* FBY *gale of wind* FBY *the space of*—yields only this exact storm pushing Dion's ship from Sicily to Libya in

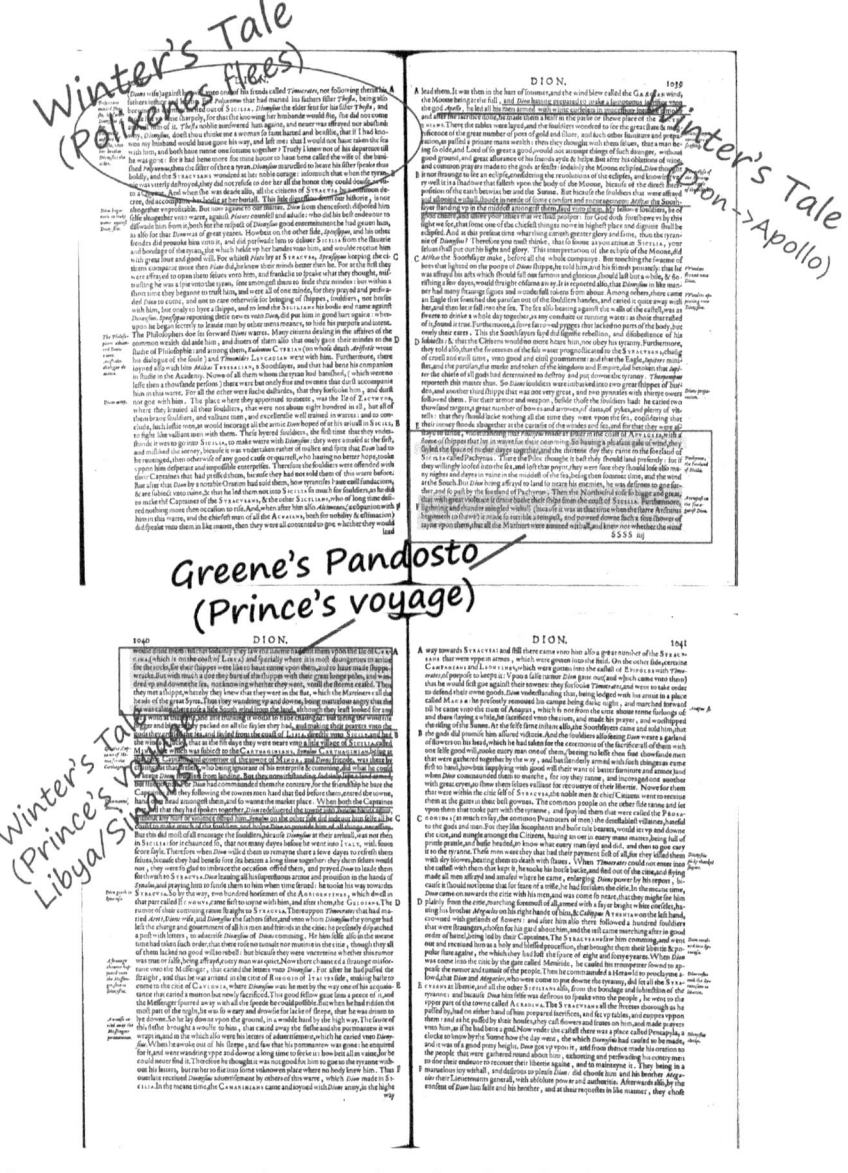

Figure 8.1. Four consecutive pages of North's *Plutarch's Lives* (1038–1041) showing passages used for both *The Winter's Tale* and Greene's *Pandosto*.

Table 8.11

North's *Plutarch Lives*	Prince's Voyage as described in Greene's *Pandosto* and Shakespeare's *Winter's Tale*
So having a pleasant gale of wind, they sailed the space of twelve days . . . Then the North wind rose . . . with great violence . . . so terrible a tempest . . . that all the Mariners were amazed withal, and knew not whether the wind would drive them: till that suddenly they saw the storm had cast them . . . on the coast of Libya . . . until the storm ceased . . . the sea was calm, there rose a little South wind from the land . . . and making their prayers unto the gods they crossed the sea, and sailed from the coast of Libya, directly unto Sicily, and had the wind so lucky, that at the fifth day they were near unto a little village of Sicily, called Minoa, the which was subject to the Carthaginians. Sinalus Carthaginian, being at that time Captain and governor of the town of Minoa . . . —1039–1040	so lucky a gale of wind for the space of a day and a night . . . the winds to rise . . . with the violence of the wind . . . The tempest continued three days, all which time the Mariners every minute looked for death . . . could not tell by his compass in what Coast they were. But upon the fourth day about ten of the clock, the wind began to cease, the sea to wax calm . . . —*Pandosto* F3–F3v Florizel: She came from Libya. Leontes: Where the warlike Sinalus, That noble honored lord, is feared and loved? Florizel: Most royal sir, from thence, from him, whose daughter His tears proclaimed his, parting with her. Thence, A prosperous south wind friendly, we have crossed . . . —*Winter's Tale* 5.1.152–61

Shared Terms:
So pleasant/lucky a gale of wind . . . the space of . . . day(s) . . .
Wind(s) rose/rise . . . with-violence . . .
Tempest . . . all the Mariners [were terrified]
knew not whither (could not tell) . . . [what] Coast . . .
cease(d) . . . the sea calm
Libya, south wind, crossed, Sinalus

So having a pleasant gale of wind, they sailed the space of twelve days	so lucky a gale of wind for the space of a day and a night
Then the North wind rose that with great violence	the winds to rise with the violence of the wind
so terrible a tempest . . . that all the Mariners were amazed withal	The tempest continued three days, all which time the Mariners every minute looked for death
wind so lucky	so lucky . . . wind
until the storm ceased . . . the sea was calm	the wind began to cease, the sea to wax calm

North's *Plutarch's Lives* and Dorastus' storm in Greene's *Pandosto*. Again, a search of both Google and Google Books for *so* AROUND(10) "*gale of wind*" AROUND(10) "*the space of*" yields only these same two passages of North and Greene. This unique connection is then followed in both works by a series of peculiar events, all of them similarly worded (1) **wind-rose/rise** . . . **with-violence**, (2) **tempest** . . . **all** . . . **the Mariners** (astonished), (3) the Mariners *knew* **not** *whither* (*could* **not** *tell*) *what coast* they were blown to, (4) the storm then **cease**(***d***)—**the sea, calm.** In *Plutarch's Lives*, this is then followed by the *Libya, Sinalus, south wind, crossed* passage, which is indisputably the source of the corresponding passage in *The Winter's Tale*.

Importantly, Greene's *Pandosto* has none of the other Plutarchan names and no other Plutarchan elements. As Greene apparently takes nothing else from the tome, there is no reason for him to decide to flip through the pages of *Plutarch's Lives* to find a description of a sea storm. And even if he had, the text refers to dozens of other squalls—and includes the term *storm* or *tempest* eighty-nine times. So why would he turn to this particular passage, running from the bottom of 1039 and extending to 1040, to borrow the wording of a description of a storm that he could have easily written himself? And even if we choose to believe that Greene did act in such a manner and did randomly choose that page, how would it have been possible that, twenty-five years later, when Shakespeare adapted Greene's *Pandosto*, he would at the very start of the play, again like Greene, turn to these same pages of *Plutarch's Lives*, 1038–1040, and start assigning characters' names from these pages—Polixenes, Dion, and Sinalus? Then, at the point in the story where Greene borrows the description of a storm, Shakespeare has Florizel start talking about a voyage from Libya that begins on page 1040 right where Greene's source passage ends. And why is there no explanation for how Florizel was blown from Sicily to Libya? This is all the more inexplicable given that this Plutarchan passage describes a storm that blows ships from Sicily to Libya!

None of this could have occurred by chance. No, Greene and Shakespeare did not—at precisely the same moment in their shared storyline—borrow different halves of the same long passage in *Plutarch's Lives*. Rather, both Greene and Shakespeare were following the same source play, and it is this work that had all the Plutarchan elements and Northern language from these pages, some of which ended up in Greene's tale, some in Shakespeare's play. Thus, this earlier Northern version included this same storm from *Plutarch's Lives* that blew ships from the coast of Sicily to Sinalus's Libya. In other words, in North's version, when Leontes asks about the dangers of sea travel and "the dreadful Neptune," Florizel does not just oddly change the subject with "She came from Libya." He first describes the storm that carried him from Sicily to Libya, then he discusses his interaction with Sinalus and the meeting of Perdita, his "daughter." Then North's Florizel—as with Shakespeare's Florizel—discusses the "prosperous **south wind** friendly" with which they *crossed* the sea. Shakespeare cut out the first half of this description, perhaps because there was another description of a sea storm earlier in the play (3.3), but Greene kept the storm. The result is the ostensibly fantastic circumstance of two authors, writing twenty-five years apart and both working independently on the same storyline, both seemingly opening up a third text and borrowing two different parts of the same passage when relating the same event.

All this evidence supplied by Greene's *Pandosto* is probative. Though writing during different reigns, Greene and Shakespeare both appear to have borrowed independently from (1) Herberay's *Amadis de Grecia*, (2) North's *Dial*, and (3) North's *Plutarch's Lives*. North's *Dial* is the origin of the Isle of Delphos error in both Greene's prose work and Shakespeare's play, and each work includes different elements and language from North's Oracle-related stories. From North's *Plutarch's Lives*, both works incorporate different halves of the same passage to describe the same voyage. Again and again, we find facts that admit only one explanation: North, shortly after his trip to Rome, wrote two plays on Henry VIII's divorce of Katherine—one a straightforward history, the other an allegory based on his continental journey. Half a century later, Shakespeare reworked these plays as *Henry VIII* and *The Winter's Tale*.

MEASURING "THE LANDS AND WATERS 'TWIXT YOUR THRONE AND HIS"

As we have seen, *The Winter's Tale* corresponds with the life of Mary in dozens of peculiar details. But two of the most interesting may be those parallels during the time of reconciliation of the two estranged kings and their nations, which, in turn, represent the reconciliation of England with Rome. Table 8.12 provides an example of how both North's journal and *The Winter's Tale* describe the celebrations that ensued.

Both passages refer to the bonfires that celebrate the union, the foreign arbiter (Oracle/Church of Rome), and the wonders too numerous or marvelous to describe.

But one of the more intriguing correspondences to Marian history is Florizel's claim that the king "had himself / The lands and waters 'twixt your throne and his / Measured to look upon you, whom he loves" (5.1.143–45)—a comment that immediately prompts the question: Does this also fit the facts?

162   *Chapter Eight*

Table 8.12.

North's Journal: On the moment that England is reconciled with Rome	*The Winter's Tale:* On the moment Bohemia is reconciled with Sicily
They made **great bonfires** in Rome because we were reconciled to the church of Rome, and the castle shot off much ordnance. We saw a world of relics, very ridiculous and incredible . . . Cum multis aliis que [nunc] prescribere longum est [with many other similar things, too long here to be described] —16 June	Second Gentleman: Nothing but **bonfires**. The oracle is fulfilled; the King's daughter is found. Such a deal of wonder is broken out within this hour that ballad makers cannot be able to express it. —5.2.23–26

Did someone really travel from London to Rome and back again, on a mission for Philip and Mary, and actually measure the exact distance over both land and water between their court in London and Rome? Remarkably, that answer seems to be yes, and the person who carefully measured and then calculated this distance was Thomas North.

The beginning of every entry in North's journal is noticeable in that it keeps careful track of each mile he travels. Even when he does not write an entry for a stopover, North never forgets to mark the distance the delegates had just traveled. At the very end of his journal, he adds these up—including the distance "From Calais to Dover by sea— 30 miles."

> Transcript:
> From Calais to Dover by sea—30 miles.
> We embarked ourselves at one o clock after midnight and arrived at Dover, the next day being the 22, about nine or ten o clock in the forenoon, and there rested ourselves all that day.
> From Dover to Canterbury—12 miles
> From Canterbury to Dartford—32 miles
> From Dartford to London—12 miles.
> And so ended our Romish Journey.
> The number of the miles from Rome to London through Germany, accounting the leagues from Trento to Worms at five English miles the piece, amounteth to 1100 and one.

North saw the bonfires and the wonders of the reconciliation of England and Rome—and North was the one who measured the distance over "the lands and waters 'twixt" the kingdoms.

SUMMARY

The original purpose of both *Henry VIII* and *The Winter's Tale* has now taken form: as an ambitious young writer, Thomas North would naturally feel drawn to celebrating the wondrous history of his new queen, who was the dedicatee of his *Dial* and had just sent him on his mission to Rome. His study of George Cavendish's unpublished manuscript and Edward Hall's history of the life of Henry VIII—both of which he had consulted for his journal—encouraged him to write a history play on the de-queening of Mary's mother, and then an allegory on the same subject.

While this tragic story of Katherine provides the basic plot outline for both plays, North's visits to Mantua and Rome explain many of the plays' striking images and exotica. In *The Winter's Tale*, this includes North's eye-opening experiences with the lavish palaces in the realms of Ferdinand and Charles V (i.e., the Kings of Bohemia and Sicily); the lifelike painted statues in a chapel dedicated to the Virgin Mary and decorated by Giulio Romano; striking scenes of faith in miracles, especially a poignant prayer for a resurrection in the blizzards of a barren mountain; con artists displaying fake popish relics, including a horn-ring in lawn; his interaction with a very honest Camillo at a wedding celebration; a banquet at the Sala di Psyche at Palazzo Te in Mantua, with Giulio Romano's frescoes of a pastoral feast of the petty gods, with Flora, dressed as spring, distributing flowers, fire-robed Apollo dressed as a humble swain, porters carrying sacks of goods from the spice trade, multiple satyrs, Jupiter changing into a beast to seduce a mortal woman, Proserpine and Dis, Juno, and Cythera. All of these seemingly impossible and fantastic elements—all of the striking visions that make *The Winter's Tale* seem so otherworldly—all this we find in North's trip to Rome.

And these are not commonplace experiences. For many years, various scholars have assumed Shakespeare got his information about Giulio Romano from some traveler to Mantua. But though many have searched, no one has been able to place a Shakespeare-era Englishman in Santa Maria delle Grazie—let alone one expressing astonishment at its lifelike wax figures. According to Rita Severi and our own research, North is the only known traveler prior to 1610 to provide a description of the chapel's interior. He then follows this with a visit to Giulio's most extraordinary achievement: the Palazzo Te. Similarly, some scholars find the notion of the realization of a resurrection in a chapel so outlandish that they contend Hermione never died. Yet North witnessed just such a prayer for a miraculous resurrection of a dead body—and did so among the perpetual storms of barren mountains, just as described by Paulina. After visiting Mantua, North enjoyed the grand international banquets of the Duchess in Pesaro followed by a stay in Rome, where he describes a fabulous procession of cardinals and the pope sitting in his consistory. These served as the basis for similar scenes in *Henry VIII*.

To those familiar with both *Henry VIII* and *The Winter's Tale*, the relevance of various descriptions in North's journal is quite conspicuous. Still, we have also enlisted the aid of forensic linguistics and its associated research tools to unearth additional evidence that Thomas North originally wrote these plays that, decades later, Shakespeare adapted. Through the use of digital search engines and plagiarism software, we have uncovered the ways in which texts by William Thomas, George Cavendish, and Edward Hall served as sources for North's journal. And many of these same source passages that North used for his journal, he then used in *Henry VIII*, even connecting the same widely separated source passages that North had juxtaposed in his journal. At the same time, the playwright frequently veered from the historical source text to incorporate North's language and experiences—including the conflation of the descriptions of the consistory and cardinal parade and adding the costumed women of carnival to Anne's procession. Finally, we have shown that North's *Dial of Princes*, also written between 1555 and 1557, was the origin of many elements and passages in both *The Winter's Tale* and *Henry VIII*.

NOTES

1. In October 2019, Michael Blanding, via email, alerted us to the similarities in the stories of Antigonus in North's *Dial of Princes* and Antigonus in *The Winter's Tale*. At that point, we had not made the connection. But it is now clear that this is the origin for the character's name and various elements of the play's subplot.

2. An EEBO search for *Antigonus* NEAR *Noble** AND *roaring* NEAR *the bears* yields only *The Dial* and *The Winter's Tale*.

3. The translation of the story of Scylla and Charybdis comes from A. S. Kline, *Poetry in Translation*: https://www.poetryintranslation.com/PITBR/Greek/Odyssey12.php.

4. An EEBO search for *she* FBY *before her time* FBY *delivered* results in only seven works at any time. One is Shakespeare's First Folio, two are North's editions of *The Dial*, and one is quoting North's *Dial*. In other words, North and Shakespeare are responsible for four of the seven. Remarkably, *a goodly babe* was even rarer, resulting in only three works at any time, and North and Shakespeare are responsible for two of the three. Both of these extremely peculiar phrases regarding the birth of Perdita are Northern.

5. "Camillo" in The Cross Reference Project (Crossref-it.info): https://crossref-it.info/textguide/the-winters-tale/10/1185.

6. William Elton, "Two Shaksperian Parallels," *The Shakespeare Association Bulletin* 22.3 (1947): 115–16.

7. J. Christopher Warner, *Henry VIII's Divorce: Literature and the Politics of the Printing Press* (Suffolk: The Boydell Press, 1998), 125.

8. John Heywood, *The Four P.P.*, in *"The Pardoner and the Friar," "The Curate and Neighbour Pratt" (c. 1533), "The Four P.P." (c. 1540)*, ed. John S. Farmer (London: Gibbins & Co., 1906). While Farmer suggests *The Four P.P.* was written about 1540, EEBO's date for Heywood's publication is 1544.

9. John S. Farmer, Introduction to *"The Pardoner and the Friar," "The Curate and Neighbour Pratt" (c. 1533), "The Four P.P." (c. 1540)*, by John Heywood, ed. John S. Farmer (London: Gibbins & Co., 1906), viii.

10. Richard Burt, *Licensed by Authority: Ben Jonson and the Discourses of Censorship* (Ithaca: Cornell University Press, 1993), 95.

11. Geoffrey Bullough, *Narrative and Dramatic Sources of Shakespeare, Vol. 8, Romances: "Cymbeline," "The Winter's Tale," "The Tempest"* (London: Routledge & Kegan Paul/New York: Columbia University Press, 1976), 133.

12. Louise Wilson, "The Publication of Iberian Romance in Early Modern Europe," in *Translation and the Book Trade in Early Modern Europe*, ed. José María Pérez Fernández and Edward Wilson-Lee (New York: Cambridge University Press, 2014), 201–206; 205.

13. Malcolm C. Smith, *Ronsard & Du Bellay Versus Bèze: Allusiveness in Renaissance Literary Texts* (Geneve: Librairie Droz, 1995), 99n53.

14. Peter Sharratt, "Du Bellay and the Icarus Complex," in *Myth and Legend in French Literature: Essays in Honour of A. J. Steele*, ed. Keith Aspley, David Bellos, and Peter Sharratt (London: The Modern Humanities Research Association, 1982), 73–92; 80.

15. Sir Sidney Lee may have been the first to connect Autolycus's poem with Ronsard's *L'Alouette*. See Sidney Lee, *The French Renaissance in England: An Account of the Literary Relations of England and France in the Sixteenth Century* (New York: Charles Scribner's Sons, 1910), 245. Ronsard's poem is available online on many websites, including "The LiederNet Archive," http://www.lieder.net/lieder/get_text.html?TextId=12133 and "Bartleby.com," which quotes *The Oxford Book of French Verse*, http://www.bartleby.com/244/71.html. The translation is ours.

16. The Folio version of *The Winter's Tale* has "thrush" here, while the New Oxford Shakespeare Modern Critical Edition opts for "throstle cock."

17. John Heywood's nephew, Stephen, attended Lincoln's Inn with Thomas North, and both North and Heywood were master of revels there in 1556 and 1557, respectively. John's son, Jasper, also wrote favorably about Thomas North in the young Heywood's translation of *Thyestes* (1560). George Ferrers, author of the source work "The Fall of Robert Tresilian" in *A Memorial of Such Princes* (1554), was admitted to Lincoln's Inn in November 1534 (see H. R. Woudhuysen "George Ferrers," *Oxford Dictionary of National Biography*, https://doi-org.ezproxy.lafayette.edu/10.1093/ref:odnb/9360).

18. H. Thomas, *The Talorian Lecture 1922: Shakespeare and Spain* (Oxford: Clarendon Press, 1922), 22.

19. Terence Spencer, "Shakespeare's Isle of Delphos," *The Modern Language Review* 47.2 (1952): 199–202; 199. The conventional view is that Shakespeare based

his *Winter's Tale* on Greene's *Pandosto*, and Spenser suggested that this is also where the dramatist picked up the Isle of Delphos error. But, again, we confirm this cannot be the case. An EEBO search for *Ile of Delphos* FBY *Oracle of Apollo* [or *Isle of Delphos* FBY *Oracle of Apollo*] yields only North's *Dial* prior to Greene's *Pandosto*. Clearly, Greene and Shakespeare were not both independently borrowing from North's *Dial* when working on the same fable. Instead, they were both borrowing these elements from North's play.

20. Robert Greene, *Pandosto: The Triumph of Time* . . . (London: Thomas Orwin for Thomas Cadman, 1588).

21. Kelly A. Quinn, "Sir Thomas North's Marginalia in His *Dial of Princes*," *The Papers of the Bibliographical Society of America* 94.2 (June 2000): 283–87.

22. In the First Folio, *Sinalus* is spelled *Smalus*, but this is clearly the printer's misreading of *in* for *m*. *Smalus* occurs nowhere else in EEBO, and scholars have been unable to connect the name to any other known person in history—let alone a Libyan governor. The New Oxford Shakespeare edition of *The Winter's Tale* corrects the name to Sinalus. In quoting the passage from Bevington, who uses *Smalus*, we amend the spelling to *Sinalus*.

Epilogue
The Lost Playwright

Thomas North's travel journal presents significant new evidence on the origins of many of the most mysterious elements of *The Winter's Tale* and *Henry VIII*, indicating North wrote early versions of these plays during the reign of Queen Mary. Nonetheless, we also need to ask whether there is biographical evidence to suggest that North, the great translator, was also a playwright. Our answer, of course, is yes: North's documentary life is consistent with his having begun writing plays in the 1550s and having continued writing plays throughout the 1570s and 1580s, especially for Leicester's Men, the theater company of his powerful patron, Robert Dudley.

That this was not discovered until now should not be surprising. There were far more plays and playwrights in the Tudor/Stuart era than many commonly suppose. In their introduction to *Lost Plays in Shakespeare's England*, David McInnis and Matthew Steggle estimate that, between 1567 and 1642, roughly 3,000 plays were staged in the commercial theaters, and of that number, only 543, or a little more than 18 percent, survive.[1] The main reason so many plays are now lost is not that they were published and then perished but that they were never published in the first place. But as low as this number is, it is inflated by the percentages of the first half of the seventeenth century, when plays became increasingly popular. If we focus just on the sixteenth century, the percentage of printed plays is lower. The business records of the Elizabethan theater manager Philip Henslowe, for example, show that only thirty of the 280 plays that he recorded between 1592 and 1603—a shade over 10 percent—are extant.[2] If we examine the decades in which North mostly wrote—from the 1550s to the 1580s—we find the percentage of printed plays was even lower. Necessarily, then, if thousands of plays from the era are lost, we can rightly assume that a number of early playwrights are lost as well.

Thomas North, who is known for his four major translations and for the excellence of his prose style, entered Lincoln's Inn in 1556, shortly after his return from Italy. In 1557, at the age of twenty-two, he became master of revels at Lincoln's Inn, which placed him in charge of entertainments. The appointment, J. Christopher Warner suggests, indicates that North "could also indulge in songs and plays."[3] Indeed, for young writers, the Inns of Court were a welcoming venue.

In 1560, Jasper Heywood, in a Preface to his translation of Seneca's *Thyestes* (1560), spoke of how the ghost of Seneca visited him in a dream, urging him to translate his works into English. Responding with humility, he noted that there was a group of young tragic writers at the Inns of Court who would be far worthier. Heywood placed North at the top of the list, marking him first among writers who had a "painful pen," writers who, it would seem, Melpomene, the Muse of tragedy, "had taught them for to write":

> In Lincoln's Inn and Temples twain, Gray's Inn and other mo',
> Thou shalt them find whose painful pen thy verse shall flourish so,
> That Melpomen thou would'st well ween had taught them for to write
> And all their works with stately style and goodly grace t'indite.
> There shalt thou see the self-same North, whose work his wit displays,
> And **Dial** doth of **Princes** paint, and preach abroad his praise. . . .[4]

For emphasis, and because the allusion to North is significant, we provide a modern translation:

> At Lincoln's Inn, Inner and Middle Temple, Gray's Inn and others,
> you, Seneca, shall find writers whose skill at tragic writing ("painful pen")
> would be best suited to translate your tragedies into English.
> Indeed, you would think that Melpomene (the Muse of tragedy) had taught them how to write
> and did imbue their works with stately style and grace.
> There (at the Inns of Court), you will see an example of such a tragic writer,
> North, whose work reveals his wit
> and whose *Dial of Princes* earns him praise abroad.

Heywood singled out North both for his translation of *The Dial of Princes* (published in 1557) and as one of a group of tragic writers at the Inns of Court—a tragic writer who has already demonstrated his skill as such.

Heywood's Preface seems to have influenced the young writers he praised. The next three students he names after North—Thomas Norton, Thomas Sackville, and Christopher Yelverton—would all attempt Senecan-style tragedy. Norton and Sackville would write *Gorboduc* (1561), and Yelverton would be credited with the epilogue to George Gascoigne's *Jocasta* (1566) and, much later, the dumb shows for *The Misfortunes of Arthur* (1588). And the self-same North would write yet another tragedy.

In a 2014 paper for *Shakespeare Survey 67*, we provided evidence that in 1560–61 North wrote *Titus and Vespasian*, which became the source play for Shakespeare's *Titus Andronicus*. As we proposed, North likely wrote the play for the same reasons fellow students Norton and Sackville wrote *Gorboduc*: to respond to the renewed attention Heywood brought to Seneca and to please Robert Dudley by advising against Elizabeth's marriage to Erik XIV, King of the Swedes and Goths.[5] This explains why the detestable villains of Shakespeare's tragedy are the Goths—and why the play underscores, in a horrific manner, the disastrous consequences that befall a nation when a monarch marries one. It also explains why the end of the tragedy pays homage to Heywood's *Thyestes*, the very work that gave North his first known, favorable review.

North was to receive another "favorable review" in 1576, when George North, likely a cousin, wrote the dedication to "A Brief Discourse of Rebellion and Rebels," offering praise for Thomas, who, he stated, excelled "both for invention and translation"[6]—and *invention* can only refer to original work. George dedicated the manuscript to Thomas's brother, Roger, 2nd Lord North, also mentioning that "I knew your L[ord] to take great delight" in Thomas's works.

Importantly, Roger North's household account book links his younger brother with Leicester's Men, at times documenting payments to both Thomas and the theater troupe after a performance.[7] For 9 and 10 November 1578, Roger records paying both Leicester's players and his brother the same amount, forty shillings.[8] In the following January, Roger documents Thomas's bringing apparel for minstrels and a player to London.[9] In one very important receipt, in 1580, Roger pays both Thomas and Leicester's Men for a play performed at court, giving Thomas the traditional fee and reward, down to the very penny, granted to playwrights and producers of court plays.

Specifically, Lord North gave the theater troupe forty shillings, his standard payment for a performance, and Thomas £3.6s.8d. (Stowe MS 774, pt. 1, 126v). This followed an earlier payment to Thomas of £6.13s.4d. (Stowe MS 774, pt. 1, 125v). These two specific payments—£6.13s.4d. with an additional reward of £3.6s.8d.—are the exact amounts given to the playwrights and producers of court plays, including Sebastian Westcott, Richard Farrant, William Elderton, Richard Edwards, William Hunnis, Richard Mulcaster, Robert Wilson, John Lyly, Anthony Munday, and William Rowley. Each of them received his fees of £6.13s.4d. for his play, and some also earned a reward of £3.6s.8d. Also, in his magisterial *British Drama 1533–1642*, Martin Wiggins indicates that within the "drama-related expenses" for the queen's 1574 progress "the authorities of Bristol paid [Thomas] Churchyard £6.13s.4d. for writing the text." Likewise, in 1591, Robert Greene notoriously sold his play of *Orlando* twice: first to the Queen's Men for a fee of £6.13s.4d., then to the Admiral's Men for the same price. Finally, the Revels records a payment to Shakespeare, Kemp, and Burbage for two comedies performed at court at Greenwich on 26 and 28 December 1594 for £13.6s.8d. with a reward of £6.13s.4d. in total. This again amounts to a payment of £6.13s.4d. and a reward of £3.6s.8d. for each play. As Lord North places both the payment for Leicester's Men's play performance and North's reward together in a single receipt and adds them up, there is no doubt the payment was for North's work on that court play.[10]

Robert Dudley first began supporting a theater troupe even before he became Earl of Leicester, as early as 1559. His players then continued performing—in London, in the suburbs, at court, on tours throughout the English countryside, and even in continental Europe—until their patron's death in 1588. But what plays were they staging over those nearly thirty years, and who was writing them? Sadly, as Terence Schoone-Jongen remarks, "little information about Leicester's repertory survives."[11] Nonetheless, sixteenth-century documents support what all other evidence reveals: Thomas North was not only a translator; he also wrote plays, first for Lincoln's Inn and then for Leicester's Men.

NOTES

1. David McInnis and Matthew Steggle, "Introduction: *Nothing* Will Come of Nothing? Or, What can we Learn from Plays that Don't Exist?," in *Lost Plays in Shakespeare's England*, ed. David McInnis and Matthew Steggle (New York: Palgrave Macmillan, 2014), 1.

2. Neil Carson, A Companion to Henslowe's Diary (Cambridge: Cambridge University Press, 1988), 82–84.

3. J. Christopher Warner, *The Making and Marketing of Tottel's Miscellany, 1557: Songs and Sonnets in the Summer of the Martyrs' Fires* (Burlington, VT: Ashgate, 2013), 22.

4. Jasper Heywood, Preface to *The Seconde Tragedie of Seneca entituled Thyestes faithfully Englished by Jasper Heywood fellowe of Alsolne College in Oxforde* (London: In Fletestrete in the hous late Thomas Berthelettes, 1560). Citation follows *Elizabethan Seneca: Three Tragedies*, MHRA Tudor and Stuart Translations, vol. 8, ed. James Ker and Jessica Winston (London: Modern Humanities Research Association, 2012), 142–43.

5. Dennis McCarthy and June Schlueter, "A Shakespeare/North Collaboration: *Titus Andronicus* and *Titus and Vespasian*," *Shakespeare Survey 67* (2014): 85–101.

6. See Dennis McCarthy and June Schlueter, *A Brief Discourse of Rebellion and Rebels by George North: A Newly Uncovered Manuscript Source for Shakespeare's Plays* (Cambridge: D. S. Brewer in association with the British Library, 2018), 101.

7. Roger North, *Lord North's Household Book, 1576–1589*, British Library, Stowe MS 774, pt. 1, fols 79v, 80, 126v; pt. 2, 40.

8. Roger North, *Lord North's Household Book, 1576–1589* (9–10 November 1578), pt. 1, 80: "given my L. of Lesters plaiers 40s . . . to my brother 40s." See also fols 79v, 126v; pt. 2, 40.

9. Roger North, *Lord North's Household Book, 1576–1589* (11–13 January 1578–79), pt. 1, 85v. Roger writes "to my brother going to London **in money** viii li **beside** apparel to minstrels ii s to player ii s vi d." Roger's use of the words *in money* and *beside* necessarily confirms that he considered the apparel for the minstrels (and likely player) as part of North's gift. As an example, for Tuesday, 29 June 1585, Roger writes, "Sent my brother to London by the carrier on Tuesday velvet hose, a satin gown guarded w[ith] velvet and a mare cost v li and **in ready money** v li" pt. 2, 93v. Again, here Roger obviously considers the gown, hose, and mare as part of a gift given to Thomas—along with the "money."

10. See Martin Wiggins, *British Drama 1533–1642: A Catalogue, Volume 2: 1567–1589* (Oxford: Oxford University Press, 2012), 106, 109, 115, 160, 162–63, 212–15, 221–23, 244–49, 257–58, 308, 310, 311, 313. See also Martin Wiggins, *British Drama 1533–1642: A Catalogue, Volume 5: 1603–1608* (Oxford: Oxford University Press, 2015), 36, 78, 218. See also John Tucker Murray, *English Dramatic Companies, 1558–1642* (London: Constable and Company, 1910), 1:106.

11. Terence Schoone-Jongen, *Shakespeare's Companies: William Shakespeare's Early Career and the Acting Companies, 1577–1594* (Burlington, VT: Ashgate Publishing, 2008), 175.

The Transcript

The Lambeth Palace Library manuscript may be viewed online at http://images.lambethpalacelibrary.org.uk/luna/servlet/s/r9qik9

PRACTICES EMPLOYED

In transcribing the Lambeth Palace Library manuscript, we employed the following practices:

- Corrected names of towns, cities, rivers, and other places named in the journal. In transcribing these, we gave the spelling North used, followed by the corrected spelling in brackets: e.g., St. Lyes [Chantilly], Equam [Château d'Écouen]). To maintain consistency and for ease of reference, if the town is mentioned again, we used the corrected name.
- Normalized and modernized spelling, punctuation, and capitalization.
- Disregarded lines that were crossed out, transcribing only the surviving text, often interlined. (The deleted material may be seen on the above-mentioned website.)
- Silently expanded brevigraphs and abbreviations and added accented characters.
- Copied numbers as expressed in the manuscript. These are usually Arabic but are at times written out; on the few occasions when North uses lower case Roman (xii), we converted these to Arabic (12). When North states the days they remained at a particular town, he might say 9, 10, and 11; so as not to confuse these with dates, we have added a superscript th (or st, nd, or rd as appropriate). For ease of reading, we did not include the periods

The Journey of the Queenes Ambassadour
unto Roome Anno. 1555. The Reverend father
in God the Bisshopp of Ely, and Vicount
Montague then Ambassadours: who sett owt
of Calleis in Picardy on Wednesday, being
Wednesday the 27. of February a[nn]o
p[re]d[ic]to.

February.
27.
in Boulogne.

Boulogne — leages 7.
from Calleis to Boulogne passinge by Sandyforde
Abbey, and Fevenghm Morgyson, n[ow] the new forte
destroied by King Henry theight.

28.
Monstruell.

Boulogne to Monstruell — leages 7.
from Boulogne to Mountrell passing by Hardillo
Castle, w[hi]ch standeth vpon a great marysh
i[n a] wood on th[e] one syde of it. Mongerrell
standeth high as [Boulogne] doth. Bulleyn sitting
on the north easte and sowth syde of it a marysh.
At o[ur] being theer they were fortifieng and inlarging
of the toowne. It was better manned by much
then Boulogne.

Marche.
1.
in Abbeville.
some fl[ood].

Monstruell to Abbeville — leages 10.
from Mounstrell to Abbeville conteyning a towne named
Bue on the right hand. This towne standeth very
strongly, [for] [it hath a] water of many sli groundes about it, and
for the [harb]our of Some passing by it.

conventionally enclosing a number, and we deleted the "a" that precedes it (*a .1000. crowns = 1000 crowns*).
- Provided, in brackets, the names of those who, in 1555, held the titles mentioned in the journal.
- Provided, in brackets, the meaning of an obsolete or obscure word; occasionally provided an endnote for a longer explanation.
- Retained North's underlinings, which may indicate items to which he intended to return when creating a fair copy.
- Occasionally consulted the British Library manuscript or the Huntington Library transcript to recover a word or two that the binding of the original obscured.

MARGINALIA

Along the left side of each page of the Lambeth Palace Library manuscript—but not the manuscript in the British Library—is a roughly one-inch wide column in which North, in italic hand, indicates the date, the town, and at times the river (fl. = flumen) associated with that town alongside the corresponding narrative. These notes, present in both parts of the journey, provide a shorthand telling of the delegation's progress; useful as manicules, they direct one's attention to experiences treated at greater length in the narrative. North's marginalia may be seen in the online facsimile noted at the head of this chapter. Below, we provide a summary that reveals the kind and character of those entries we consider substantive.

The most prominent of the patterns that emerge in the marginalia is North's interest in Roman Catholic relics and miracles. As early as the fourth day of travel (2 March), as the embassy was heading south from Calais, North writes in the margin "St. John's head at Amiens." On 6 March, at Saint-Denis, where the Englishmen saw St. Denis's head, a rood of clean gold, and a piece of the holy cross, he records these (and a unicorn's horn) in the margin. On 2 May, in Bologna, where the delegates saw the bodies of St. Dominick and St. Katherine, along with a piece of Christ's crown of thorns, a marginal note points to the relics. And on 16 June, North inventories the relics they saw at La Scuderia just prior to their departure from Rome, including a nail from the crucifix, the Last Supper table, and Christ's crown of thorns, which North's marginal note calls "wonderful relics." But by "wonderful," North means "full of wonder," and this does not imply his faith in them. In fact, the journal frequently makes clear that North is skeptical about the authenticity of such relics: his 2 May note in the margin does not simply say "relics"; the entry reads "foolish relics."

In France, Italy, and Austria, the Englishmen also heard of Roman Catholic miracles. North's entry of 25 April, near Mantua, describes men flagellating themselves and, in the chapel of Santa Maria delle Grazie, figures of men pitifully tortured or awaiting execution but saved by the Virgin Mary. In the margin, he writes "miracles." On 31 March, North tells the story of an encounter with an old woman looking for life in a stillborn, hoping it will come alive again or, failing that, bleed so it could be christened. In the margin he writes "A fond superstition about a dead born child." Alongside the narrative on 26 May, in Perugia, concerning Our Lady's first ring and the cleansing of children who are "miraculously fed by the Holy Ghost," he writes "A foolish superstitious ceremony devised upon a supposed ring of Our Lady."

On 19 July, in Seefeld, Austria, North hears the story of the arrogant knight who refused to kneel to receive Communion and who demanded a larger piece of the Host. In response, the earth opened, about to swallow him up, but he repented and was saved. The handprint he left upon the altar as he was sinking was still visible in 1555, nearly 200 years after this Eucharistic miracle, which also involved the bleeding of the Host. Here North writes in the margin "A miracle of the Sacrament." Moreover, he interrupts his narrative by writing and underlining "Soodeldom. Soodeldom." And in the margin, he writes it twice more. We have had little luck in uncovering the meaning of this term, but he seems to have been emphatically signaling a story to which he wanted to return.

North's marginalia become more detailed when the delegation reaches Rome and meets the pope. In the narrative and, in brief, in the margin, North speaks of the gift that Cardinal Carafa sent to the lords (9 June), the lords' repair to the court and audience with the pope (10 June), the pope's receiving of the lords in the conclave, sitting in state, the cardinals about him (noting the similarity to the English Parliament in Westminster) (10 June), and the fact that the lords dined and supped with the pope (16 June). Clearly impressed, he records in the text, and briefly in the margin, the manner of the pope's going to the chapel (12 June) and the order of the pope's going in procession (13 June). Of course, he also notes the news the embassy twice received: the death of Pope Julius III (31 March) and, a few weeks later, of Marcellus II (2–14 May). In his 6–7 June entry, and in the margin, North points out that three popes reigned in succession during their six-month progress: Julius III, Marcellus II, and Paul IV (6–7 June).

The twenty-year-old who was impressed with the ritual surrounding the pope was also intrigued by wild beasts. In Rome, he saw an ostrich (11 June); two more ostriches appear in his narrative and in the margin (7–10 July), as do a young partridge (1 April), a tortoise a yard long (27–28 April), and a tiger (25 April), not to mention unicorn horns, one at Saint-Denis (6 March) and one in Mantua (25 April). Other items intrigued North as well: the bell in Notre Dame that weighed 33,000 pounds (6 March), trees called oppie (18 April), the fine knives of Cremona (22 April), the oranges, lemons, and pomegranates growing in Moulins (19 May), an eighteen-foot-long bone of a man (19 May).

North highlighted particular people too: a man at St. Mathurin's who healed mad people (12 March); men drowned in the snow, one eating snowballs to stay alive (2 April); the Duke of Piacenza and Parma, who had been slain in his own house some eight years before (19–21 April); Hippolita, the fair beauty they saw in Mantua (25 April); men in Spoleto who were given to murder and sodomy (28 May); the grave of Polydore Vergil (25 June). And he inserted marginal notes alongside the two edited (though not materially) accounts of Masters White and North: "Master White fell down the hill and his horse both" (28 March); "Master North in danger of killing" (7 April). (It is in this latter entry that North temporarily switches from first person to third.)

Although the practice was unusual, North thrice used the margin to record information not in the narrative. On 12 July, the travelers arrived in Bozen-Bolzano in northern Italy and, judging from the marginal note, met a number of fellow Englishmen there: "Here we met with Lords Turnebull, Martin, Matthew Carewe, William Hussey, Justin Tallern, Fitzwilliams, and alderman Chester's son of London."[1] Similarly, on 23 March, when the embassy traveled from Tarare to Lyon, North inserted this seemingly unrelated marginal note concerning someone he may have met in Lyon: "Signior Giovanni Ambrosio Lavagna [Lavagno] [called] Amitino. He gave me his letters of commendation unto his brother Signior Giovanni Baptista Lavagna [Giovanni Battista Lavagno] in Milano, alla Doana." Also incidental to the narrative, though related, is a marginal note on the day (13 June) that the pope went to Mass in the chapel of St. Peter's church, stating that each year on St. Peter's Day (29 June), the King of Spain (Philip II, who was also England's king) presented the pope with a white horse and 7,000 crowns because Naples embraced the church of Rome.

In the narrative, North repeatedly borrows from Cavendish's *Life of Wolsey* and Hall's *Union*. He also twice refers to William Thomas's *History of Italy*: on 5 June he speaks of the bath or therme of Julius Caesar, and on 13 June he states that it is needless to write anything of Rome's antiquities since they are "truly and very notably set forth" in Thomas's book.[2]

Also, several weeks before he tallies the number of miles the delegation traveled, he notes in the margin that every Dutch mile is five Italian miles (11 July), a note suggesting how challenging a task he had, given that the metric changed from region to region. North does, nonetheless, conclude that the trip from London to Rome covered 1,158 miles, the return trip 1,101 miles; in all, the delegation traveled 2,259 miles in six months, with a two-week stay in Rome.

The Journey of the Queen's Ambassadors unto Rome Anno 1555. The reverend father in God the Bishop of Ely and Viscount Montague, then Ambassadors, who set out of Calais in Picardy, on Wednesday, being Ash Wednesday the 27th of February, a° predicto

February 27

From Calleis [Calais] to Boulogne [Boulogne-sur-Mer], leagues 7, passing by Sandyforde [Saint-Inglevert] Abbey, and through Morgyson [Marquise],[3] which were both destroyed by King Henry the eight.

February 28

From Boulogne to Monstruell [Montreuil], leagues 7, passing by Hardelot Castle, which standeth upon a great marsh and a wood on the one side of it. Montreuil standeth high as Boulogne does, Boulogne having on the northeast and south side of it a marsh. At our being there they were fortifying and enlarging of the town. It was better manned by much than Boulogne.

March 1

From Montreuil to Abbeville, leagues 10, leaving a town named Biu (Rue) on the right hand. This town standeth very strongly by reason of marsh grounds about it and the river of Some [Somme] passing by it.

March 2

From Abbeville to Amiens, leagues 10, passing by a castle of Monsieur de Rions of Flanders and a bridge named Pont de Remy and by a house of the vidames called Pinckeney [Picquigny],[4] leaving always on the left hand of us the river of Somme. Amiens standeth upon the river of Somme in a marvelous even ground, the town being walled about and some few English miles in circuit. The water of Somme runneth in seven streets of the town. In this town we saw the relic of St. John's head very richly enclosed in gold and many precious jewels, the church very beautiful and adorned with cunning workmanship. The ambassadors were lodged in the Duke of Vendôme's [Antoine, from May 1555 King of Navarre] house. There is also a place called St. Dennis [Saint-Denis] churchyard, which is thicker beset with sundry fashioned crosses than any man can well number and very great devotion there customably shown of all sorts.

March 3

From Amiens to Brotuill [Breteuil], leagues 7. In our way we saw the first vineyards.

March 4

From Breteuil to Clermont, leagues 7. There we saw 6 pictures of gentlemen hanged upon the gibbets standing in the midst of the marketplace, but the gentlemen themselves were fled away. There is very good wine at Clermont.

March 5

From Clermont to Luzarche [Luzarches], leagues 7, passing through a town named St. Lupe [Saint-Leu-la-Forêt]. We passed also over the river Oyze [Oise] in a ferry boat. This river parteth Picardy and France.

March 6

From Luzarches to Paris, leagues 6, leaving on our left hand the constable's [Anne de Montmorency] house, called St. Lyes [Chantilly] [Château de Chantilly], with a very great pool adjoining to it. We saw also another house, which the said constable had but lately built, called Équam [Château d'Écouen], which was praised for the fairest house in France. This house standeth upon a pleasant large hill yet in the middle of a great plain; the one side is employed to corn and the other full of vineyards. The hill is full of wood on every side saving the very top, where the house standeth. Yet is there no tree but that beareth fruit, the greatest sort chestnuts, walnuts, pine or fir trees, the smaller figs, cherries, almonds, peaches, and others, which was to the beholders a marvelous sight and pleasure.

This house is built in a quadrant form to the height of two stories plain and the roof with gable windows cast out for a third, the foresaid gable windows being of a marvelous greatness, answering to the others beneath in number, fashion, and quantity. The whole house is of freestone, so white, so great and fair as may be seen; the covering is of blue slate, the roof (as through all France) more raised up than our buildings, the which gives much beauty to their houses. The gate is made extant with pillars and thrice vaulted, and in the uppermost vault standeth St. George on horseback, wrought also in freestone to a marvelous greatness, the pillars likewise being Tuscan work. In the inside of the said gate, two of the lowest pillars are of blue and fine marble, answerable to a like couple right over against them on the farthest side, there being a like front and extant to that galleries before. Of the four sides of this quadrant, the gate side, with that over against it, are appointed to two galleries, the other couple to chambers. The gate galleries is of a lower roof than the other three and therefore hath but his gallery above of a high vaulted roof, and his terrace beneath, open to the court or quadrant. This gallery is 21 foot broad, and 80 in length: the pavements are very broad and like even, stained with the arms of the crown and peers of France, the king's poesy being *Donec totum impleat orbem* [Till he replenish the whole world]. The roof within is gilt, the ridge tiles without are also gilt. The ceiling within is of walnut. The other gallery was hanged with rich arras, where was also a chart of the holy land, made of divers woods and of natural colors, set in small pieces, as the demonstration of the said places required, and seemed rather to have been done with the pencil than otherwise. At the end of the gallery, under the same roof, is the chapel, the ceiling whereof is like workmanship to the chart afore named, of Brazil, Ebony, walnut tree, and other like woods, joined in the figures of the Apostles, and other curious works. The table of the altar, with the images thereabout, be of white marble, with two pillars of fine jet. The chambers are not great but very well conveyed, having a narrow gallery to convey you to every one of them apart; but the gallery is close and appeareth not outward to them that be in the court. The chimneys stand 2 foot out of the wall into the chambers and yet seem not to hurt the room nor the sight thereof because they be raised in the midst of the side of the chamber, having a side light of the window, and, again, they keep even largeness to the roof of the chamber, all above the marble, painted with pleasant works and in oil colored. In the court standeth an huge great horse of copper, which shall be set upon the gate, with the image of the king upon the back of him.

Within 2 leagues of this house is Saint-Denis, where all the kings of France be buried and sometimes crowned. But the appointed place of coronation is at a city called Reims in Bryttayne [Brittany[5]] [sic—Champagne].

The town of Saint-Denis is neither fair nor large, but the church is great and the treasure also. In this church we saw the shrine of St. Denis made of silver and gilt and a great rood of clean gold, lacking but one arm, the which Francis [Francis I], the French king, took away to maintain his wars [the Hapsburg-Valois wars, which continued until 1559], adjoining instead thereof for recompense one of silver and gilt. There is also one whole unicorn's horn, which was almost 2 ells long, grown taper wise and wreathed, as we see it commonly painted. This horn is but slender to the length, yet notwithstanding massive and heavy. There was also St. Denis's head (*ut dicitur* [as said]) richly enclosed in gold and beset with precious stones and orient pearl. Likewise a piece of the holy cross and one of the nails wherewith Christ was nailed thereto, set in gold. We were also brought into the treasury there, where we saw relics in another place with ornaments of the king and queen's coronation. And first I saw these relics: a piece of the holy cross in a cross of gold; the finger of St. Thomas that he put into the wound of our Lord; a griffin's claw trimmed with silver, as great as a hunter's horn of the middle sort; St. Benedict's head; St. Denis's penner and inkhorn; a cup that was Solomon's; and one other made of an agate of a marvelous greatness and riches. I saw also the crowns of the king and the queen: upon the king's crown, a ruby as big as a walnut, and on every part set with rich stones. Also the sword and scepter of the kings set with massy gold, the knob thereof being set with diamonds and pearl. Also the king's spurs of gold and the portraitures of Nero, Charlemagne, and other emperors.

March 7, 8

Between Saint-Denis and Paris, there are divers crosses, much like to churching crosses but not so big altogether nor so high, where (as it is said) St. Denis rested after he was beheaded.

Thus rode we towards Paris, whereas Mons[ieu]r le beaue Dolphin [René de Laval-Bois-Dauphin] met the ambassadors in the highway to Paris, which city standeth somewhat low upon the river of Seine which divideth the university from the town, compassing round about the city, which lieth between them both as an isle, and yet is Paris altogether of a round form. It is very fair and great and full of merchandise, but the streets be very foul by reason their houses be very high and the streets very narrow. The city alone hath 19 churches in it, with the great church of Notre Dame, in the steeple whereof hangeth a bell weighing 33000 lbs. The French king hath a house there called the Louvre. I saw in Paris the wonderful instrument of Orontius [Orontius Finnaeus/Oronce Finé], then alive,[6] wherein was to be seen the course of the seven planets presently moving, with the aspects the one to the other. I also saw the coining house, with the new coins so perfectly stamped that in my judgment no man is able to counterfeit the same. The mill that standeth in the midst of Seine serveth to draw forth the bullion, and the work is so speedy that putting in a lathe of bullion an inch thick and a foot long, he bringeth it quickly to the thinness of a French sous and the thickness sufficient to the stamp is, when the lathe will enter in a little notch that is in a steel shiner[?]. We tarried there the 7th and 8th day.

March 9

From Paris to Melun, leagues 10, leaving on the left hand, one league from Paris, a castle of the kings, built by King Henry the 5th, King of England, named Boys Vintcens [Bois de Vincennes], where all the prisoners taken in the wars against the emperor do lie in hold, and so passing through two towns, the one called Pont Shalentine [Charenton-le-Pont] and the other Ville neufe de St. George [Villeneuve-Saint-Georges]. At Pont Charenton there meeteth two rivers, Marne and Seine, and so runneth to Paris. Almost at the gate we went out of standeth a castle called the Duke of Bedford's castle and the Bastillion without the gate, where the Frenchmen now build a pace. In Melun standeth a castle environed with the river of Seine, built by Englishmen.

March 10

From Melun to Fontebleaue [Fontainebleau], leagues 4, where the French king's [Henry II] court lay. Two miles off the court, certain gentlemen of the king's house met our lords and courteously entertained them and brought them the nearest way to the court, where they were lovingly received, and led up into a gallery, where they had each of them a very fair lodging appointed, costly hanged, and set forth with as rich beds as might be seen. The house is called Fontainebleau, for the goodly fountain that is in the house and the fair water thereof. This house is both beautiful and larger than any I had before seen in France or England. I may resemble the state thereof to the honor of Hampton Court, which, as it passeth Fontainebleau, with the great hall and large chambers, so is it inferior in outward beauty and uniformity, which praiseth all kind of building most, for the covering thereof is blue slate and all the rest of freestone. There is an out-court or quadrant whereof one side is a gallery to walk in, being in length 600 foot. There is also on the south side a garden, having in it a great pond, the walks and alleys shadowed with pine and cypress trees. At the end of one of the alleys is a vault curiously counterfeited as out of the rock natural, whither they do repair to refresh them in hot weather. There is another garden more privy, set full of antiquities of copper. In the face of the great lodging rises a fountain fair, as I have said, spouting with 5 spouts upright out of a natural rock or else, very naturally wrought. This house standeth in a valley, compassed about with rocky hills but not very great; and the country is forest, full of wild deer, wolves, and wild boars. The name of the forest is [La] Barre; the house standeth 3 leagues within it every way. The lords came to the court about 4 of the clock and within one hour after were brought to the king's presence, who received them very gently and embraced as many gentlemen of the train as came unto him. After the lords had had some talk with the king, they were brought unto the queen's chamber of presence, where the French queen [Catherine de' Medici], accompanied with the Queen of Scots [Mary, not yet 13], and two of her own daughters, were ready to receive them. From thence they departed to their lodgings, where were ready to wait upon them divers of the French king's gentlemen, being appointed to attend them dinner and supper during their abode there.

March 11

[From Fontainebleau to St. Mathurin (Basilique Saint-Mathurin, in Larchant), 4 leagues.[7]] The next day after, being the 11th day, the rest of the train that could not be lodged at the court came thither and desired certain Scottish gentlemen they might see the Queen of Scots, who being told of their desire to see her grace, she very courteously came forth out of her privy chamber into her chamber of presence among us all and said unto us she was very glad to see us, calling us her countrymen. About 4 of the clock this afternoon, the French king came from hunting the wild boar, and then the lords went and took their leave of him and the king embraced them, and as many of their gentlemen as came unto him. That done, the same night they departed from the court and rode to St. Mathurin's. The king is a goodly tall gentleman, well made in all the parts of his body, a very grim countenance yet very gentle, meek, and well beloved of all his subjects.

March 12

We remained all this day (the 12th) at St. Mathurin's. This St. Mathurin (as they say) is a holy man that can help mad men and women, within 9 days space if they do this that follows. The priest, when Mass is done, must call for the madmen or women to come and kneel before the altar, and, when he had said certain prayers, he must come and lay flannel upon their heads and say certain words over them. That ended, they rise, and go round about the altar 4 times, and at every time kiss the four brazen pillars that stand about the altar. Then must they offer up unto St. Mathurin a pottle pot full of wine, 3 loaves of bread, and a French sous in money, which in value of our English money is ijd. ob. q. [2 denarii (2 penny), obulus (half-penny), quadran (quarter-penny)], and, doing this for the space of 9 days together, they say they shall have their right wits again.

March 13

From St. Mathurin to Montargis, leagues 8. This town standeth so well for wood, water, and meadow, as I have not seen the like in all France before.

There standeth a castle, fair for all lodgings but of no force, the which sometime (as they say) was in the keeping of my Lord Talbot [John Talbot, 1st Earl of Shrewsbury]. The house is of great receipt and very stately. The hall hath a pair of stairs 56 steps going up to it. It hath also 6 chimneys in it. It is 65 paces long and 20 paces broad. There is both a guard chamber and a chamber of presence, the which I have not seen in other places in that country.

March 14

From Montargis to Briare, 9 leagues. By this town runneth the greatest river in France, called Loire, leaving it always upon our right hand. It parteth the duchy of Berry from Nivernais [now Nièvre] and from Barbois.

March 15

From Briare to Cone [Cosne-Cours-sur-Loire], 8 leagues, through a town called Bonny [Bonny-sur-Loire].

March 16

From Cosne to La Charité [La Charité-sur-Loire], 8 leagues, leaving on the right hand of us, over the river of Loire, a town called Sancerre, with a castle in it of great force, which town of late is named Young Geneva, of divers men, because of their religion.

March 17

From La Charité to Nevers, 5 long leagues. As we rode by the river of Loire, we saw water mills standing upon boats in the main river, to be removed by the millers to any other place they like better, as they list. At Nevers is a bridge 25 score paces over, upon the which we passed the river of Loire and there left it.

March 18

From Nevers to St. Pierre le Monastier [Saint-Pierre-le-Moûtier], 5 long leagues. This is a little walled town, where the justices of the country sit and keep their sessions.

March 19

From Saint-Pierre-le-Moûtier to Molins [Moulins], 7 leagues, through a town called Ville neufe [Villeneuve-Saint-Georges], leaving the river Allier on our right hand, the which runneth into Loire. This town of Moulins is the chiefest town in Bourbonnais, where is a great and ancient house of the Duke of Bourbon, commodious for conduits and gardens. There is a conduit having out of the midst of the cistern an artichoke bearing 4 ripe, as it were, and one seeded, and out of the leaves springeth water as rain, very artistically wrought in copper and gilt. Here we saw oranges, lemons, and pomegranates growing by labor and diligence of men; for the trees be growing within barrels filled with good earth, and in the winter be removed under terraces and houses made for the purpose and are ever brought out against the spring into the garden again. In the garden, be two goodly banqueting houses; the one of them hath water round about it and the other a great many of singing birds in it of divers sorts, and at every corner of it a great hart's head standing, with many other goodly commodities. There is a bone of a man to be seen, whose length was 18 foot and found in Vienne in Dolphinois [Viennois in Dauphiné]. Furthermore, I saw there the proportion of divers cities, with the walls, churches, and bulwarks carved in wood very curiously.

March 20

From Moulins to la Palice [Lapalisse], 10 long leagues. This town standeth upon a hill, the country round about it being forest and heath.

March 21

From Lapalisse to Rouane [Roanne], 8 long leagues, passing a small mountain. There we passed over the river of Loyre [Loire] as we go out of the town towards Italy.

March 22

From Roanne to Tarare, 6 long leagues. This town standeth in a deep bottom, the hills hanging over on every side, and is watered with a narrow stream but so swift that within the space of 200 yards 4 mills are driven, 2 for corn, 1 to saw timber, another to bench the hemp. The corn mill grinds with a flat wheel, the water being forced to one side of it. The saw mill is driven with an upright wheel, and the water that maketh it go is gathered whole into a narrow trough, which delivereth the same water to the wheel. This wheel hath a piece of timber put to the axletree end, like the handle of a broch [a hand organ], and fastened to the end of the saw, which, being turned with the force of the water, hoisteth up and down the saw that continually eateth in, and the handle of the same is kept in a riggle [groove] of wood for [from] swerving. Also, the timber lie as it were upon a ladder which is brought by little and little to the saw with another vice. The hemp mill is much like the cider mills we have in England, where a stone is rolled about in a vault or vessel where the hemp lieth.

March 23

From Tarare to Lion [Lyon], 6 long leagues. Lyon is a goodly city, and a strong, by means of the rocks on the one side of it, and the waters on the other side. We came into the town on Lyon's side, a mile before we came to any bridge, and then we passed a bridge over the river Soâne, and, going out of the town, we went a long mile in [the] Dauphiné side and passed a long bridge over the river of Rhone. The greatest part of the town is as it were in an isle, at the end thereof both the rivers being joined together. Upon the north side of the town is the new fortification and the castle upon the very rock. Upon the south side is the church of St. Henry, his corpse and sepulcher; the pillar whereunto Christ was bound, of blue marble with white veins; and, on the east side, a valley or plain, very fruitful. It is evil dwelling there for those that will perjure themselves, for they shall [be] burned with a fire called St. Anthony's fire. We tarried two days at Lyon. Here we had great entertainment of Madame La Cheveriere, a great lady in Lyon.

March 26

From Lyon to Burgoing [Bourgoin-Jallieu], 5 leagues. This town standeth under a great hill having a good soil, with wood and water enough.

March 27

From Bourgoin to Pont beauvessin [Pont-de-Beauvoisin], 5 leagues, through a town named La Tour du Pine [La Tour-du-Pin], passing a great wood of chestnuts. Through this town [i.e., Pont-de-Beauvoisin] runneth the river of Arte [L'Arc] that cometh from the mountains. The one side of the water is Dauphiné and the other is Savoy. There is also a mill to make oil of walnuts.

March 28

From Pont-de-Beauvoisin to Chamberi [Chambéry], five long leagues, which by the way we passed over Mont D'Aigubeteto [Mount d'Aiguebelette], a great mountain and very dangerous, 1 league high and more, all upon rocks and very narrow passages. Here, Master White (whose father [Thomas White] was master of the requests to Queen Mary[8] and a gentleman of Master Carne's train, ambassador leger to Rome), taking hold of the head of his horse to pull him near the rock side to keep him from falling down the hill, his horse, going back, pulled his master after him, and both together tumbled down the hill, one over the other, a great way, notwithstanding (as God would) bushes stayed them, and neither horse nor man hurt. This is the chiefest and best town of all Savoy and hath a fair great castle in it, but of no force; it standeth in a valley full of corn, woods, and pasture, plenty of fruits, as figs, almonds, &c. We being almost at the foot of the hill and thinking we had had but one English mile to the town, we found it 5 long miles ere ever we came at it, and the way very straight.

March 29

From Chambéry to Aigubele [Aiguebelle], 8 long leagues, through Montmélian, a pretty town in the which standeth a notable strong castle upon a rock that keepeth the passage between the mountains, the which is thought impregnable but by famine or treason. By this town runneth the river of Isère and, through Aiguebelle, the river Arc that joins with Isère. It is called aqua bella of the fountains, but the river is exceeding foul. The church of Aiguebelle was founded by a Bishop of Hartford called Petrus de Aqua Blanca.[9]

March 30

From Aiguebelle to S. Jehan de morienne [Saint-Jean-de-Maurienne], 6 long leagues, riding between the mountains of a very great height all that journey, upon which mountains was plenty of corn and vines, with very many dwelling houses and cottages, as we call them, and some of them thought to be a league high. That day we passed over the river of Lyzere [Isère] 4 times. Upon these mountains was great store of snow lying. This town standeth very barrenly upon the river of Arc, the which falling from the mountains is so swift and maketh so great a noise that it is able to make a man deaf, and hath no fish in it.[10] We rode along this river 5 days' journey. In these mountains be wild boars; their hogs are all black; their sheep likewise great and long legged, with crooked snouts; very many goats.

March 31

From Saint-Jean-de-Maurienne to St. Andrews [Saint-André], 4 long leagues, still between the mountains, and those higher to my seeing than the other. There was such noise of waters beating upon the rocks, and such monstrous mountains to behold, of a huge height, being always in danger of some stones falling upon us that it seemed rather a hell than a highway for men to pass by. Upon the right hand on the other side of those mountains, all the way is Dauphiné.

At Saint-André I, coming into a church about 4 a clock at afternoon, spied a young child lying dead upon a board before the image of Our Lady, and an old woman sitting, watching and praying by it, having also a tallow candle burning and a great many of peas and beans in a little tray, the which she had offered up to Our Lady. I asked her in French what she meant to do so. And she made me answer again that the child was born dead and that she looked for life of it, or at the least to burst out of bleeding in some place of the body. And thus they do for the space of 15 days together until it stinked. If it be so that it bleed, although it receive not life, it is christened; if not, then it is cast into the river. In this town news came for a certainty that Pope Julius Tertius [Pope Julius III, Giovanni Maria Ciocchi del Monte] died at Rome, the 23rd day of March.

April 1

From Saint-André to Lunebourg [Lanslebourg-Mont-Cenis], 5 long leagues, passing by a town called Tresignon [Termignon, now part of Val-Cenis], over a great mountain, yet there accounted as none, by reason of the inestimable height of the other mountains. This day we had great rain and snow, and, coming under the steep of a cliff, a great gulf of waterfall (as great as the throw of a mill) fell down and in falling suddenly from the cliff was turned to snow and had made there a mighty heap on the which we trod, the snow falling continually and thick, and yet the space from the fall to the ground could not be judged above 20 fathom. Among these mountains we saw on the 28th day of March a young partridge. I being tired among these mountains was drawn in a sled[11] a great part of the way for the value of 2d [tuppence].[12] The way is made out of the rocks and mountains by men's hands. The diet there of the common people in Lent is nothing else but peas and herbs, oil and chestnuts, and yet they be very fat withal.

April 2

From Lanslebourg to Susa, 6 long leagues, passing over the great mountain Cenis, the which is 2 leagues to the top, and, when we are come to the top, then we have a great plain to go, which is 2 long leagues and a half. Then had we 3 foot of the mountain (as they call it) to go down, that were half leagues apiece, 2 of them, and the 3rd was a whole league. We all passed without danger, thanks be to God, to the great admiration of them of the country, and no less, I assure you, to them that should hear the truth. After we got to the top of the mountain, which we came unto with great pain, for I was fain to hire one to lead my horse up before me and I to come after holding him by the tail for fear of falling backwards, it was so steep up to the top. By the way I did see a poor man lie almost drowned in the snow, making round balls of snow and eating of them for very hunger.[13] After we came at the top of the mountain, going our way towards the chapel named La Chapelle de Trancizes [Transis] (to wit, the chapel of the dead) being half a league: this chapel lieth full of dead men's skulls that have died upon that mountain for extreme cold and other misfortunes, and there seem to be more than 1000 persons, whereof 18 Launceknights [Landsknechte] [German mercenary soldiers] were thrown in there in March before.[14]

From thence we went to the post house, called La Tavaro, an inn, being half a league off. We had no other ground to go on but only snow that was but two foot broad and hardened with the continual frost that is there almost always, so that in this way the snow was thought to be at the least a spear depth and more, the which doth, if there be any heat at all, sink every 2 hours. The very same day that we passed over this mountain, there were 4 persons drowned by going a little out of the way; we were in the more hazard by reason of the great wind that blew and the abundance of snow that fell so fast from the elements that one of us could not see another, being but a small way asunder, and such was all the way on the plain of the hill. Descending off the plain, we turned upon the way as though we had been going down a pair of stairs, having at every corner under us valleys of snow, some 10 fathom deep, and some more. In my going down I fell willingly above a dozen times, only to stay myself. What the knights said that it was I will not write lest I should be counted a liar; but the truth is, no man will believe the danger of the hill but such as know it. And in this wise did we turn at every 10 or 12 fathoms for half a league, until we came to a place called the hospital. Then turned we in like case upon the rocks half a league, until we came at a town called Feriere [La Ferrière], the first town of Pyemont [Piedmont], and from thence to another town named Novalese [Novalesa], the which payeth monthly to the French king 22 crowns.

April 3, 4

From thence to Susa all the way upon great stones, but not so evil as before. This town Susa payeth in like case monthly unto the French king 100 crowns. The 26th of April [sic—March] were 5 men drowned upon this Mount Cenis, and 3 weeks before that were 3 of the Prince of Salerno's men drowned in snow. The same day that we went over Mount Cenis, it was told us that the number that have been drowned there within this half year is above 50 persons, by report of the inhabitants thereabouts, and yet in the months of July and August the snow is melted quite away from the plain of the mountain, besides some other, so that you shall see as good ground there as is in all Savoy. Furthermore, the town of Susa is not strong but yet kept with a garrison of men to keep the passage between Savoy and Piedmont. Doctor [William] Benet, sometime Archdeacon of Salisbury and ambassador from King Henry the eighth to the pope, lieth buried in Susa.[15] Upon the north side of Susa is a mountain called Rochemelune [Rochemelon], by estimation 10 leagues high, upon the top whereof standeth a chapel of Niges [Notre Dame des Nieges/Our Lady of the Snows], the which was built by a Jew that made his vow: he would build a chapel upon the top of the highest mountain in Europe, this being counted the highest mountain of all others. The Duke of Bourbon [Charles III] went thither before he went to the sacking of Rome to offer up his harness there to Our Lady of the Snows. It was so high that he made 2 days' journey to the very top of it. We remained at Susa two days, the 3rd and 4th. Upon Mount Cenis there appeared the way that was cut out of the rock by Hannibal when he entered into Italy.

April 5

From Susa to Avigliana, 5 long leagues, through 3 towns, the first called Borsling [Bussoleno], the second St. Ambrose [Sant'Ambrogio], the 3rd St. George [San Giorgio]. This town standeth very pleasantly and hath a castle of great force in it, the which payeth monthly to the French king 500 crowns.

April 6

From Avigliana to Porein [Porino] 15 miles, leaving Turin [Torino] on the right hand of us, which is the chiefest town of Piedmont. It seemeth to be very fair and strong and standeth upon the river of Po. It was our right way to have gone through it, but we could not be suffered to come within it because their enemies lay so near unto it. There the wars were set between the French king [Henry II] and the emperor [Charles V]; they skirmished every day one with the other. Turney [Turin/Turino] is the French king's town. We passed through a town named Ravole [Rivoli], which payeth 600 crowns a month to the French king, and by a fort of the French king's called Mount Calier [Moncalieri], a very strong fort, over the river of Po, the which is the greatest river (as they say) in all Italy. We left also on the right hand of us, as it were a league from us, a very strong town named Chier [Chieri], a town of war of the French king's also. Porino hath been a very strong town but decayed by the wars and is now a neuter town. There, for lack of lodgings, we were fain to lie in barns and stables all that night in our hoods.

April 7

From Porino to Aste [Asti], 12 miles, the which being the march or frontier town of both parties, and we being to pass by the holds and castles of either party, who had daily skirmishes together, we were conducted by a French trumpet and a Spanish drum by a town called Villa nova D'Aste [Villanova D'Asti], French, and another called Valfranera Imperiall [Valfenera Imperial], the towns round about us being all spoiled and burnt. Half a mile on this side the town of Asti, the captain of the town, accompanied with 300 men of arms, met the lords and brought them to the town with great rejoicing, and they so curvetted their great horses that some of them, horse and man, lay in the ditches; and when we came to the town, they gave the lords a great volley of small shot and some great ordnance shot off the walls.

[Heavily edited and interlined passage:] As we were coming near the town, M. Thomas North, my Lord North's younger son and my Lord of Ely's page, in danger to have been slain by a scout sent to discover the lords' coming, who, being upon him ere he was ware, with his pistol in his hand, cried, in Italian, *Chi Viva* [Who goes there?],[16] whereupon he answering they were Englishmen the horseman wheeled about and so left him, galloping away to bring news of the lords' coming.

About 4 a clock in the afternoon, there was a general procession in the town, in token of rejoicing (as it seemed) at our coming, supposing the lords' journey had been as well to have treated a peace betwixt the emperor and the French king as for any other matter besides. In this procession there were 13 crosses and such a number of friars as I never saw together in all my life before, and above 2000 people I am sure. The women went strangely appareled, fitter in my judgment for maskers and players than for women.[17]

This is the first town of the emperor's. Here the lords had very great presents given them. The town of Asti is not very strong of itself, but it is very well guarded with men of war. The Frenchmen gave alarum to the town this night, we lying there. The next day the captains and men of arms conveyed the lords in like manner, out of the town, as they brought them in, and with as much bravery as they could devise. For in 3 several places as we departed out of the town, all the soldiers of the town made a guard in very good order and gave the lords a volley of shot to the number of 200. Then, when we came out of the gate, we saw 200 shot marching before us in good array, which went along with us a good mile out of the town. And when the lords came nigh unto them, they blew off their pieces, and took their leave of the lords, and so departed back to the town in like order as they came out.

April 8

From Asti to Alexandria [Alessandria], 20 miles, passing by the castle of Nonven, which, when we came over against it, shot off very friendly, and, as we passed through small towns, they rang the bells in token of rejoicing. At the gates of Alessandria, the captain of the town, with a great number of gentlemen, came and entertained the lords very courteously and brought them to their lodging, the fairest house of the town. As we entered into the house, there was a great peal of squibs shot off with a train, which made a very great report, that to our thinking we took them for great pieces of ordnance. That night there came to the lords from the emperor's camp a gentleman of Spain called Signior Andrea Rodovico with a great troop of horsemen and lay that night in the town to keep the lords company, the emperor's camp being but 8 miles off the town. Here the lords and all their train were clearly defrayed at the knights' costs and charges for all things, for not eight days before our coming thither the captain of the town was taken prisoner of the Frenchmen. The French king had then taken Casale and the whole state of Mountferrat, which is the inheritance of the Duke of Mantua, enjoining 300 holds and small towns to them. There runneth a goodly river on the west side of Alessandria, with a fair bridge over it, and divers mills.

April 9

From Alessandria to Vogera [Voghera], 20 miles, being accompanied with Rodovico, before named, and his troop of horsemen, passing over the river at the town's end in a boat. There met us a small number of horsemen, but excellently well appointed, which went forward with us. Riding 2 or 3 miles further, we were met with a great garrison of soldiers, which brought us through a town called Tartano [Tortona], with trumpets blowing as they rode. And as we were passing through the town, the castle played with their great shot. When they had brought us through the town, many of the horsemen returned to the camp again. Then, when we came within a mile of a town called Pont Crooke [Pontecurone], soldiers of another garrison came to attend the lords and went forward with us. And being within half a mile of Voghera, a gentleman of the town, well accompanied, met the lords and brought them to their lodgings, where they and all the train were defrayed by the king. I never saw better horses, nor better appointed, than those that met the lords by the way this day.

April 10

From Voghera to Pavia, 15 miles, ferrying over the river of Po and Granelanuke[?] within a mile of Pavia. Being over the river, the lords and gentlemen of the town met our lords and brought them to the city, passing a bridge at the town over the river Tessine or Ticinium [Ticino]. Upon which bridge stood a great number of soldiers in good order and well appointed, and among them 300 shot, which gave the lords a brave volley. And so, after they had brought them to their lodging, being the house of Signior Hierolymo Sacco, there the state of Millane [Milan] defrayed the lords' charges and all their train, appointing divers gentlemen officers to attend upon them as . . . Signior Aloisio Marliani[18] and Signior Christophano Apiano, and a knight to carve [to help or serve] the lords called Cavalliero Contientia, a knight of the order of St. James. All the foot bands of the garrison came marching by the lords' lodgings in the afternoon, five in a rank, passing bravely armed and appointed as ever I saw. Here the lords were very sumptuously feasted and entertained at the king's charges. Pavia is an old ancient city and a county and was in times past a kingdom. Lombardy is a goodly plain country and very rich. Pavia is an university and very pleasant for gentlemen to lie in. In the great church there [San Pietro in Ciel d'Oro], we saw the lively image of St. Augustine and his tomb of white marble, very rich; the tomb also of Liutprand, the last King of Pavia; the tomb of Boethius Severinus; the tower of Fazen the lawyer, which he built with the head upward upon a certain oration. At our going out of the city, to give the lords their farewell they shot off their great ordnance and small shot gave them volleys.

April 11–17

From Pavia to Milano [Milan], 20 miles. Five miles from Pavia, we were brought to La Certosa di Pavia [Charterhouse of Pavia], where the lords dined, and were greatly feasted. It is the goodliest and best built house of all Europe. It was founded by Gian Galeazzo Visconti, [1st] Duke of Milan, who lieth there interred in a tomb of white marble; the 2 coffins and the table of the altar are all of ivory, with such workmanship that it is a spectacle to all Lombardye [Lombardy]. There is a cloister 40 foot quadrant; the doors, desks, and stools be so garnished with such notable histories, all of cut work, of divers kinds of woods, that no man possibly can paint them out more finely and lively. The marvelous works that be there, as well of the elephant's tooth, as of all other kinds of wood, I think be nowhere else to be found in Europe; howbeit it is not yet all finished.

By the way we saw the field where the French king was taken prisoner.[19] Betwixt Pavia and the Charterhouse, the duke enclosed a piece of ground with a great high wall, four square and 15 miles in compass about. This he called his garden, having within it divers several enclosures for bears, wild boars, red and fallow deer, wolves, and all other kinds of beasts of venery; which garden, at the battle when the French king was taken prisoner, was spoiled by divers breaches that he had made into the same. All the monks of this Charterhouse be nobly born and descended. The revenues of the said Charterhouse per annum is 25000 crowns.

The lords were very honorably received into Milan and lodged in a nobleman's house called Il Signior Constancio de alta, where they were highly feasted at the king's [Philip II's] charge. Thither came to salute the lords: Il Conte Giovanni Battista Borromeo, being 18 or 19 years of age, one of the chiefest and noblest houses of Milan; Il Conte l'Andriano; divers nobles and gallant gentlemen of the city. Here the lords had all the pleasures that could be shown them, as well by instruments of music as otherwise.

The city is called Milano la greate [Milan the great], being by estimation 7 or 8 miles about. The form thereof is like unto a heart and hath 6 gates and to every gate two noblemen of the city appointed, and every gate is bound to marry 12 poor maidens yearly, being at certain charges in their bridals and apparel. Upon Easter Tuesday we saw 12 maids married, every one of them led with 2 noble women, they themselves being clad in white. When they are married, there is given each of them a purse with 20 ducats in it, one suit of apparel besides that on their backs and their dinner also. The walls of the city are exceeding strong, but not all together finished, and the castle also, for provision and strength, is to be wondered at, as for artillery, munition, corn, wines, oil, bacon, powdered beef, and Parmesan cheese. They make great store of armor within the castle, but no townsman may come in at the gate. This castle is of such force as none in all Europe is to be compared unto it.

The church is an huge thing all of white marble, growing within their own duchy, at a place called Lago di Como [Lake Como]. They bore us in hand, that the covering shall also [be] of marble, but it is unlikely to be finished in our time, notwithstanding they have daily 100 laborers a work upon it.[20]

There is an hospital that may dispend 25000 crowns a year, the provision whereof passes all other. For at that present time we saw 100 fat oxen in a stable, 100 vessels of wine, every one containing 5 tons, in one cellar. The diet so cleanly and daintily prepared for the sick as can be by the recourse of surgeons and physicians, that it is a goodly thing to see. In this hospital are 800 nurses to look to the sick and to bring up children. Many hospitals more there are, some for men and some for women and some for children, besides a house built without the town for such as shall [be] infected of the plague, having 365 chambers several.

This city is notable rich and full of merchandise and artificers, very wealthy; for there is almost no artificer's wife but she weareth a chain of gold about her neck or middle.[21] The noblemen and gentlemen of Italy lie always in the great towns and never in the country. The lords tarried at Milan 6 days, viz, the 12th, 13th, 14th, 15th, 16th, and 17th.

April 18

From Milan to Lodi, 20 miles, passing through a town called Marignano [San Giovanni in Marignano], where the Marquis hath a goodly house, and the lords were made a great banquet there, the Marquis Marignano [Gian Giacomo Medici] himself being at that time general for the emperor, and lay before Siena, besieging the town against the French king.

All the way betwixt Milan and Lodi, we rode as between gardens; and to speak truth, my eyes never saw any soil comparable unto it for beauty and profit. They make hay there thrice a year. Their grounds for tillage bear them also vines and fuel; for their vines are grown up by certain trees called oppie, that are of a quick growth, and therefore loppable every 3 years; from one of these trees to another, they pull the main branches of the vines as stiff and straight as a cord so that they hurt not the ripening of their corn. And thus their vines and trees growing in order, there is a space left to the plough and so intermix the corn with the ranks of vines. There are no woods of such timber as we have, but these only: willows, witch hazels, and poplars, all set by line in their meadows, pastures, and grounds for tilling, so that you cannot see from you any way half a quarter of a mile. They bring their water in every ditch round about their enclosures and make them to run continually like little rivers of either side of the ways and have none other defense than that. And for their commodity, they make their waters so to run one over another and contrary to each other because the evenness of the ground helpeth them much thereto. Their kine be great and good, and they eat a meat [dish] called lattimel or fiorita.²² Their cheese is the best in the world, and also their veals.

Marignano is a pleasant castle but of no force; it standeth upon the river of Olon [Olona]. The lords were received into their lodging very honorably, with shot both great and small. They were lodged in the house of the most noble Lodovico Vestarino, then general of the camp in Piedmont in Novara. This Lodi standeth upon a hill very strongly and hath a castle in it of great force.

April 19–21

From Lodi to Piacenza, 20 miles, passing by a little pile [a stronghold] where was shot off ordnance both great and small; the lords had a banquet in this pile and after passed the river of Po with boats. Being all over the river, the lords were received as before and so passed by the town walls a long while ere ever they came to their lodgings, they being lodged in the house of Signior Francisco Baratiero in the street called Santo Nazaro (la Signora Hippolita *sua moglie* [his wife], Signior Cesare et Hercole *suoi siglioli* [his children], Signior Alberico Alessandro, et [and] Camillo Baratiero *nipoti del detto* [nephews of the same] Francisco Baratiero).

This city is very strong and hath a river coming to it called Trebia [Trebbia]; it hath also a castle in it of great force but not yet fully finished. This town did belong to the church of Rome, Paulus Tertius being a Roman born, and of the noble house of the Farnese and pope, who, willing to advance his own blood, created his son Peter Aluige [Pier Luigi Farnese], Duke of Piacenza and Parma, who, for his cruelty and rigor shown to his subjects, was slain in his own house [in 1547]; and because he that did kill him was afraid of the pope, the town's men delivered their town into the emperor's hands, the which he hath exempted unto the duchy of Milan.²³ This Peter Aluige, the first Duke of Piacenza and Parma, married the base daughter of Francis the French king and had by her 3 sons and one daughter. His daughter [Vittoria Farnese—see also 19 May] is married to the Duke of Urbino, and his eldest son named Octavio [Ottavio Farnese] is now Duke of Parma. The other two brethren be cardinals, the one called Cardinal [Alessandro] Farnese, who is now chancellor of Rome, and the other Cardinal St. Angelo [Ranuccio Farnese], they both being in great estimation with the Pope Paulus Quartus [Pope Paul IV, Gian Pietro Carafa] that now is; so that it is thought they will procure and stir up war against the emperor for recovery of Piacenza for the Duke of Parma. Here the lords remained two days, the 20th and 21st.

April 22

From Piacenza to Cremona, 18 miles, where we passed over the river of Po. This city is great and rich and payeth yearly to King Philip of Spain (now our king), without tax, 50000 crowns. There is an high steeple in the town from whence this proverb rises, "Una Torre in Cremona, Un Porto in Ancona" [a tower in Cremona, a port in Ancona]. They make excellent good knives at Cremona. Being passed over the river of Po, the lords were received and feasted as before. It is the last city of the dukedom of Milan and is a great circuit about; a very fair town and rich of merchandise but of no great force. It hath a notable strong castle in it. There is no ordnance in any town through the whole dukedom as we rode, but all in the castle that I could perceive. The lords viewed this castle, but no Italian was suffered to go in with them, 3 or 4 only of the chiefs excepted that did accompany them. At their going out, the castle shot off their great and small pieces. We tarried here the 23rd day. This day Il Conte Despesiano Porzenno married the sister of Signior Camillo Stanga, a very honest gentleman. Divers of the lords' gentlemen were bidden thither by this young count to dinner and supper, and there danced with the ladies. This country and dukedom is wonderful pleasant, and so well replenished with corn, vines, fruit, pasture, and meadow, all the ground being so level and so well watered that the like is not to be seen in one country again so long together. In this town is a notable strong castle. There is no ordnance in any town through the whole dukedom as we rode but three, else all in the castle. The lords viewed this castle and at their coming out of it, there was store of great and small shot, to give the lords an honorable farewell. No Italian could be suffered to come into the castle save only 3 or 4 of the chiefest that did accompany the lords.

April 24

From Cremona to Caneto [Canneto Sull'Oglio], 22 miles, through a town named Salvaterra, passing over the river of Olio [Oglio] by boat. This river parteth the dukedom of Milan and the dukedom of Mantua. In this town the lords lay at the duke's charges.

April 25

From Canneto to Mantua, 20 miles, over the river of Chiese, through a town called Acqua Negra [Aquanegra Cremonese], where we saw men whip themselves with chains, going after a procession. We passed also through a town named Redondesco and by Our Lady of Mantua, her chapel [Santa Maria delle Grazie], where is the greatest offering in those parts of Italy. There they show pictures of men which she preserved (as they say) that were stricken into the brains and hearts and in at the backs with swords and daggers and where is also such wonderful works of wax as I never saw the like before. Mantua is a notable strong city, environed with great lakes and marshes. The duke [of Mantua, Guglielmo Gonzaga] met with the lords in the city and brought them to their lodgings, which was in an old palace of the duke's [Palazzo Ducale]. This duke is very young [age 17], and looks a little asquint. Here the lords were greatly feasted at the duke's charge. After supper, they went to the court [Palazzo Te] to deliver the queen's letters, and there we saw the duke's grandmother [Anne d'Alençon, age 63], his mother's sister [Eleanora Gonzaga, Duchess of Urbino, age 62], the wife of Gonzago [i.e., the widow of Frederico II Gonzaga and the current duke's mother, Duchess Margaret Paleologa Gonzaga, age 45], and his daughter[24] [Frederico's daughter, Isabella Gonzaga, age around 20], [25] and one other lady called Hippolita, one of the fairest ladies of the world [possibly Ippolita Gonzaga, daughter of Ferrante Gonzaga, widow of Fabrizio Colonna, married to Antonio Carafa, Duke of Mondragone]. After complement of salutations, the lords had a banquet [Sala di Psyche, Palazzo Te], in the which were green almonds, the first that ever I saw. We were brought into the duchess's jewel houses, which exceeded in rich jewels as agates, sapphires, diamonds, an unicorn's horn, a tree of red coral one ell long. Here we saw also a beast called a tiger.

April 26

From Mantua to Ostia, 20 miles, over a bridge at Mantua, a quarter of a mile long, passing by the end of the river of Musone, running into the river of Po, upon the which this town standeth. On the other side of the river standeth a fair town of the Duke of Ferrara called Renahe [Rovere].

April 27–28

From Ostia to Ferrara, 30 miles, riding 12 miles by the river of Po, and then passed it in a boat and dined that day in a posthouse, being 10 miles on this side of Ferrara. After dinner riding towards Ferrara, within 2 miles of it, an earl of the country met with the lords and brought them to within the gates of the city. Then the prince met with them and conveyed them to their lodgings to a fair house of the duke's, richly furnished and hanged. The pavements of the house were of such curious works of white marble, red, and black that it is impossible to find fairer. The borders of the house chambers and chimneys [are] of such fine jasper stone that one might looking upon them see all that was done in the chambers. There is also a closet wherein are such curious works of all kind of marble and other stone and all of the duke his father's own doings, as they cannot be mended. This city is very strong, for they may drown the country round about them. The town walls are very thick and the ramparts 25 yards broad. There be 2 castles in the city, the one in the midst of the town and the other standing upon the river of Po, both of great strength. The town ditch is 100 yards over. There are 3000 Jews in the city and above, having a temple and school after their own laws. They keep the Saturday for their Sabbath. Their market is kept upon the Sunday, with fish, herbs, and other things till 12 a clock at noon. Upon the Sunday they eat nothing but fish and that which was dressed the day before; neither do they touch any money that day. Here the ambassadors were honorably feasted at the duke's charge and lodged in his palace, the prince keeping them company all the time. The duke himself was at Rome at the consecration of the pope. The streets of this town be very wide and full of excellent good building. There was a camel in this town to be seen. The 18th day before dinner the lords and gentlemen being mounted on the duke's horses, excellently well trimmed, the prince and gentlemen rode about one part of the wall showing them the commodities of the town. After dinner they were brought about the other part of the walls, where they saw such wonderful pleasures and strange things that it was wonderful to behold, after the which they had a very notable banquet. The heavenly noise that was there, as well with strange instruments of music, as otherwise I cannot declare. The truth is our entertainment here did far exceed the best entertainment the lords had other where. The duke's name is Hercules [Ercole II d'Este, Duke of Ferrara, Modena, and Reggio], and the prince his son Alphonso [Alphonso II d'Este, later 5th Duke of Ferrara], who is as worthy a prince as may be seen and of as goodly a personage. Here we saw a tortoise a yard long and more and half a yard broad. We met the duke coming homewards to Ferrara, who, when he met the lords, saluted them very lovingly and said he was sorry he was not at home to make them better cheer. The lords stayed at Ferrara the 28th day.

April 29

From Ferrara to St. Petro [San Pietro, in Casale], 20 miles, over the river of Po, riding but 6 miles within the Duke of Ferrara his liberties. After that we came into the pope's dominion, where the vice legate sent a gentleman to provide for the lords and their train at his charges. It is but a small town insomuch that the train was dispersed this night in 3 several places, some 2 miles, some 3 miles off, the lodgings there were so scant. Pope Marcellus Secundus [Pope Marcellus II, Marcello Cervini degli Spannochi] was then alive.

April 30

From San Pietro to Bononia [Bologna],[26] 10 miles, being met with several trains of noblemen and gentlemen with trumpets and drums and so brought into the town. But before we could recover the town gates, a mighty tempest of rain poured down upon us. At the gates of the town the vice legate and the Bishop of Bononia [Giovanni Campeggio] with a great company of horsemen met the lords and brought them to the vice legate's house, where they were lodged. Notwithstanding this extreme shower of rain, the trumpeters stood over the gates of the vice legate's house and blew a long time, until we were all alighted. And when the ambassadors went to supper there was excellent music of lower instruments.

May 1

The next day being the first of May, there was in the morning brought in a brave May with a number of shot and pikes, well appointed, marching into the market place, all being the vice legate's men, to the number of 60. About 10 a clock this forenoon there was an officer brought in, according to the custom of the town, who is, as it were, the president of the council there. There are 24 of the council, whereof the president is chosen at the end of 24 days and enters not into his office till the end of 48 days. You shall understand that when he enters into his office, he is fetched from his own house very honorably by him that occupied the place before him, with all the rest of the council, as also with the vice legate's guard, and so brought into the palace, where he is put into a chamber, having but 2 men to wait upon him and to abide there to the end of 2 months without coming out of his chamber door and in all that time neither his wife, his children, friends, nor servants may speak with him. He is largely allowed for his diet and keepeth a good table, being as well served and lodged as if he were in his own house.

May 2–14

The second day a post came from Rome that brought the lords word of the death of Pope Marcellus Secundus and that he died the last of April. A sight of worshipful relics to be seen in Bononia.

The body of St. Dominick, the body of St. Katherine, and a piece of the crown of thorns wherewith Christ was crowned.

To this city cometh a small river called Rheno [Reno]. The town is great and hath 13 gates in it. It is fair built and with such vaults that in the greatest rain and foulest weather men go dry and are also defended from the heat of the sun. The vice legate is Bishop of Genoa [Gerolamo Sauli] and hath a guard of Launceknights well appointed for his guard. Other soldiers there be none in the town, except when it is *sedia vacante* (to say when there is no pope). The pope being dead, 10 of the 12 gates of the city are kept shut, and 800 soldiers appointed to watch and ward, in divers places of the town, for at that time misdoers and offenders think themselves without law. As for example, when Julius Tertius died, there came a banished man to the city with 400 soldiers, supposing to have found the town without soldiers and to have done much mischief there; he was let into the town, himself taken and beheaded, and all his men slain and taken. The lords were greatly feasted at the pope's charges all the time they lay in Bononia, and so were they invited to noblemen's houses of the city and greatly entertained. Two noblemen of the town (Pillades and Malvachall)[27] were at deadly wars. We remained at Bononia 13 days together.

May 14

From Bononia to Imola, 20 miles, over the river of Reno,[28] leaving San Pietro, a town on our right hand which hath a castle in it but of no great strength. The lords, viz, the Bishop of Ely [Thomas Thirlby] and my Lord Montague [Anthony Browne], they took their journey to see Fiorenza [Florence]. Lord Kearne [Sir Edward Carne], the leger ambassador for Rome, he with all the carriages and the greatest part of the train, departed from the lords and took his way through La Romagna [now Emilia-Romagna], to Rome.[29]

May 15

From Imola to Faenza, 10 miles, over the river Lammon [Lamone], which keepeth no certain course but sometimes very great, another time very small, passing by Castel Bolognese, an old walled town. The lords of the town met my lord ambassador 2 miles without the town and brought him to the pope's palace, where he was lodged, with trumpets and drums before him. Some shot both great and small was also bestowed upon him; the town defrayed him and all the train at their charges. The commodity and profit of this town standeth by making of cotton and many sundry things in fine metals of earth.

May 16

From Faenza to Forli, 10 miles, being met without the town as before and lodged in the palace at the town's charge. In the market place, when the ambassador came unto it, there were *arquebus à croc* [hook guns] and other shot discharged. There is a very strong castle in the town standing upon the river of Mountaine [Montone], the which cometh from the mountains. The castle hath great lodgings in it and store of great ordnance. It was built by Julius Caesar and is called after his name, Castello Julio.

May 17

From Forli to Cesena, 10 miles, passing over the river Runcke [Ronco] with a boat and by a castle named Frampole [Forlimpopoli], leaving a strong town standing on the right hand upon the side of a hill with a castle on the top of it called Bartonere [Bartinore]. The leger ambassador was received into this town as before and lodged at the palace at the town's charges. There is a castle in this town situated upon a hill adjoining to the palace; there cometh a river called Vrtycon [Rubicon]. The boys of the town, being a great number, met my lord ambassador without the town gate, crying, "*Viva Inghilterra*" (as much to say, "God save England"), every one of them with an olive bough in their hands.

May 18

From Cesena to Rimano [Rimini], 20 miles, leaving a town called Archangelo [Santarcangelo di Romagna] on the right hand. Here the ambassador was received and lodged as before at the palace at the charge of the town. It standeth upon the sea named Il Golpho di Venetia [the Gulf of Venice] and hath a small haven pertaining unto it. The town itself is of no force, but the castle in it is very strong.

May 19

From Rimini to Pesaro, the first town of the Duke of Urbino [Guidobaldo II della Rovere], 20 miles. The young prince (the Duke of Urbino's son [Francesco Maria II della Rovere]) was determined to have met the ambassador, but, being prevented by his sudden coming, he met with him at the stairs' foot of the hall and then received him very honorably and brought him up to his lodging, which was very richly hanged, and there we were notably feasted, all at the duke's charges. After dinner the duchess, his mother [Vittoria Farnese], sent for all the gentlemen of our train, into a withdrawing chamber, where we found her sitting in a rich chair, the prince her son standing by her and a great number of ladies and gentlewomen sitting about her. After we had all done our humble duties unto her grace, as many of us as could speak Italian or French went to entertain these ladies and gentlewomen. The rest of us that had no language to entertain them with yet sat down amongst them to behold (as *spectatores formarum*) the glory of their surpassing beauties. This heavenly angelical troop of ladies being thus accommodated and we greatly graced by their honorable presence, on the sudden we were presented with the music of the virginals, lute, and viol. Then the young prince stepped forth and took one of his play-fellows by the hand and danced the pavane with him and afterwards a galliard, which being ended the prince entreated our gentlemen that could dance to take out a lady or gentlewoman to dance withal; and so they did. The dancing ended, a great banquet was made for us, which ended we departed out of the chamber and there left the duchess with her ladies. This young prince is not passing 10 years of age [age 6], but he is well favored and excellently made in all the parts of his body. The town is not strong, yet wanting no ordnance, of small circuit but very well built, and paved with brick throughout. It standeth upon the forenamed sea, having a pretty haven and a pleasant country joining unto it.

May 20

From Pesaro to Fossembrone [Fossombrone], 26 miles, leaving Fano, a fair town on the left hand, by the seaside. The ambassador was lodged at the duke's palace in Pesaro and there defrayed by the duke. The town standeth between mountains. Betwixt Fano and Fossombrone there runneth a river called Il Metro [Metauro], where is a goodly plain, and there was a great battle fought betwixt the Romans and the Africans, where were slain 53000 Africans and 9000 Romans.[30]

May 21

From Fossombrone to Cantiano, 20 miles, riding through a park of the duke's with fallow deer in it 3 miles from Fossombrone, which was the first park that we saw in all Italy before. From the park to Il Furlo [the Furlo Pass] *dove è la veggie* [where it is seen], 2 miles, passing through a rock smoothly cut out and close over our heads, made by man's hand for Hannibal to bring his army that way against Scipio Africanus. So to Acquilania [Acqualagna], 5 miles, and thence to Caglie [Cagli], 5 miles, through the town, and so to Cantiano, 5 miles further, all the way of an huge height between mountains and rock, 20 miles. This town is but little, standing amongst the mountains. Here all our charges were defrayed by the duke.

May 22–24

From Cantiano to Sigillo, 12 miles, over a great mountain, passing by Sichara [Scheggia], the last town of the Duke of Urbino's, 2 miles from Sigillo. This town is the pope's; there we tarried the 23rd and 24th.

May 25

From Sigillo to Perugia, 22 miles, very ill and dangerous way. Here the lords met all 3 together again. The pope's vice legate—there more for shame than for any good will he bore to the lords—met them without the town gates and brought them to the abbey of St. Augustine's without the town, where they were lodged. The town is very great and hath a marvelous strong castle in it, built by Pope Paulus Tertius [Pope Paul III, Alessandro Farnese]. The people be all French in their hearts. For three nights together fires were made, as well upon the walls of the castle as in other places in the town, only for joy of creation of the new Pope Paulus Quartus. The great pieces of ordnance and small shot shot off bravely, and great fireworks besides in the air. The cause of this their great joy of these was supposed to be because the pope was French in heart and enemy to the emperor, notwithstanding he was a Neapolitan born.

May 26

Here we remained the 26th day. On this day all the trumpeters and drummers of the town came to visit the lords and began to play. But answer was sent from the lords that with what friendship they were received and lodged, with the like they should receive their reward. Then they departed in great despite and anger, striking upon their drum heads as hard as they could lay on, they being 12 drums in number. That day at 5 a clock at night, the vice legate sent a present to the lords, viz, three dozen and a half of capons, 6 dozen of rabbits, 15 wethers and lambs, a veal, and 32 sacks of barley, and oats for their horses. But forasmuch as it was known to the lords that the legate had intelligence of their departure the next morning following, and considering how ungently they had been used before, they refused the present, rendering few thanks. This evening the vice legate sent the soldiers of the town (being 500) marching in rank to the lords' lodging, and there to honor them they gave 3 several volleys of shot, and so departed without reward given them.

Here we saw a special relic, forsooth, of Our Lady's ring, the first (they stick not to say) that ever she did wear, which is not shown (I tell you) without great ceremony. This ring is a great ring, all of black horn, and hangeth in a pyx within a tabernacle, being clad with 2 or 3 fold of lawn [linen]. That is seen in mystery, as all of her relics be. When it is shown to anybody, there is wonderful much blessing, kissing, kneeling, and knocking; and upon either side of the tabernacle is a great basin, in the which two children of 5 or 6 years old do sit and are let down in the basin; then the ring is to be shown to anybody. They make us believe, forsooth, that these children live not by meat [food] nor drink but are miraculously fed by the Holy Ghost.

May 27

From Perugia to Foligni [Foligno], 18 miles, leaving a town on our left hand called Assisi. There was a great market fair at that time that we were there. The town of Foligno standeth in a fair plain, having great mountains on both sides of it.

May 28–June 3

From Foligno to Spoleto, 12 miles, leaving a town named Trevi on the left hand. Spoleto hath a castle in it, standing upon a high hill, which commandeth the town and people. Here the lords remained 5 days, even till the 3rd of June, on which day they went from thence. The 29th the lords received letters out of England dated the 14th of May. This town standeth between the mountains, as far east as can be travelled that way. The Cardinal of Perugia [Fulvio Giulio della Corgna] is governor of this town. The people are very proud and beggarly and of no civility; great boasters, but of no activity; and much given to secret murder and privy sodomy. The villainy of them is such, and they so much borne and maintained in it that a boy being, as they term it, dishonored and buggered by his like, he will ever after seek the death of his dishonorer. As for example, at our being in the town two school boys, one of them bearing malice to the other before, coming into the school and finding there the other boy, his enemy that had dishonored him, he suddenly cast a ball of lead at him and hit him on the head withal that he amazed him, and, presently having brought a dagger for the monster to school with him, he stabbed the other boy to the heart and killed him dead. This fact was not unpunished, as I did learn afterwards of certain. Oh what good justice is executed in this town and offenders punished to the uttermost, as ye may hear, to the good example of other.

June 3

From Spoleto to Narni, 18 miles, through a town named Terni, 12 miles on the way. A mile without the town, the Bishop of Sullino [Salina?] met the lords with 400 soldiers, who was sent of purpose to bring them to the place where they should dine, at the pope's charge; there the soldiers blew off their pieces and departed. After dinner the lords were brought out of the town in like manner as they were received into it. The river of Negro [Nera] runneth on the south side of the town. This town is well stored with great ordnance and small shot; the castle in it standeth upon a very high hill, and the town upon the side of a hill, a goodly plain of the one side of it and great mountains on the other side. When we came near to Narni, the legate met the lords a mile without the town in like manner as before and brought them to their lodgings, lying at the pope's charges, and had a present sent them from the lord of the town. In the time of *sedia vacante* (which is when there is no pope) Narni and Terni be at great wars together.

June 4

From Narni to Rignano [Rignano Flaminio], 20 miles, passing over the river of Tiber with a boat to a town named Borgetto [Borghetto], where the lords dined at the pope's charges. This town of Rignano belongeth to the Cardinal Farnese, but we lay at the pope's charges. The lords' train were lodged in field inns and could not be suffered to come within the town gates, but the reason of it I could never yet learn.

June 5

From Rignano to Rome, 22 miles, passing through a town called Castello Novo (eight miles from Rignano), and so forth to La Prima Porta, 7 miles, where the lords dined at the pope's charges, and thence to Rome, being 7 miles. This Prima Porta hath the name of the first old gate of Rome, when Rome flourished, as appeareth by the old ruins of the walls.

After dinner, within a mile of Rome, we passed over a bridge called Ponte Mole [Ponte Molle], over the river of Tyber [Tiber], and rode to a house without the city which Pope Julius Tertius built, where the lords rested themselves and had a small banquet. This house is of such an excellent building and hath such a notable commodity in it, all of white marble, so curiously wrought, so replenished with strange fruits, and furnished with antiquities that be daily dug up in old Rome, and some found in the river of Tiber, in such sort that it doth far exceed all the buildings that ever I saw except the Charterhouse beside Pavia. Amongst which antiquities there are 2 marble pillars of such mixture of colors, white and black, being 5 cubits long and a yard about in the greatest part, which two pillars, Pope Julius Tertius, by report, would not have given for one million of gold and are of many men esteemed at 100000 crowns.

After that the lords had rested themselves in this vineyard 3 or 4 hours, there came now one nobleman, then another, and sometimes 5 or 6 together, so that there were a 16 bishops. The cardinals they sent their pledges, riding upon their mules, having their masters' hats hanging behind them on their backs, their mules being bravely furnished, and they were in number 35. The pope sent also the officers of his court to the number of 32, all in scarlet gowns and black velvet coats, to bring in the lords into the city, besides his guard to wait upon them; and last of all came a bishop that represented the pope's holiness, who was accordingly honored of the lords. So about 6 a clock at night the lords were brought into Rome in very good order and so conveyed to their lodgings, trumpets and drums before them, in a fair palace, having in train, by estimation, 1000 horses and mules, and so conveyed to their lodgings in a fair palace where Cardinal [Giovanni] Poggio lay, which he rented of the Duke of Parma [Ottavio Farnese], and removed himself, leaving it unto the lords. Here the lords lay at their own charges.

This palace was in old time the bath or therme of Julius Caesar (as in William Thomas's book of the description of Italy you may read there of thermes, or baths.) [31]

June 6, 7

The two former popes (Julius Tertius, and Marcellus Secundus) had made great provision for the lords in the palace of St. Mark, the which provision this new-created pope, Paulus Quartus, did spend and eat himself. The eighth day at night, the lords were sent for and had secret audience, but no Englishman suffered to come into the chamber. The ninth day in the morning Cardinal Carafa (the pope's nephew, newly made cardinal on the 7th day) sent the lords a present: 3 veals, 3 great Parmesan cheeses, 10 Roman cheeses made in Rome, 3 dozen of capons and chickens, 52 spades of bacon, 10 torches of virgin's wax, 24 pounds of candles of virgin's wax, 10 sugar loaves, 6 tons of wine, and 50 quarters of barley and oats for their horses.

June 10

The 10th day the lords went to the court accompanied with divers bishops, noblemen, and gentlemen and there had open audience. As they passed by the castle of St. Angelo [Castel Sant'Angelo], the lords were saluted with a great peal of ordnance. The pope sat in the conclave (or consistory), where he was chosen in a great high chair, having a very rich cope upon him and a miter of a wonderful price upon his head. The place where he sat was railed in that the people might not come in to trouble the orator. The cardinals sat upon benches within the rails, round about the pope's holiness, the bishops underneath them, and the pope's servants lay upon the ground. After my lord, my master, the Bishop of Ely had ended his oration made to the pope, then all the Englishmen of the lords' train were called for and let come within the rails to kiss the pope's holiness's foot, who had a crimson velvet slipper on that had a cross of silver laid upon it. That done, the pope blessed them, and so they departed sanctified.

June 11

The 11th day the lords visited divers of the cardinals, and at the Cardinal of Pisa his house I saw a live ostrich and plucked a white feather from it.

June 12

The 12th day in the morning the lords heard a dirge Mass at the Spanish church for the emperor's mother, where we had every one of us a taper given us to hold all Mass time in our hands. This day the lords dined with Cardinal Carafa at a place called Belvidere [Belvedere], as much to say, as fair to look on, so called for that it standeth in such a pure good air and hath the most pleasant prospects of all the palaces within Rome.

After dinner the lords went to visit other cardinals which lay in the pope's court, and so went up to the chamber of presence to wait upon the pope, that came out to evensong. When they came first into the presence, they found but one cardinal there, who very courteously entertained them. Afterwards there came 2 of the cardinals together, and sometime 3, and so came in stile till they made the number of 30, and ever as they came over the bridge of St. Angelo, whether it were one, 2, or 3 cardinals together, so many as they were, so many pieces of ordnance were shot off the castle for an honor that the pope is bound to observe to his well-beloved brethren, when-so-ever they pass the bridge,[32] whether they come to the court or no. Also, as the cardinals do come to the outer gates of the pope's palace, a drum and fife do give warning of their coming.

Within half an hour after, all the cardinals were come into the presence chamber, there came the pope's holiness out of his privy chamber among them.

They all rising up at the sight of him bowed themselves, ducking friar fashion, and the pope likewise to them again. And then he being led by 2 cardinals to a little side table in the chamber, they both did help him to put on his robes pertaining to his holiness. His robes being put on him, he went in this manner towards the chapel to evensong, attended upon as follows: first, the officers of his household, being a great number, before him, all in scarlet gowns; after them followed two, carrying each of them a miter, and two officers next them with silver rods in their hands; then the cardinals, having a cross borne before them, and every cardinal his several pillar borne next before himself; after them cometh the pope's holiness in a chair of crimson velvet wrought with gold, very rich, the which was carried upon 8 men's shoulders, having 16 more spare men waiting upon the chair. Thus going to the chapel, two servants going before him crying still *Abasso! Abasso!* (which is to say, kneel down, masters), he sitting, blessing all the way as he went to evensong, which being done the pope returned in the like manner to his chamber again.

June 13

The next day being the 13th, his holiness went through St. Peter's church [Basilica Papale di San Pietro] to Mass to the chapel of St. Peter's in like manner as before, saving that he had then 2 triple crowns borne before him, of an inestimable value, which he had not before. So Mass being said, he went in procession, in this order following: first, went the friars, and every parish by themselves with their cross, all having white torches in their hands; next to them followed the pope's officers, all in scarlet gowns and black velvet coats; then the priests and singing men of the pope's chapel; then bishops to the number of 58, all of them having miters of white linen cloth on their heads and copes on their backs; after them followed the cardinals, having miters of white damask and tunicles upon their backs, with their crosses and pillars borne before them, as above said; then came the pope's holiness; and next before him went the guard, being a great number, the pope being carried in his chair as before mentioned, having a little table before him whereupon stood the Sacrament, and two men going before him with great broad fans made of peacock tails to keep the sun and flies from his holy face. The most part of his cardinals had also the like fans before them. After the pope followed a troop of light horsemen to the number of 64, well armed and appointed. And thus was the order and number of the pope's going in procession. Now, at the pope's setting out of the gates of his palace with the procession, all the pope's trumpeters stood there and sounded. Then was there a warning piece shot off to the castle of St. Angelo, whereupon the castle gave a great peal of ordnance, which continued a long time.

To write anything of the antiquities of Rome I thought it needless, considering that they are truly and very notably set forth in William Thomas's book of the description of Italy.[33] (We remained in Rome 14 days.)

June 16

The 16th day the lords dined and supped with the pope at the palace of St. Mark. After dinner they went to visit those cardinals they had not spoken with before, and the same night they took their leave of the pope, who gave my Lord Montague a table diamond with a ring esteemed at 2000 crowns, and my Lord of Ely, my master, a cross of gold. They made great bonfires in Rome because we were reconciled to the church of Rome, and the castle shot off much ordnance.

We saw a world of relics in a place called La Swaderia [La Scuderia], very ridiculous and incredible, viz, the picture of Christ, lively as he was upon the earth; one of the nails that Christ was nailed with to the cross; the stairs Christ went upon going to be examined and judged of Pilate, upon which stairs he had a fall and, with his elbow to save himself, he made a great hole in the stairs, the which is covered over with a grate of silver, unto the which there is made a great offering; the table that Christ made his last supper upon with his disciples; the crown of thorns wherewith Christ was crowned when upon the cross. *Cum multis aliis que [nunc] perscribere longum est* [with many other matters that it would now be tedious to write about fully].

Note here that the whole number of miles from London to Rome, accounting the leagues in France 2 English miles a league and those in Savoy and Piedmont at 3 every league, though some miles in Savoy be more, yet because the Italian miles be shorter than the English, I let them borrow of the leagues in Savoy, accounting all as English miles, by which account all together make up the full number of a 1158 miles.

The End of our Journey to Rome.

Our Journey back again from Rome through Germany, and so to London.

June 20

From Rome to Rignano, 20 miles.

June 21

From Rignano to Narni, 20 miles.

June 22

From Narni to Spoleto, 18 miles.

June 23

From Spoleto to Foligno, 12 miles.

June 24

From Foligno to Sigillo, 24 miles; to Nocera [Nocera Umbra] to dinner, 12 miles.

June 25–26

From Sigillo to Urbino, 22 miles, and to Cagli to dinner, 17 miles. This town [i.e., Urbino] is the principalest town of the duke's and standeth upon the top of a high hill but of no great strength. The duke was in the town at our coming thither. There we saw Polydore Vergil's grave, who died not passing a month before we came thither. Here the lords remained one day, which was the 26th.

June 27

From Urbino to Rimini, 24 miles, through a town called Montefiore [Montefiore dell'Aso] to dinner, 12 miles.

June 28

From Rimini to Cesena, 20 miles.

June 29

From Cesena to Imola, 30 miles.

June 30–July 1

From Imola to Bononia [Bologna], 20 miles, where we stayed the first day of July.

July 2

From Bononia to Crocetta, at the sign of the Spread Eagle, the post house, 14 miles, by a castle named St. Zuan [St. Zuan de Conca], of great force and well watered.

July 3

From Crocetta to Concordia [Concordia sulla Secchia], 25 miles, passing over the river of Panaro upon a bridge in a little village called Bon porto [Bomporto], riding a long time by the river of Secchia, which cometh to this town and meets the Po 10 miles from Concordia at a town called Sacketta [Sacchetta] and then cometh into the Po. This town belongeth to the Earl of Mirandola [Ludovico II Pico] and was burnt 3 years past by the Pope Julius, with other men, for displeasure.

July 4

From Concordia to Mantua, 22 miles, passing the river of Secchia, riding through a town called S. Benedetto [San Benedetto Po]; after that we passed the river of Po. There we inned at the Black Morian. The Duke of Mantua his revenue by year was but 1000 ducats. But afterwards the duke his father [Federico II Gonzaga] increased it 30000 ducats more by marriage with a nobleman's daughter in Italy, an heiress [Margaret Paleologa, Marquise of Montferrat]. The duke that is now [Guglielmo Gonzaga] was but the second brother. He is very uncomely of person, squint-eyed, crook-backed, and but 15 [sic—17] years old. His elder brother [Francesco III Gonzaga] was drowned by misfortune, being a fishing in a boat in the lake that is about the town. The third brother [Louis Gonzaga, Duke of Nevers] was put to the French king's court to learn French, but the French king will no more let him come home as yet. Some think he will marry him to one of his daughters, that after the decease of the duke his brother, he, being the next heir, might enjoy the dukedom of Mantua. The fourth brother [Federico Gonzaga] is a bishop. The duke's uncle [Ercole Gonzaga], being Cardinal of Mantua, is governor of this town. Here I saw a mill to weave silk, which was a notable piece of work.

July 5

From Mantua to Bosolingo [Bussolengo], 22 miles, through a town called Villa Franca [Villafranca di Verona],[34] a strait by the which they must pass that come from Mantua to Venice by land or from Mantua to Trento, in the which strait are such exceptions to passengers as I have not known before.

For no man can pass that way but he must pay the value of an English penny, and yet is it not gathered for the repairing of an highway or bridges.[35] There be two men that farm this strait of the Venetians yearly for 150 crowns. By this town runneth the river of Adese [Adige], the swiftest river that ever I saw, which falls into the Gulf of Venice.

July 6

From Bussolengo to Vawe [Vo], 22 miles, passing over the river of Adige and riding through two towns, Sereing [Ceraino] and Bergetto [Borghetto sull'Adige], standing both between mountains upon the river of Adige. At Ceraino is a strait called La Chiusa [Ceraino's lock], having notable rocks of the one side of it and the river on the other side, being well fortified with ordnance and munition, as the Venetians have all their forts for the most part, so that there is very hard passing without license. These two towns, Borghetto and Vo, belong to the King of the Romans [Ferdinand I, brother to Charles V].[36] The Cardinal of Trento is governor of them.

July 7–10

From Vo to Trento, 22 miles, riding all the way by the river of Adige and between mountains, passing through a goodly town of the King of Romans called Rovero [Rovereto], where we dined at the sign of the Star. It hath a very strong castle in it standing upon a rock. Trento standeth upon the river of Adige, but it is of no force, neither great nor much fair building in it, his own palace or castle excepted, which is wonderful beautiful and very richly furnished. The cardinal is absolute lord and governor of this town; he hath a guard of 50 men to wait upon him, besides a great number of gentlemen and other servitors. He is a Dutchman born and cometh of a very noble house, but in his housekeeping he showeth himself an Italian, to keep bare cheer and a mean table; notwithstanding, this cardinal is more honorably served in his house for the cheer he keepeth than any other that I have seen and is very rich. I saw 2 ostriches at his house, the one russet and the other black color. Here we saw a child whom the Jews had martyred many years past, all his body pricked with needles. We inned at the sign of the Rose and remained there 3 days: the 8th, 9th, 10th.

July 11

From Trento to Neumark [Neumarkt], called in Italian Enea [Egna], 4 Dutch miles.[37] We lay at the sign of the Crown.

July 12–13

From Neumarkt to Boczen [Bozen (German), Bolzano (Italian)], at the Golden Spread Eagle, 3 miles; a fair town and as big as Trento. Here we stayed the 13th day, and our lords came hither to us in post from Rome. Within a mile of this town the mountains are divided into three parts. From the west mountains cometh the head of the river of Adige, and from the mountains on the east side cometh the river called Flicke [Eisack],[38] and runneth into Adige.

July 13

From Bozen-Bolzano to Brixin [Brixen], at the sign of the Spread Eagle, 6 miles, through a town called Culma [Colma], halfway, where we dined. There the King of Romans hath a goodly palace, built with fair brick and painted white and red. Over the gate is written Palacio. After dinner we passed through a strait (called La Chiusa [lock] in Italian) where there is a fair castle and a pretty town belonging to the Cardinal of Trento. All this day we rode between mountains, passing 3 times over the river of Eisack upon bridges. In this journey much of our way was made out of the rocks with lime and stone and so kept continually or else it were unpassable. The mountains be so high that the clouds rack beneath them in such sort that neither the sun nor rain have any power upon the tops of them, where lieth very much snow.

July 14

From Brixen to Stursen [Sterzing], a fair town where we dined and stayed all day at the Golden Eagle, 4 miles.

July 15–16

From Sterzing to Staine [Steinach am Brenner] [Austria], where we stayed the 16th day. 3 miles. A Dutch mile beyond the town, Ferdinando met with the emperor his brother when he came out of Spain.[39]

July 17

From Steinach to Innsbrooke [Innsbruck], 4 miles. This is a goodly town of the King of the Romans, standing between mountains, very well built but little. The river of Ise [Isar] cometh to it and runneth into the river of Danubie [Danube]. Here we were lodged at the Golden Eagle; hard by the gate runneth the river called in Latin, Enus flumen [Aenus flumen], and in Dutch, I[nn]. The head of it is 14 Dutch miles from Innsbruck. We passed over this river

[Inn] upon a fair bridge at the town's end. An English mile out of the town is a house where are made very fair pieces of ordnance. We saw also all the pedigree of the house of Austria cast in brass, with many other pictures so lively and notably wrought that I am not able to describe them. Every picture cost 1000 crowns. When they be all made they shall set in the monastery which the King of Romans is now a building in the town.[40] This town hath no walls, but the houses be built so uniformly together, all of one fashion, out of the town ward, being very high and thick together that every man may defend his own house. In this town be water mills to grind both corn and malt. Here we tarried the 18th.

July 19

From Innsbruck to Metoualde [Mittenwald], at the Golden Lion, 6 miles, through a town called Cefeld [Seefeld], halfway to Mittenwald, where we dined at the Black Eagle. This Seefeld is the last town of the county of Tirol [Tyrol]. In this Seefeld, God showed a marvelous miracle by the Sacrament at the time of Easter when the people do of custom use to receive the same.

A man of the same town came to the church to receive the Sacrament, and when it should have been ministered unto him he was so proud that he disdained to kneel down as the rest did, but he would stand up near the altar, for which pride the ground did open to swallow him up. But to save himself he clapped his hand upon the altar, the print whereof remains there till this day. <u>Soodeldom. Soodeldom.</u> As he was sinking, the priest took the Host out of his mouth and put it into the pyx again. But in short space after, it putrefied; then the priest took it out and scraped it with his knife. But after he had scraped it, it fell a bleeding.

Mittenwald is but a small village and is the first town of the Duke of Bavaria [Albert V]. There is such abundance of snow lying for seven months' space together that no person can pass that way without great danger. In that time the inhabitants there cannot go out of their doors, and therefore they make all their provision in the summer. We found the weather as cold there in our travel those ways as in the month of November in England.

July 20

From Mittenwald to Ambrige [Ammergebirge or Ammergau Alps], at the Black Eagle, 6 miles, through a town called Zoyen [Soien], halfway, where we dined at the Golden Star. At Ammergau we left the mountains. A mile off from Ammergau there is a goodly abbey called Ethall [Ettal]. They be black friars of the order of St. Benedict. This abbey was built by the Duke of Bavaria and is situate upon the top of an hill, very fair and commodious.

July 21

From Ammergau to Schonge (Schongau), at the Golden Star, 4 miles. It is a pretty walled town and standeth in a fair plain one league from the Alps. By this town cometh a river called Lewher [Lech].

July 22

From Schongau to Lansbourg [Landsberg am Lech], at the sign of the Golden Bell, 4 miles. To this town cometh the river of Lech. In this town my Lord of Ely, my master, overtook my Lord Montague, for my lord remained at Rome 13 days after my Lord Montague's departure from thence, having only 6 persons to attend him.

July 23

From Landsberg to Ausburge (or Augusta) [Augsburg], 6 miles, very short, riding all the way upon such a goodly plain as I never saw the like before. They made hay of the most part of this ground except it were a 2 miles from Augsburg where was as goodly corn as need to be. The lords of the town sent our lords for a present 20 trouts and 60 gallons of wine. In this city are 6 churches of Protestants and 7 of Catholics. But although the churches of the Protestants be fewer in number than the churches of the Catholics, yet in the Protestant churches you shall find 10 to one of them of the Catholics. In time of service and prayer, I did see in one such church both the Communion and Mass having but a bare partition of boards between them. The town is a commonwealth of itself and payeth tribute to no man. This notwithstanding, all forfeits be preserved and kept for the emperor and are presented to him when he cometh thither, and if he come not thither at all yet the treasure remains untouched. The King of Romans lay in this town when we were there, to desire aid of the Germans against the Turks, who were already entered into Calabria. Here we remained the 24th day. The Duke of Savoy [Emmanuel Philibert] came thither in post from the camp, whom the lords went to salute. That done we departed.

July 25

From Augsburg to Tilling [Dillingen an der Donau], 6 long miles. A pretty town where the Cardinal of Augusta [Otto Truchsess von Waldburg] hath a goodly house and castle where we lay that night. Half a mile from his house on the left hand there is a pretty town called Herstreete [Heretsried], which is belonging to the Earl Palatine. Half a league from this town on the southwest side standeth a fair town called Loging [Lauingen], the which is the Duke of Bavaria's. Half a mile from the cardinal's house we passed over the river of Danube. This Dillingen is the first town of the duchy of Swabia. The King of the Romans hath the honor and name of it, but the city of Augsburg hath the profit of it.

July 26

From Dillingen to Hedingham [Heidenheim], 3 long miles. This town is the Duke of Württemberg's [Christoph von Württemberg] and the chief town of his country. He hath a fair castle in it for lodgings but of no strength. He himself in person lay in it this night. This duke is one of the greatest princes of Germany, a great Protestant, and so be most of his subjects.

July 27

From Heidenheim to Gipping [Göppingen], 4 miles. In this town be many baths for men and much sought too; the water of it that cometh out of the mountains tasteth like alum.

July 28

From Göppingen] to Canstet [Cannstatt, now Bad Cannstatt, part of Stuttgart], 4 miles. We rode to Esling [Esslingen am Neckar] to dinner, 3 miles, a great town and strong. There beginneth plenty of vines. This town is free but environed with the Duke of Württemberg's country. It is subject to the mountains. This duke's father won the town and would have restrained their liberty, compelling them to have been subjects unto him, whereupon many other of the free states made wars with him and took the town from him and restored the people thereof to their former estate again, and so they remain at this day. By those two towns runs the river of Necker [Neckar] and there be all the Neckar wines made. The people of the town be all Lutherans.

July 29

From Cannstatt to Prett [Bretten], 5 miles. We rode to Foyne [Pforzheim] to dinner, 3 leagues. Two English miles on our right hand as we rode, we saw a notable strong castle of the Duke of Württemberg's called Ankesbridge [Altenburg], the which the emperor won from his father and kept it 5 or 6 years. But the duke that now is redeemed it again for the sum of 6000 dollars. This town Pforzheim hath a goodly castle in it. After dinner we went from Pforzheim to Bretten two miles off, by a town called Nulle [Neulingen], the which standeth in the halfway. Two English miles from Bretten endeth the duchy of Württemberg, and there we enter into the country of Frederick the Palsgrave of the Rhine, Count Palatine, and Prince Elector. He is a Protestant but dareth not profess it openly, as other princes of Germany do, for fear of the emperor's displeasure for that he had married his sister's daughter [Charles V's niece, Dorothea of Denmark]. Yet notwithstanding, in his own house he doth as other princes do. Philip Melanchthon was born in this town of Bretten.

July 30

From Bretten to Rheinehouse [Reinhausen], 4 miles. We rode to Brossell [Bruchsal] and dined there, 1 mile. We passed through a town called Adeze[?], which is the Bishop [of] Spire's [Speyer] [Rudolf von Frankenstein], and then after dinner went to a small village called Reinhausen, 3 miles, which taketh the name of the river of Rhine that runneth by it. On the further side of the Rhine we left the Palsgrave's country for a time, where the wines be made called Rhenish wines, which be brought into England. The lords would have been at Speyer, the which is but a mile from the Rhine, but that they died there of the plague.

July 31–August 1

From Reinhausen to Wormes [Worms], 6 miles, through Speyer, which is a very fair town. All the country that we passed this day is divided between Speyer and Worms, both free towns. Upon the left hand of us we left the mountains that divided Swabia and Germany. We remained at Worms the first day of August, where be more Protestants than Catholics. The bishop of the town dareth not come within the town because he is a Catholic. There is no building in the town praiseworthy but it is double walled, and the outer wall of a great compass. From this town forward the miles be smaller than they were before.

August 2

From Worms to Mentz [Mainz], 6 miles. We rode to Opinham [Oppenheim] to dinner, 3 miles. This is the Palsgrave's. After dinner we rode to Mainz, 3 miles. Mainz standeth upon the river of Rhine. The town is free and hath much good building in it. The streets are narrow yet accounted a strength to the town. The Bishop of Mainz [Daniel Brendel von Homburg] is one of the electors. In this town was the first invention to make guns and to print books.[41]

August 3

From Mainz the lords went to Collen [Köln, Cologne] by water with a small train, but the whole company went to Sanckiware [Sankt Goar], 9 miles. We rode to Bacharach to dinner, 6 miles, passing through two towns, the one named Ingelom [Ingelheim am Rhein] and the other Bingen [Bingen am Rhein], standing both upon the Rhine. There cometh another river to Bingen named Dannowe [sic—Nahe], which runneth into the Rhine. We passed over this river upon a bridge. The bishop hath a fair castle for lodgings. The palsgrave is the only lord of this town. No boat doth pass here but it doth pay great custom as the manner is upon all this river. There are the best wines made that be called Rhenish wines.

After dinner from Bacharach to Sankt Goar, 3 miles, through a town called Wesell [Wesel], which belongeth to the Bishop of Treves [Trier] [Johann von Isenburg-Grenzau], one of the electors, where he hath a fair castle standing upon the river's side. We rode all this day for the most part by the river's side between mountains, where we saw many towns that seemed fairer than they were indeed, as it did appear by those we were in. Although we saw nothing but mountains in the most part of this journey, yet were they so well replenished with wines that they have very much profit by them, for it is their whole living. Sankt Goar is the first town of the landgrave, in the which standeth upon a rock a very fair castle.

August 4

From Sankt Goar to Andernach, 9 miles. We rode to Coens or Confluence [Coblenz, now Koblenz] to dinner, 6 miles, riding all the way by the Rhine between mountains, passing by a town called Properte [Boppard], the which is the Bishop of Trier's. This journey for the most part the way is so straight that none but one could pass at a time. Within a mile of Koblenz, there cometh the river of Delowe [Lahn] into the Rhine. To this town cometh a great river, Mosel [Moselle], which runneth into the river of Rhine. This town is the Bishop of Trier's. After dinner, from Koblenz to Andernach, 3 miles, passing over the river of Moselle, riding all the way in a champaign country [a plain]. This town, Andernach, a goodly city, is the Bishop of Cologne's [Adolf III of Schauenburg].

August 5

From Andernach to Bonn, 6 miles. We rode to Remagen to dinner, 3 miles. The Bishop of Cologne and the Duke of Cleves [William, Duke of Jülich-Cleves-Berg] are both of them lords of this town. We rode through a town called Winter [Königswinter], being the Bishop of Cologne's, which seemeth much fairer on the outside than it is indeed in the inside.

August 6–7

From Bonn to Cologne, 4 miles. This town is a free town and indifferently strong. It is very great and hath much fair building in it and is well replenished with merchandise. The bishop is of great power and one of the corvesters [electors]. In this town be the relics of the 11000 virgins and of the three kings. There is a nunnery in this town which passes all that ever I saw, for there is never a nun in that house under the degree of an earl's daughter. They be religious in the forenoon and have the liberty women desire in the afternoon. They be the beautifulest creatures that ever I saw and the goodliest women. In the great church called the Duomo [Cologne Cathedral], the chancel is very fair both within and without, but the church itself is neither fair nor worthy of praise. The town standeth upon the Rhine; there are in this town as many churches, chapels, chantries, and religious houses as there be days in the year. We rested here the 7th day.

August 8

From Cologne [Köln] to Gulick [Jülich], 6 miles, through a town called Bergham [Bergheim], halfway to Jülich. Within 3 or 4 miles of Cologne beginneth the duchy of Jülich, the which the Duke of Cleves hath. He is now a building a very goodly house a little without the walls of the town, where he maketh also a notable strong fort. This town was burnt of late by casualty of fire, but there is much of it very well built again. The duke sent the lords a peck of wine and 10 sacks of oats.

August 9

From Jülich to Maestrickt [Maastricht], 7 miles. We rode to Aachen to dinner, 4 miles. This town is the emperor's, a very old town of no force nor much inhabited. King Charlemagne is buried in the great church there. The emperor is first crowned here with an iron crown. Next he is crowned at Milan with a crown of lead. The third and last time he is crowned in Rome with a crown of gold. There are many hot baths in this town by nature having places to let water in and out as they will. After dinner we rode to Maastricht, 3 miles. Through this town runneth a great river, Meuse, the which divideth Luke [Liège/Luik] and Brabant. The town is very old and well built on Luik's side, but on Brabant's side it is not to be dispraised. It is of force but they be now building a bastillion on the north side, which will be very strong when it is finished. From Maastricht over to Calais all is the emperor's.

August 10

From Maastricht to Sanctron [Sint-Truiden/Saint-Trond], 6 miles, a great town and a goodly city and belongeth to two persons: the Bishop of Liège and the abbot of the town. The town is ruled by 14 citizens of the town: 7 for the bishop and 7 for the abbot. The abbey was built by St. Trudo, bishop of that town, whereof the town taketh her name. The revenues of the abbey are 20000 crowns per annum.

August 11

From Sint-Truiden/Saint-Trond to Louen [Leuven], 6 miles, through a town called Lyne [Linter], halfway. Leuven is very great within the walls but much of it not inhabited. It is of no force. There are but few scholars remaining at the colleges but such as be very poor. There cometh a small river to this town which beareth a great vessel, and it runneth to Andwarpe [Antwerp]. It is made deep by policy of man and therefore hath no name.

August 12–13

From Leuven to Brusselles [Brussels], 4 miles. Half a mile out of the town we were met with Sir John Mason, knight, Queen Mary's ambassador leger for England; the Earl of Devonshire [Edward Courtenay]; and a great company of gentlemen of the emperor's court, and so brought the lords to their lodging. This town is very great but of no strength. It hath many fair streets in it and a park of white and fallow deer. Here the emperor lieth for the most part. There cometh a river to this town which runneth to Antwerp and beareth a great vessel but hath no name because it is made by industry of man as many others are also in this country. We tarried here the 13th day, and then the lords spoke with the emperor in a little house in the park, where he lieth for the most part very solitary.

August 14

From Brussels to Dendermonde, 5 great miles. This is a fair town and well built but of no strength. A river cometh into it by man's hand as before and hath no name. A little without the town runneth a great river called Scheldt.

August 15

From Dendermonde to Gendt (also Gawnte) [Ghent/Gent, earlier Ganda], at the Golden Head, 5 miles. This is the first city of Flanders and the greatest and therewith of an invincible force without treason. The emperor built a castle in it, that for strength may be compared with any in Europe. It hath so fair streets and such excellent building that, Antwerp excepted, I have not seen the like. This town is the stronger because of the rivers that come to it, whereby they may drown all the country round about them if they will. They have 60000 fighting men out of the town and yet the town furnished nevertheless. Here in this town was the emperor born. By the report of the people, there are no less than 400 windmills about it, for paper, oil, and corn and other things. It is 6 leagues' compass to pass about by the ditch. The river of Scheldt, which cometh from Antwerp, runneth through Ghent. There are 2 other rivers also which pass through the town called Leco fl. [Lesse] and Lyse fl. [Lys/Leie].

August 16

From Ghent to Bruges at the Golden Star, 8 long miles. This town is well walled and double ditched and reasonably strong, a very fair town and right. It hath no river to it but one forced by men's hands and yet is such a one that they have their wares brought from 2 ports of the sea, that is, from Ostend and the sluice, and may go by water by many places in the land if they will. This river within the town is dispersed in and through so many streets of the town that there is no dweller there but he may have his provision brought by water within 100 yards of his house. And for the more ease of the people to pass the next way to and fro, there are 132 bridges in that town, whereupon the town was named Bruges.

August 17

From Bruges to Neuport [Nieuwpoort], 8 miles, through two towns, Adenburg [Oudenburg] and Ostend. Oudenburg is a pretty town, and 3 miles from Bruges. Two miles from Oudenburg is Ostend, a fair haven town by the sea side and standeth well for the coast of Norfolk by reason whereof corn masters frequent it much, when they find a good vent for their corn at Ostend. Within this 26 years it stood 3 leagues from the sea and now the water cometh to the town. Ostend hath 32 fishing craiers [small trading vessels] belonging to it, all of them indifferently well furnished with ordnance. All the partners of them be sworn one to the other to take like parts and to make him account of that they get, and at their coming home their goods be divided, part and part-like. Also, if any of them sustain any loss they all bear like part, so that by this means there is no man but may well bear his part without any prejudice or hindrance. They were wont to have a master whose negligence many times was the cause they fell into their enemies' hands. Nieuwpoort is a fair haven town indifferently strong and standeth all by fishing. When the emperor hath any wars, Nieuwpoort findeth him 2 ships well appointed at their own charges.

August 18

From Nieuwpoort to Dunkirk, 5 miles. It is a haven town, fair and well built, meetly strong, and hath 200 pieces or ordnance in it.

August 19–20

From Dunkirk to Calais, 6 miles, through a town called Gravelin [Gravelines], halfway. A little of this town parteth Flanders and the ground that belongeth to Calais. This is a poor town and of no force, but towards the English pale there is a castle built of great force. In this town all that come out of Flanders that way towards England are searched. Calais is of such force and hath such store of munition in it and is kept in so good order that it passeth all that ever I saw. We stayed in Calais the 20th day.

August 21–22

From Calais to Dover by sea, 30 miles. We embarked ourselves at one a clock after midnight and arrived at Dover, the next day being the 22nd, about 9 or 10 a clock in the forenoon, and there rested ourselves all that day.

August 23

From Dover to Canterbury, 12 miles.

August 24

From Canterbury to Dartford, 32 miles.

August 25

From Dartford to London, 12 miles.

And so ended our Romish Journey.

The number of the miles from Rome to London, through Germany, accounting the leagues from Trento to Worms at 5 English miles the piece, amounteth to 1100 and one.

NOTES

1. Most of the names are elusive, owing either to North's spelling or to the ephemeral nature of history. But we did find two references stating that Mathew Carewe and Thomas Fitzwilliams were in Padua in August 1554. See Thomas Hoby, *The Travels and Life of Sir Thomas Hoby, Kt. Of Bisham Abbey, written by himself, 1547–1564*, edited for the Royal Historical Society by Edgar Powell (London: Offices of the Society, 1902), 117.

2. William Thomas, *The historie of Italie, a boke excedyng profitable to be redde: Because it intreateth of the astate of many and divers common weales, how thei have ben, & now be governed* (Imprinted at London: In Fletestrete in the house of Thomas Berthelet, 1549). Thomas was clerk of the council to Edward VI.

3. North is not the only early Tudor Englishman to refer to Marquise as *Morgyson*. This particular name for the French town also appears in *The Maner of the Tryumphe at Caleys and Bulleyn* (London: Wynkyn de Worde, 1532). It is possible that North, who perused other historical texts on important Henrician events, got the name of the town from this text.

4. An ecclesiastical official charged with protecting an episcopal see; the vidame de Picquigny represented the Bishop of Amiens (in 1555, Nicolas de Pellevé).

5. North may have been confusing it for Rennes, a large city in Brittany.

6. As Oronce Finé would not die until 8 August 1555, this confirms that North would not write this entry until at least five months after its 8 March date. The implication is that he compiled the journal from notes or from an earlier draft after he returned home.

7. The 11 March entry actually begins with "The next day after." The customary way of beginning an entry—here "From Fontainebleau to St. Mathurin, 4 leagues"—is written in the margin.

8. This is a heavily corrected entry in which North crossed out an original parenthetical identifying Master White as "son to Master White one of the masters of the requests" and replaced it with the parenthetical "whose father was master of the requests under Queen Mary." This again implies that his original work on the journal occurred during Mary's reign but that he made this correction (and probably others too) after Mary's death in November 1558.

9. Leland mentions Petrus de Aqua Blanca in *The Itinerary of John Leland the Antiquary*, Vol. the Seventh, In two Parts. 3rd ed. (Oxford: Printed at the Theater for James Fletcher, Bookseller in the Turl; and Joseph Pote, Bookseller at Eton, 1769).

10. Other early modern travelers provide similar descriptions. In 1588, for example, Jacques de Villamont, who crossed at Mount Cenis, noted that "it is very dangerous to pass . . . since in the plain there are precipices, which, being covered with snow. . ., one can easily fall in, and be sure to never come back out." He also speaks of "swirls of mountain wind" that "lift the snow in such great quantity that . . . it carries with it any passers-by and overtakes and buries them piled up on top of them." Jacques de Villamont, *Les Voyages du Seigneur de Villamont de l'ordre de Hierusalem, Gentilhomme ordinaire de la chamber du Roy* . . . (Paris: Claude de Montr'oeil and Jean Richer, 1600), 7.

11. The drawing or carrying of travelers over the ridge of the Cenis Pass in a sled—actually a chair on runners—was a common service offered by local guides known as "marrons." Four marrons would carry the traveler to the top of the mountain and then hand him off to marrons on the other side. Michael de Montaigne also hired this service when he crossed Mount Cenis in 1581. In many cases, only two marrons were required for the descent, one in front and one behind, and they typically guided the chair down the slope like a toboggan. This, of course, was a precursor to sledding and eventually skiing; not surprisingly, Lanslebourg-Mont-Cenis now has a ski resort at this same location. See *Oeuvres de Michel de Montaigne avec Notice Biographique*, ed. J.-A.-C. Buchon (Paris: A Desrez, Libraire-Editeur, 1837), 756. See also E. S. Bates, *Touring in 1600: A Study in the Development of Travel as a Means of Education* (Boston and New York: Houghton Mifflin, 1912), 294–95.

12. François Vinchant, writing of a 1609–1610 journey across the Alps, describes such a sled as driven by a marron "who, placing himself in front and between two poles that he holds on each side, allows himself to slide on the snow, holding himself upright, in a channel dug long ago in the rock, and pulls in this fashion the person sitting on the sled, who must remain calm and not be afraid, fearing the losing his vision or falling into the precipices that one sees at times at one's side." François Vinchant, *Voyage de François Vinchant en France & en Italie du 16 septembre 1609 au 18 février 1610* (Bruxelles: Société générale d'imprimerie, 1897), 186–87. Though travelers disliked the marrons' high prices, the guides were indispensable. Vinchant is also quoted in Richard E. Keatley, "Alpine Cannibals: French Renaissance Representations of the Alps and Their Residents," in *Monsters and Borders in the Early Modern Imagination*, ed. Jana Byars and Hans Peter Broedel (New York: Routledge, 2018), 85–100; 92–93.

13. Villamont notes that some travelers and some guides drink "snow water," which is "very dangerous to drink" and causes their "swollen throat" [goiters], which is "very monstrous to see." Villamont, *Les Voyages du Seigneur de Villamot*, 6v.

14. Other sixteenth-century journalists have also described the Chapelle de Transis as a place that was continuously replenished with the bodies of unfortunate travelers. In 1578, Nicolas Audebert recorded eighteen bodies at the church. E. S. Bates writes, "After heavy snowfalls the monks of the neighbouring hospice of St. Nicolas used to send out search parties; corpses discovered were examined for proofs of orthodoxy, beads, for instance, failing which the bodies were left to the beasts of prey." See E. S. Bates, *Touring in 1600*, 296. Villamont also tells of such a chapel at the top of Mount Cenis, where there were many dead bodies. And Richard E. Keatley references Michel Bideaux's remark on "the marker at the height of the Mont Cenis . . . In a small chapel travelers could view the frozen victims of avalanches and cold that were thrown into the chapel through a small hole." Richard E. Keatley, "Alpine Cannibals: French Renaissance Representations of the Alps and Their Residents," 90–91, referencing Michel Bideaux, ed., *Voyage d'Italie* (1606) (Geneva: Slatkine, 1982), 38.

15. North may have learned about William Benet's death and other details from Sir Edward Carne. Carne had also been one of Henry VIII's ambassadors to Rome and was traveling with Benet back to England when the latter died in Susa on 26 September 1533.

16. Hugh Percy Jones writes about the interesting connection between the calls of French and Italian sentinels: "The cry of French sentinels when on guard was, until the sixteenth century, *Qui va là*, 'Who goes there?' It is said that the expression *Qui vive* has nothing to do with *vivre*, 'To live,' but is derived from the Italian *Chi viva*, which is itself a corruption of *Chi vi va*, 'Who goes there?'" See Hugh Percy Jones, ed., *A New Dictionary of Foreign Phrases and Classical Quotations* (London: Charles William Deacon, 1900), 327n.

17. Asti remains famous today for its masks and carnival. This is clearly an allusion to a carnivalesque celebration that the locals threw for the Palm Sunday procession and the welcoming of the English visitors.

18. For commentary on Aloisio Marliani, a "learned man who can cure any ailment," see Monica Azzolini, "Anatomy of a Dispute: Leonardo, Pacioli and Scientific Courtly Entertainment in Renaissance Milan," *Early Science and Medicine* 9.2 (2004): 115–35; 119.

19. On 24 February 1525, Francis I was taken prisoner by the Imperial Spanish Army at the Battle of Pavia.

20. This is the world-famous Duomo of Milan. To help him with its description, North turned to Thomas, *The historie of Italie*, 188v–189.

21. North also got this tidbit from Thomas, *The historie of Italie*, 188v.

22. *Fiorita* is Italian for "bed of flowers," but it is unclear what the food item is. Lombardy is, however, well-known for the first dish: "That Lombardy likes rich desserts might be guessed from the fame of its whipped cream (*lattemiele*) . . . Milan also makes a variety of cream chilled puddings: *bonett de latimel*." See Waverly Root, *The Food of Italy* (New York: Vintage Books, 1992), 295.

23. North found the story of Paul III and his son Peter Aluigi in Thomas, *The historie of Italie*, 212v–214.

24. The young duke had no wife or daughter at this time, so "the wife of Gonzago and his daughter" must refer to the wife and daughter of Frederico II Gonzaga. Similarly, the young duke's "mother's sister" must signify his mother's sister-in-law, Eleanora Gonzaga, Duchess of Urbino (1494–1570)—the only woman alive at the time who fits this description. Eleanora's husband, Francesco Maria I della Rovere, had been murdered in his seaside villa in Pesaro in 1538 in a novel way: poison was poured into his ear. Source scholar Geoffrey Bullough considers this the inspiration for the similar murder described in Hamlet's play-within-a-play, *The Murder of Gonzago*. It is perhaps interesting that North also uses the same incorrect spelling—*Gonzago*. On 19 May, North and the train would stay in Pesaro, the site of the murder, as guests of Guidobaldo II, son of Francesco Maria I and Eleanora. See G. Bullough, "The Murder of Gonzago: A Probable Source for *Hamlet*," *The Modern Language Review* 30.4 (1935): 433–44 and Geoffrey Bullough, *Narrative and Dramatic Sources of Shakespeare, Vol. 7, Major Tragedies: "Hamlet," "Othello," "King Lear," "Macbeth"* (London: Routledge & Kegan Paul/New York: Columbia University Press, 1973), 32–33.

25. At her wedding in 1554, they played Ignanni by Curzio Gonzaga, the source for *Twelfth Night*.

26. North uses the Latin for Bologna.

27. We were unable to find any references to these two Bolognese noblemen.

28. North writes "Wafreno" and, in an earlier entry, "Rheno."

29. North now travels with Carne.

30. Battle of the Metaurus River, 207 B.C.E., which ended Hannibal's hopes of conquering Italy.

31. Thomas, *The historie of Italie*, 28–28v.

32. North here is closely following Thomas's description of the cardinals passing the bridge of Saint Angelo. Thomas, *The historie of Italie*, 37v.

33. Thomas, *The historie of Italie*, 22–37.

34. Verona was made a tax-free town in 1185. Shakespeare's Prince references the town in *Romeo and Juliet*: "To old Freetown, our common judgment-place" (1.1.102).

35. Apparently, such tolls were in place in Germany. See Erasmus, "A Pilgrimage for Religion's Sake," in *Collected Works of Erasmus (Colloquies)*, Vol. 40, trans. Craig R. Thompson (Toronto: University of Toronto Press, 1997), 633.

36. As the Holy Roman Empire comprised much of modern day Germany, Bohemia, and Austria (figure 6.1), the title "King of the Romans" designated Ferdinand ruler of this region and next in line for Holy Roman Emperor, the title then held by Charles V. Eventually, the King of the Romans became known as the King of Germany.

37. A Dutch mile had various definitions, but when North adds up the total distance of the trip, he approximates the Dutch mile as equal to five English (or Italian) miles. This is close to an Austrian or Prussian mile, which was equal to a little more than 7.5 km (or 4.7 miles).

38. North's mistake of *Eisack* for *Flicke* is more likely an error of the eye than the ear. The studious North likely misread some document that he is using for place names.

39. North's use of *Ferdinando* and his allusion to "the emperor when he came out of Spain" echoes the Latin inscription of a monument built near Gries in the Brenner Pass to commemorate the 1530 reunion between Charles V and Ferdinand (see Chapter 6).

40. The Hofkirche in Innsbruck now contains 28 bronze statues of alleged ancestors of Ferdinand and his wife Queen Anna of Bohemia and Hungary surrounding the cenotaph of Ferdinand's grandfather, Maximilian I (1459–1519).

41. Johannes Gutenberg, who introduced printing to Europe, was born in Mainz and perfected his printing press there. We have been unable to determine why he believed guns were also invented there.

Index

The index includes all of the historical individuals mentioned in North's manuscript (as well as in our own narrative). But we have been selective with the towns recorded in the journal, omitting those of little consequence to the traveler. Similarly, because press style is not to index endnotes, which contain numerous citations of scholarly work, we have not included the names of scholars mentioned in our narrative. Page references for figures are italicized.

Aachen, 8, 221
Adige (river), 213–14
Admiral's Men, 170
Adolf III of Schauenburg, Bishop of Cologne, 220
Aenus/Inn (river), 214
Aiguebelle, 187
Albert V. *See* Bavaria, Duke of
Alderman Chester's son of London, 177
Alessandria, 3, 192
Alessandro, Alberico, 196
Allier (river), 185
Alps/mountain[s], 3, 6–8, 45, 83, 122–24, 163, 185–90, 202–6, 213–19
Altenburg, 218
Amiens, 1, 2, 175, 178–79
Ammergau, 215
Amyot, James, 18
Ancona, 197
Andenach, 219
Anne d'Alençon, 198
Anne de Montmorency, 179

Anne of Bohemia, Queen of England, 92–93
Antigonus, in North's *Dial*, 139–43; in North's *Doni*, 143; in the *Odyssey*, 142; in *Winter's Tale*, 89–90, 127, 139–43
Antigonus, in North's *Dial*, 139–43; in *Winter's Tale*, 89–90, 127, 139–43
Antoine. *See* Vendôme, Duke of
Antwerp, 221–22
Apiano, Christophano, 193
Apuleius/Lucius Apuleius, *Metamorphoses* or *The Golden Ass*, 128
Aqua Blanca, Petrus de, Bishop of Hartford, 187
Aquanegra Cremonese, 4, 198
Arc (river), 123, 186–87
Archidamus, in "The Life of Agis and Cleomenes," in *Plutarch's Lives*, 155–56; in *Winter's Tale*, 155–56
Arden of Faversham, 126

229

Arthur, Prince of Wales, 86, 90
Assisi, 205
Asti/Astigani, 3, 55, 70–71, 73, 191–92
Astle Forlimpopoli, 202
Augsburg, 6, 7, 93, 107, 216–17
Austria, 6, *6*, 7, 12, 91–92, 176, 214–15
Avigliana, 70, 190

Bacharach, 219
Balbi di Correggio, Francesco (arquebusier), 107
Banchetto rustica/rustic banquet, *129*, 130–31, 133, 151
Baratiero, Camillo, 196
Baratiero, Cesare, 196
Baratiero, Francisco, 196
Baratiero, Hercole, 196
Baratiero, Hippolita, 196
Basilica Papale di San Pietro/St. Peter's Church, 209
Basilique Saint-Mathurin, 183
Bavaria, Duke of (Albert V), 7, 215–17
Belvedere, 208
Benet, William, Archbishop of Salisbury, 45–46, 90, 96, 190.
Bentinck, Margaret Cavendish. *See* Portland, Duchess of
Bergheim, 220
Bible, 22, 85
Bingen am Rhein, 219
Blackfriars, 7, 27, 48, 55, 97, 216
Blanding, Michael, 17
Boccaccio, Giovanni, *De Casibus Virorum Illustrium*, 65, 85
Bodleian Library, 17
Boethius Severinus, 193
Bohemia, 7, 34, 36, 83–84, 87–90, *91*, 91–95, 107, 141, 151, 153, 155–57, 162–63
Bohemia, King of, and Holy Roman Emperor (Rudolf II), 7, 34, 84, 88–90, 92–94, 155–56
Bohemia, King of, and King of the Romans (Ferdinand I), 7, 34, 83–84, 88–91, *91*, 92–94, 107, 155–56, 163, 213–14, 216–17

Boileau, Giles, Claude Colet, and Jacques Gohorry, *Florisel de Niquea*, 147
Bois de Vincennes/Wood of Vincennes, 182
Boleyn, Anne, Queen of England, 53–56, 68, 72–74, 108, 110, 164
Bologna/Bononia, 4, 6, 45, 66, 175, 200–201, 211–12
Bomporto, 212
Bond, Edward A., 13
Borghetto sull'Adige, 213
Borromeo, Giovanni Battista, Count, 194
Boulogne-sur-Mer, 46, 178
Bourbon, Duke of (Charles III), 2, 46, 123, 185, 190
Bourgoin-Jallieu, 186
Bozen/Bolzano, 214
Brabant, 221
Brende, John, *The History of Quintus Curtius*, 36, 86
Brendel, Daniel von Homburg, Bishop of Mainz, 219
Brenner Pass, 7, 91, 92
Bretten, 8, 218
British Library/British Museum, 11, 13–18, 21–22, 175
Brixen, 214
Brooke, Arthur, 34
Brooke, C. F. Tucker, 22
Browne, Anthony, Viscount Montague, 1, 4, 5, 7, 11–13, 45, 66, 178, 201, 210, 216, passim (as lord[s]) in Transcript
Bruges, 8, 222–23
Brussels, 6, 8, 221–22
Burbage, Richard, 170
Bussolengo, 212–13

Calabria, 7, 107, 156, 216
Calais, 1, *2*, 3, 6, 8, 11, 46, 162, 175, 178, 221, 223
Cambridge University, 18
Camillo, in *Winter's Tale*, 36, 90, 95, 108–9, 143–45, 154, "Camillo as Sir Thomas More" 108–9. *See also* More, Thomas; Stanga, Camillo

Campeggi, Lorenzo (Campeius), Cardinal-protector of England, 27, 45, 51, 70
Campeggio, Giovanni, Bishop of Bologna, 200
Canneto/Canneto sull'Oglio, 4, 144, 197–98
Cannstatt, 8, 217–18
Canterbury, 8, 29, 48, 162, 224
Cantiano, 203–4
Carafa, Alessandro ("Cardinal Nephew"), 176, 207–8
Carafa, Antonio. *See* Mondragone, Duke of
Carafa, Gian Pietro. *See* Paul IV (pope)
Carewe, Matthew, 177
Carne, Edward, 1, 4, 12, 45–46, 66, 90, 96, 187, 201–1
carnival, 55–56, 66, 70–73, 164
Castel Sant'Angelo/Castle of St. Angelo, 207, 209
Castiglione, Baldassare, Count of Casatico, 85, 116–17; *Il Cortegiano*, 117
Castiglione, Hippolita, Countess of Casatico, 116
Castlemain, Earl of (Roger Palmer), 11
Catholic miracles, 7, 16, 83–84, 87–88, 97, 106, 118–19, 121–22, 125–26, 135–36, 163, 175–77, 204–5, 215
Catholic relics, 2, 4, 6–8, 36, 84, 125, 145, 147, 162–63, 175, 178, 180–81, 200, 204–5, 210, 220
Catholic/Catholicism, 1, 4, 6, 7, 11–13, 36, 43, 45, 63–64, 70, 79, 83–84, 87–88, 90, 92–97, 103, 106–8, 116, *116*, 118, 119, 121, 124–27, 135–36, 145, 147, 157, 175–76, 216, 218
Cavalliero Continental, 193
Cavendish, George, *The Life of Wolsey*, 35–36, 41, 43–52, 55, 57, 63, 65, 68, 70, 74, 76–79, 86–87, 92, 101–2, 163–64, 177. *See also* Wolsey, Thomas
Ceraino, 213

La Certosa di Pavia/Charterhouse of Pavia, 3, 46, 193–94, 206
Cervini, Marcello degli Spannochi. *See* Marcellus II (pope)
Cesena, 202, 211
Chambéry, 1, 3, 187
Chantilly, 173, 179
La Chapelle de Transis/Chapel of the Dead, 3, 123, 189
Chapel of San Barbara, 120
Charenton-le-Pont, 182
Charlemagne, Emperor, 8, 181, 221
Charles III, Duke of Bourbon. *See* Bourbon, Duke of
Charles V, Holy Roman Emperor, 1, 3, 7–8, 12, 43, 46, 71, 87, 89–95, 107–8, 163, 182, 190–92, 195–96, 204, 208, 213–14, 216, 218, 221–23. *See also* Polixenes, in *Winter's Tale*
Château d'Écouen, 1, 173, 179
Chaucer, Geoffrey, 85; "Monk's Tale," 36
La Cheveriere, Madame, 186
Chiese (river), 198
Church of St. Henry, 186
Churchyard, Thomas, 170
Clement VII (pope), 45–46, 86, 90. *See also* Oracle of Apollo
Cleomenes, in "The Life of Agis and Cleomenes," in *Plutarch's Lives*, 155; in *Winter's Tale*, 90, 96, 109, 152, 156.
Clermont, 179
College of Cardinals, 29–30
Colma, 214
Cologne Cathedral (Duomo), 220
Cologne, 8, 71, 219–20
Colonna, Fabrizio, 198
Concordia sulla Secchia, 212
Constancio de alta, Il Signor, 194
Counter-reformation, 93, 103, 106, 125–26
Courtenay, Edward. *See* Devon, Earl of
Cranmer, Thomas, Archbishop of Canterbury, 45, 64–65, 74

Cremona, 4, 115, 118, 144, 177, 197
Cromwell, Thomas, 75–77

Danube (river), 214, 217
Dartford, 8, 162, 224
de casibus, 36, 65
d'Este, Alphonso II. *See* Ferrara, Duke of
d'Este, Ercole II. *See* Ferrara, Modena, and Reggio, Duke of
D'Ewes, Simonds, 14–15
d'Herberay, Nicholas, *Amadis de Grecia*, 86, 147–48, 150, 161; *The Dial of Princes*, 148, 150–51
della Corgna, Fulvio Giulio, Cardinal of Perugia, 205
della Rovere, Francesco Maria II, 4–5, 66, 202–3
della Rovere, Guidobaldo II. *See* Duke of Urbino
della Rovere, Hippolita, 127, 137n22, 177, 198
del Monte, Giovanni Maria Ciocchi. *See* Julius III (pope)
Delphos, "North's Isle of Delphos Error" 151–55, 161
de' Medici, Catherine, Queen of France, 2, 183
de' Medici, Cosimo I. *See* Florence, Duke of
de' Medici, Giulio di Giuliano. *See* Clement VII (pope)
Dendermonde, 222
Devon, Earl of (Edward Courtenay), 8, 221–22
Dillingen an der Donau, 7, 217
Dion, in "The Life of Dion" in *Plutarch's Lives*, 155–57, 160; in *Winter's Tale*, 90, 96, 110, 152, 156
Dionysius of Syracuse, 18, 156
Djerba, 107
Doni, Anton Francesco, *The Moral Philosophy of Doni*, 18, 55, 57, 74–79, 143, 154–55
Dorothea of Denmark, 218
Dover, 1, 8, 162, 223–24

Dragut Rais. *See* Turgut Re'is
du Bellay, Joachim, *Florisel de Niquea*, 36, 147–48
Dudley, Robert. *See* Leicester, Earl of
Duke of Bedford's castle, 182
Dunkirk, 223
Dutch/Low Countries, 8, 91, 177, 213–14

Easter (Mardi Gras, Ash Wednesday, Shrove Sunday, Shrove Tuesday, Palm Sunday), 7, 11, 70–73, 178, 194, 215
Edward IV, King of England, 8.
Edward VI, King of England, 1, 87–88, 90, 96
Edwards, Richard, 169
Egna, 213
Eisack/Eisack (river), 214
Elderton, William, 169
Elizabeth I, Queen of England/ Elizabethan, 15, 21, 64, 167, 169
Elizabeth of Schonau, 64
Ely, Bishop of. *See* Thirlby, Thomas
emperor [general], 8, 74, 221
England/English, 1, 3–8, 11–13, 15, 17–18, 20–22, 27, 29–30, 33–36, 41, 43–46, 50, 55, 63–66, 68–71, 78, 85–90, 92–95, 97, 104, 106, 117, 119, 121, 126, 145, 148–49, 157, 161–63, 167–68, 170, 175–78, 182–83, 186–87, 191, 202, 205, 207–8, 210, 213, 215, 218, 221, 223–24
Erik XIV, King of the Swedes and Goths, 169
Esslingen am Neckar, 217
Ettal abbey in Oberammergau, 7, 216
Evans, R. H., 14

Faenza, 66, 201–2
Fano, 203
Farnese, Alessandro, Cardinal Deacon of St. Angelo, 196, 206
Farnese, Alessandro. *See* Paul III (pope)
Farnese, Ottavio. *See* Duke of Parma
Farnese, Pier Luigi [Peter Aluigi]. *See* Piacenza and Parma, Duke of

Farnese, Ranuccio, Cardinal of St. Angelo [sic]/St. Lucia, 197, 206
Farnese, Vittoria. *See* Urbino, Duchess of
Farrant, Richard, 169
feast of the lesser gods, 127–37, 151, 163
Ferdinand I. *See* King of Bohemia and King of the Romans
Ferrara, Duke of (Alphonso II d'Este), 4, 198–99
Ferrara, Modena, and Reggio, Duke of (Ercole II d'Este), 198–99, 212
Ferrers, George, "The Fall of Robert Tresilian," 36, 148
Finnaeus, Orontius/Oronce Finé, 2, 21, 181
Fitzgerald, James, 33
Fitzwilliams, Lord, 177
Flanders, 8, 178, 222–23
Fletcher, John, 35, 52–53, 55–57, 64–65, 79, 144; *A Wife for a Month*, 144
Florence, 4, 45, 66, 201
Florence, Duke of (Cosimo I de' Medici), 12, 66
Florizel, in *Winter's Tale*, 84, 89–90, 93–94, 96, 106–8, 128–29, 131, 133–34, 147, 156–57, 159, 161, "Philip II: Florizel, King of Sicily" 106–8
Foligno, 205, 211
Fontainebleau, 2, 182–83
Forli, 66, 202
Fossombrone, 203
France/French, 1, 3, 5–7, 17–18, 45–46, 67–69, 71, 85–86, 107, 122, 147–48, 150, 179–84, 188–92, 194–96, 203–4, 210, 212
Francis I, King of France, 46, 180, 194, 196
Frankenstein, Rudolf von, Bishop of Speyer, 218
Frederick II. *See* Palatine, Earl [Count]; Rhine, Palsgrave of the
Furlo Pass, 203

Gascoigne, George, *Jocasta*, 168
Gay, Edwin Francis, 13
George of Austria. *See* Bishop of Liège
Germany/German[s], 6, *6*, 7–8, 12, 92–93, 107, 162, 189, 210, 214, 216–18, 224
Ghent/Gent, 8, 222
Giulio Romano, 4, 37, 85, 111, 115–16, *116*, 117–18, 120–21, 127–29, *129*, *130*, 130–31, *132*, 133, *134*, 135–36, 151, 163
Göppingen, 8, 217
Gohorry, Jacques, *Amadis de Gaul*, 86, 148, 150; *The Dial of Princes*, 150; *Florisel de Niquea*, 147–48; *Rogel de Grecia*, 147
Gonzaga, Eleanora. *See* Urbino, Duchess of
Gonzaga, Ercole, Cardinal of Mantua, 212
Gonzaga, Federico II. See Mantua, Duke of
Gonzaga, Federico, Bishop and Cardinal of Mantua, 212
Gonzaga, Federico, Bishop and Cardinal of Monferrato, 212
Gonzaga, Ferrante, 198
Gonzaga, Francesco III. *See* Mantua, Duke of
Gonzaga, Guglielmo. *See* Mantua, Duke of
Gonzaga, Hippolita [Ippolita], 127, 177, 198
Gonzaga, Isabella, 127, 198
Gonzaga, Louis [Luigi]. *See* Nevers, Duke of
Gonzaga, Margaret Paleologa. *See* Mantua, Duchess of
Gonzagas/Gonzaga family, 4, 85, 115, 117, 127–29, 131, 135
Gonzago [North's misspelling], 212
Goulart, Simon, 18
Gravelines, 223
Greece/Greek, 84, 107, 151, 156

Greene, Robert, *Pandosto: The Triumph of Time*, 34, 88, 150–55, 157, *158*, 159–61, 165; *Orlando*, 170
Grey, Lady Jane, 1
Grolier Club, 17
Guevara, Antonio de, *The Dial of Princes*, 17–18, 22, 32–33, 36, 74–75, 79, 86, 95, 121–22, 139–44, 148, 150–55, 161, 163–64, 168

Hall, Edward, *The Union of the Two Noble and Illustre Families of Lancaster and York* (Hall's *Union*), 35, 36, 41, 43, 52–54, 56–57, 63, 73, 177
Hannibal (Carthaginian general), 190, 203
Hapsburg, 1, 70, 87, 90–91, 93–95, 107, 180
Hardwicke, 2nd Lord (Philip Yorke), 11, 12, 15, 16
Harley, Edward. *See* Oxford and Mortimer, 2nd Earl of
Harley, Henrietta Cavendish. *See* Oxford and Mortimer, Countess of
Harley, Robert. *See* Oxford and Mortimer, 1st Earl of
Heber, Richard, 14
Heidenheim, 7, 217
Henry II, King of France, 1–3, 71, 181–83, 189–92, 195, 212
Henry V, King of France, 182
Henry VIII, King of England (historic figure and dramatic character), 1, 12, 32, 41, 44–46, 63, 65, 68, 85–88, 90, 92, 95, 97, 101, 108–10, 125, 143, 145, 161, 163, 178, 190
Henslowe, Philip, 167
Hermione, in *Winter's Tale*, 37, 83, 85, 87–88, 90, 94–103, 106, 108–10, 115–20, 122, 125, 127, 135, 144, 154, 163; "Hermione as Katherine and Mary as Perdita," 97–106. *See also* Katherine of Aragon
Heywood, Jasper, *Thyestes*, 63, 145, 168–69

Heywood, John, 36, 63, 145–48; *Play of the Four P's*, 34, 36, 63, 86, 145–47; *The Play of the Weather*, 145; *The Spider and the Fly*, 63, 145; *The Pardoner and the Friar*, 145
Heywood, Stephen, 63
Hoby, Thomas, 117
Holinshed, Raphaell, Holinshed's *Chronicles*, 68, 72, 76, 101–2
Homer, the *Odyssey*, 85, 89–90, 140, 142, 147
Hungary, 7, 92–93, 107
Hunnis, William, 169
Huntington Library, 13, 17–18, 21, 175
Hus, Jan/Hussites, 92, 94
Hussey, William, 177

Imola, 4, 201, 211
Inns of Court, 168
Inns and post houses: La Tavaro, 189; Spread Eagle, Black Morian, 212; Star, Rose, Crown, 213; Golden Spread Eagle, 214; Golden Lion, Black Eagle, 215; Golden Star, 215, 216; Golden Bell, 216; Golden Head, Golden Star, 222
Innsbruck, 6–7, 92, 214–15
Isar (river), 214
Isenburg-Grenzau, Johann von, Bishop of Trier, 219
Isère (river), 187
Italy/Italian, 3, 7, 11, 18, 20, 22, 27, 36, 41–43, 45–47, 52, 55–56, 63, 65–67, 69–71, 73, 75–76, 78, 85–86, 91, 93–94, 107, 111, 115–17, 121, 136, 143, 145, 147, 151, 168, 176–77, 185, 190–91, 195, 197–98, 203, 207, 210, 212–14

James I, King of England/Jacobean, 11, 34–35, 64, 88–89, 126
Jensen, Phebe, 87, 119, 126, 136
Jews, 7, 199, 213
Joan of Arc, 119, 126
Johnson, Samuel, 151

Jonson, Ben, *Every Man in His Humor*, 155
Jülich, 8, 220–21
Jülich-Cleves-Berg, Duke of (William), 220
Julius Caesar, 177, 202, 207
Julius III/Julius Tertius (pope), 1, 3, 5, 12, 176, 188, 201, 206–7, 212

Kaczynski, Ted, 33
Katherine of Aragon, Queen of England, 27, 29, 31–32, 36, 44–46, 50–52, 55, 63–65, 79, 85–88, 90, 95–103, 108–10, 122, 126, 143, 161, 163, 175. *See also* Hermione, in *Winter's Tale*
Kemp, William, 170
King's Men, 35
Kingston, William, 76–77, 92
Knights of Malta, 107
Koblenz, 8, 219–20
Königswinter, 220

L'Andriano, Il Conte, 194
La Charite sur Loire, 184
La Ferrière, 189
La Prima Porta, 5, 206
La Romagna 4, 201–2
La Scuderia 175, 210
La Tour-du-Pin, 186
Lago di Como/Lake Como, 41–42, 195
Lahn (river), 219
Lambeth Palace Library, 11, 13–16, 21, 43, 173, 175
Lamone (river), 201
Landsberg am Lech, 7, 216
Landsknechte/Launceknights, 189, 201
Lanslebourg-Mont-Cenis, 188
Lavagno, Giovanni Ambrosio ("Amitino"), 177
Lavagno, Giovanni Battisto, 177
Lech (river), 216
Leicester, Earl of (Robert Dudley), 167, 169–70
Leicester's Men, 167, 169–70

Leonidas, in "The Life of Agis and Cleomenes" in *Plutarch's Lives*, 155–56. *See also* Leontes, in *Winter's Tale*
Leontes, in *Winter's Tale*, 83–85, 87, 89–90, 93–95, 97 101, 106–10, 117, 119, 121, 124–26, 143–44, 152, 154–57, 159–60, "Henry VIII as Leontes" 109–11. *See also* Leonidas, in "The Life of Agis and Cleomenes," in *Plutarch's Lives*, 109–11
Lesse (river), 222
Leuven, 8, 221
Libya, 84, 89–90, 96, 107, 156–57, 159, 160–61
Liège, Bishop of (George of Austria), 221
"The Life of Agis and Cleomenes," in *Plutarch's Lives*, 155
"The Life of Dion," in *Plutarch's Lives*, 155
Lincoln's Inn, 63, 145, 148, 150, 168, 170
Linter, 221
Liutprand, last King of Pavia, tomb, 193
Lodi, 4, 195–96
Loire (river), 184–85
Lombardy, 193–94
London, 1, 6, 8, 11, 16–17, 73, 89, 103, 117, 162, 169, 170, 177, 210, 224
Lord Chamberlain's Men, 35
Lutheran[s]/Martin Luther, 92–93, 217
Luzarches, 1, 179
Lyly, John, 169
Lyon, 1–3, 177, 186
Lys/Leie (river), 222

Maastricht, 8, 221
Madruzzo, Cristoforo, Cardinal of Trent[o], 7, 213–14
Mainz, 6, 8, 219
Malory, Thomas, *Le Morte d'Arthur*, 22
Malvachall (nobleman of Bologna), 201
Mamillius, in *Winter's Tale*, 90, 96.

Mantua, 4, 7, 17, 85, 109, 111, 115–18, 120–21, 127, 135–36, 144, 151, 163, 176–77, 192, 197–98, 212
Mantua, Duchess of (Margaret Paleologa Gonzaga), 127, 198, 212
Mantua, Duke of (Federico II Gonzaga), 127, 131, 198, 212
Mantua, Duke of (Francesco III), 212
Mantua, Duke of (Guglielmo Gonzaga) 4, 115, 127–28, 134, 144, 192, 197–98, 212
Marcellus II/Marcellus Secundus (pope), 1, 4, 21, 176, 200–201, 207
Marcus Aurelius, Emperor, 139
Marignano, 195–96
Marliani, Aloisio, 193
Marne (river), 182
Marquise/Morgyson, 178
Martin, Lord, 177
Mary Tudor, Queen of England/Marian, 1, 12, 21, 36, 43, 45, 63–65, 74, 76, 83, 86–90, 93–97, 103–10, 119, 125–26, 143, 145, 161–63, 167, 187, 198, 221.
See also Perdita, in *Winter's Tale*
Mary, Queen of Scots, 2, 64, 183
Mason, John, ambassador leger for England, 8, 221
master of [the] requests, 21, 187
master of [the] revels, 63, 150, 168
Maximilian I, Holy Roman Emperor, 93
McArdle, Megan, 33
McMullan, Gordon, 64, 72, 97, 101
Medici, Gian Giacomo, Marquis Marignano, 195
Mediterranean, 84, 89–90, 94, 96, 107, 133–35, 156
Melanchthon, Philip, 8, 218
Melpomene, Muse of tragedy, 167
Melun, 182
Metauro (river), 203
Meuse (river), 221
Milan, 3–4, 6, 8, 41–42, 46, 56, 71, 115, 177, 193–97, 221

Milan Cathedral (Duomo), 41–42, 56
Milan, 1st Duke of (Gian Galeazzo Visconti), 4, 46, 193–94
Minoa, 156, 159
Mirandola, Earl of (Ludovico II Pico), 212
The Mirror for Magistrates, 36
Mittenwald, 6, 7, 215
Mondragone, Duke of (Antonia Carafa), 198
Mons[ieu]r le beaue Dolphin (René de Laval-Bois-Dauphin), 181
Mont Cenis, 3, 16, 188–90
Montague, Viscount. *See* Browne, Anthony
Montmelian, 187
Montone (river), 202
Montreuil, 178
More, Thomas, 63, 87, 90, 95, 108–9, 145. *See also* Camillo, in *Winter's Tale*
Moselle (river), 219
Moulins, 1, 177, 1856
Mount d'Aiguebelette, 3, 187
Mountferrat, 192
Muir, Kenneth, 34
Mulcaster, Richard, 169
Munday, Anthony, 169
Musone (river), 198

Nahe (river), 219
Naples/Neapolitan, 94, 177, 204
Narni, 205–6, 211
Neckar (river), 217
Neckar wines, 8, 217
Nelson, Alan H., 20
Nepos, Cornelius, *The Lives of Epaminondas, of Philip of Macedon, of Dionysius the Elder, and of Otavius Caesar Augustus* (*Nepos' Lives*), 18, 155
Nera (river), 206
Nevers, 1, 184, 212
Nevers, Duke of (Louis [Luigi] Gonzaga), 212

Nieuwpoort, 8, 223
North, Edward, 1st Lord North, 20, 36, 44, 191
North, George, *A Brief Discourse of Rebellion and Rebels*, 27, 169
North, Roger, 2nd Lord North, 169–70
North, Thomas, 17–228 *passim*. For North's translations, *see* Guevara, Antonio de (*The Dial of Princes*, including added chapter, *The Favoured Courtier*), Doni, Anton Francesco (*The Moral Philosophy of Doni*), Plutarch (*Plutarch's Lives*), Nepos, Cornelius (*Nepos' Lives*)
Norton, Thomas and Thomas Sackville, *Gorboduc*, 168–69
Notre Dame Cathedral, 177, 181
Notre Dame des Nieges/Our Lady of the Snows, 3, 123, 190
Novalesa, 3, 189

Obama, Michelle, 33
Oglio (river), 4, 197
Oise (river), 179
Oldcastle, Sir John/John Falstaff, 155
Olona (river), 196
Oracle of Apollo/Temple of Apollo, 90, 95–96, 98, 105, 120, 151–62
Orwell, George, *Animal Farm*, 110
Ostend, 8, 222–23
Ottoman Empire/Ottoman[s], 7, 84, 107
Oudenburg, 223
Ovid, 85
Oxford and Mortimer, 2nd Earl of (Edward Harley), 14, 15
Oxford and Mortimer, 1st Earl of (Robert Harley), 14, 15
Oxford and Mortimer, Countess of (Henrietta Cavendish Harley), 14
Oxford, 14–15, 17, 45–46, 92

Palatine, Earl [Count] (Frederick II), 217
Palazzo [del] Te, 4, 115, 127–29, *129*, *130*, 131, *132*, 133, *134*, 134, 163, 198

Palazzo Ducale/ducal palace, 4, 128, 198
Palmer, Roger. *See* Castlemain, Earl of
Panaro (river), 212
Paris, 1, 2, 21, 179, 181–82
Parliament/Westminster, 45, 47–51, 53–55, 176
Parma, Duke of (Ottavio Farnese), 196, 207
Paul III/Paulus Tertia (pope), 41–42, 56, 196, 204
Paul IV/Paulus Quartus (pope), 1, 5, 21, 176, 197, 204, 207
Pavia/King of Pavia/Battle of Pavia, 3, 46, 56–57, 193–94, 206
Peace of Augsburg, 7, 93
Perdita, in *Winter's Tale*, 37, 83, 87, 90, 93–94, 96–97, 103–7, 109, 118–20, 124–26, 127–30, 131, 133–35, 139–40, 142, 151, 156–57, 161, "Hermione as Katherine and Mary as Perdita" 97–106. *See also* Mary Tudor
Perugia, 4, 5, 45, 145, 176, 204–5
Pesaro, 66, 163, 202–3
Pforzheim, 218
Philibert, Emmanuel. *See* Savoy, Duke of
Philip II, King of Macedon, 132, *132*
Philip II, King of Spain and King of England, 1, 12, 21, 43, 87–88, 90, 93–96, 106–8, 110, 156, 162, 177, 193–94, 197. *See also* Florizel, in *Winter's Tale*
Philip III, King of Sicily, 34, 84, 88–90, 93–94, 106
Philip III, King of Spain, 34, 88–89
Philip, Francis (schoolmaster), 44
Philip, King of Macedon, 132, *132*
Phillipps, Thomas, 13–14, 17, 21
Piacenza and Parma, Duke of (Pier Luigi [Peter Aluigi] Farnese), 42, 177, 196–97
Piacenza, 4, 42, 196–97
Picardy, 11, 178–79

Pico, Ludovico II. *See* Mirandola, Earl of
Piedmont, 3, 73, 189–90, 196, 210
Pillades (nobleman of Bologna), 201
Pirie, Robert S., 11, 14
Pisa, Cardinal of, 17, 208
Plutarch, *The Lives of the Noble Grecians and Romanes* (*Plutarch's Lives*), 18, 22, 27, 84, 155–57, *158*, 159–61
Po (river), 3, 4, 190–91, 193, 196–99, 212
Poggio, Giovanni, Cardinal of Sant'Anastasia, 207
Pole, Reginald, Cardinal and papal legate, 12
Polixenes, in *Winter's Tale*, 83–84, 87, 90, 93–94, 99, 101, 121, 124, 128, 154–56, 160. *See also* Polyxenus, in "The Life of Dion" in *Plutarch's Lives*, 155–56, 160; Charles V
Pont Sant' Angelo/Bridge of St. Angelo, 42–43, 47, 56, 206, 208
Pont-de-Beauvoisin, 186
Ponte Molle, 206
Pontecurone, 193
pope, 1, 4, 5, 11–12, 21, 29–31, 42–43, 45–50, 52, 54–55, 86–87, 95–96, 98, 148, 164, 176–77, 190, 196, 199–201, 204, 206–10. *See also* popes Clement VII, Julius III, Marcellus II, Paul III, Paul IV
Porino, 190–91
Portland, Duchess of (Margaret Cavendish Bentinck), 14
Porzenno, Despesiano, Count, 143
Protestant[s]/Protestantism, 7–8, 45, 64–65, 86–87, 90, 92–95, 97, 106, 125–26, 136, 145, 216–18

Queen's Men, 170

Redondesco, 117, 198
reformation, 45, 64, 86–87, 90, 92–94, 103, 106, 119, 125–26

Reinhausen, 218
Reno (river), 4, 201
Respublica, 36, 86–87, 96, 102
Rhenish wines, 8, 218–19
Rhine (river), 8, 218–20
Rhine, Palsgrave of the (Frederick II), 8, 218–19
Rhone (river), 186
Richard II, King of England, 92–93
Rimini, 202, 211
Rions Monsieur de, of Flanders, 178
Rivoli, 3, 191
Robinson, Richard, *Gesta Romanorum*, 34
Rochemelone, 123, 190
Rodovico, Andrea, 192
Roman Catholic. *See* Catholic/Catholicism
Rome/Roman, 1, *2*, 4–6, *6*, 7–8, 11–13, 16–17, 22, 29–32, 36, 41–50, 52–54, 63, 66, 86, 91, 93–95, 97, 108, 111, 123, 126, 128, 135–36, 139, 141, 143, 145, 148, 152, 155, 161–63, 173, 175–78, 187–88, 190, 196–97, 199–201, 203, 206–8, 210, 214, 216, 221, 224
Ronco (river), 202
Ronsard, Pierre de, *L'Alouette*, 36, 85–86, 148–50
Rovereto, 213
Rowley, William, 169
Rubicon (river), 202
Rudolf II. *See* Bohemia, King of and Holy Roman Emperor
Rue (river), 178

Sacchetta, 212
Sacco, Hierolymo, 193
Saint-André, 3, 122, 124, 127, 135, 188
Saint Augustine, tomb, 193
Saint-Denis, 2, 175–76, 178, 180–81
Saint-Georges/Villeneuve-Saint-Georges, 3, 182, 185
Saint-Inglevert Abbey, 178
Saint-Jean-de-Maurienne, 123, 187–88

Saint-Mathurin, 2, 177, 183
Sala delle Aquile/Hall of the Eagles, 131, 133
Sala di Psyche/Hall of Psyche, 85, 129, *129*, *130*, 130, *132*, 133, *134*, 134, 163, 198
Salerno, Prince of (Ferdinando Sanseverino), 190
San Giorgio, 190
San Pietro in Ciel d'Oro, 193
San Pietro, in Casale, 199, 200–201
Sancerre ("Young Geneva"), 184
Sankt Goar, 219
Sanseverino, Ferdinando. *See* Salerno, Prince of
Sant' Ambrogio, 190
Santa Maria delle Grazie/St. Mary of Grace, 4, 85, 115–16, *116*, 117–22, 135, 163, 176, 198
Santarcangelo di Romagna, 202
Sauli, Gerolamo, Bishop of Genoa, 187, 190, 201
Savoy, 186, 210
Savoy, Duke of (Emmanuel Philibert), 216
Scheldt (river), 222
Schonau, Elizabeth of, 64
Schongau, 7, 216
Scipio Africanus (Roman general), 203
Secchia (river), 212
Seefeld, 7, 176, 215
Seine (river), 181–82
Seneca, *Thyestes*, 168–69
Seymour, Jane, Queen of England, 87
Shakespeare, William, 41, 170; *1 Henry IV*, 35; *2 Henry IV*, 35; *Antony and Cleopatra*, 22; *Coriolanus*, 22; *Hamlet*, 35; *Henry V*, 35; *Julius Caesar*, 22, 27; *King John*, 35; *King Lear*, 35; *The Merchant of Venice*, 34–35; *Much Ado About Nothing*, 35; *Romeo and Juliet*, 34; *The Taming of the Shrew*, 35; *Timon of Athens*, 35; *Titus Andronicus*, 169; *The Two Gentlemen of Verona*, 35

Shakespeare, William, *Henry VIII*, 22, 27–36, 43–44, 46–47, 50–57, 63–79 *passim*, 95–102, 108–10, 122, 143–44, 161, 163–64, 167
Shakespeare, William, *The Winter's Tale*, 22, 34–37, 63–64, 83–164 *passim*, 167
Shakespearean[s], 22, 27, 35, 85, 120
Shrewsbury, 1st Earl of (John Talbot), 184
Sicily, 34, 36, 83–84, 88–90, *91*, 93–97, 106–7, 110, 139–42, 151, 155–57, 159–63
Siena, 66, 195
Sinalus, in "The Life of Dion" in *Plutarch's Lives*, 155–57, 160; in *Winter's Tale*, 89–90, 96, 107, 155–57, 159–61
Sint-Truiden/Saint-Trond, 221
Soane (river), 186
Somme (river), 18, 178
Sotheby's, 11, 14
Spanish Armada, 88–89
Spain/Spanish, 1, 21, 12, 34, 84, 86–89, 91, 94–96, 99, 102, 106, 107, 143, 148, 177, 191–92, 197, 208, 214
Speyer, 8, 218
Spoleto, 5, 177, 205, 211
St. Trudo, Bishop of, 221
Stanga, Camillo, 109, 115, 118, 135, 143–44, 163, 197. *See also* Camillo, in *Winter's Tale*
Stanza del Sole/Room of the Sun, 133
Steinach am Brenner, 91, 214
Sterzing, 91, 214
Stowe, John, *The Annals of England*, 13, 76, 102, 169
Sullino [Salina?], Bishop of, 205
Susa, 3, 45, 123, 189–90

Talbot, John. *See* 1st Earl of Shrewsbury
Tallern, Justin, 177
Tarare, 3, 177, 185–86
Termignon, 188

Terni, 206
Thirlby, Thomas, Bishop of Ely, 1, 4, 5, 7, 8, 11–13, 16, 20, 22, 29, 43, 45, 63, 66, 178, 191, 201, 208, 210, 216, *passim* (as lord[s]) in Transcript
Thomas, William, *The History of Italy*, 41–43, 45, 47, 164, 177, 207, 210
Thorpe, Thomas, 14
Thyestes. *See* Heywood, Jasper; Seneca
Tiber (river), 206
Ticino, 193
Titus and Vespasian, 169
Torino/Turin/Turino, 3, 71, 190
Tortona, 3, 192
Tower of Fazen the lawyer, 193
Trebbia (river), 196
Trento, 7, 12, 162, 212–14, 224
Trump, Melania, 33
Tudor, 1, 8, 13, 36, 45, 65, 74, 85–88, 97, 102–3, 135, 148, 150, 155, 167
Turgut Re'is (a/k/a Dragut Rais), 7, 90, 96, 107, 156
Turkey/Turkish/Turks, 7, 107, 151, 216
Turnebull, Lord, 177
Turner, William, 16

Udall, Nicholas, 102
Urbino, 4, 6–7, 211
Urbino, Duchess of (Eleanor[a] Gonzaga), 127, 163, 198
Urbino, Duchess of (Vittoria Farnese), 5, 53, 66, 196, 202–3
Urbino, Duke of (Guidobaldo II della Rovere), 4, 52, 66, 202–4, 211
Urlich. *See* Württemberg, Duke of

Vendôme, Duke of (Antoine), 178
Venice/Il Golpho di Venetia/Gulf of Venice/Venetians, 202, 212–13

Vergil, Polydore, 7, 177, 211
Vestarino, Lodovico (general of camp in Piedmont), 196
Villafranca di Verona, 212
Villanova D'Asti, 191
Virgil, 151
Visconti, Gian Galeazzo. *See* Milan, 1st Duke of
Voghera, 3, 192–93

Waldburg, Otto Truchsess von, Cardinal of Augusta [Augsburg], 7, 217
Warham, William, Archbishop of Canterbury, 29, 48
Wesel, 219
Westcott, Sebastian, 169
White [Whight], Thomas, 21, 177, 187
William. *See* Jülich-Cleves-Berg, Duke of
Wilson, Robert, 169
Wolsey, Thomas, Cardinal, 27, 29–32, 36, 43–52, 55, 63–65, 67–70, 74–79, 92, 97, 100, 108. *See also* Cavendish, George, *The Life of Wolsey*
Worms, 8, 162, 218–19, 224
Württemberg, Christoph von. *See* Württemberg, Duke of (Christoph von)
Württemberg, Duke of (Christoph von Württemberg), 8, 217–18
Württemberg, Duke of (Urlich), 217
Wycliffe, John, 92–93

Yelverton, Christopher, Epilogue to *Jocasta*, 168; *The Misfortunes of Arthur*, 169
Yorke, Philip. *See* Hardwicke, 2nd Lord

About the Authors

Dennis McCarthy, an independent scholar, is the author of *Here Be Dragons: How the Study of Animal and Plant Distributions Revolutionized Our Views of Life and Earth* (Oxford University Press, 2009). With Schlueter, he published *"A Brief Discourse of Rebellion and Rebels" by George North: A Newly Uncovered Manuscript Source for Shakespeare's Plays* (D. S. Brewer in association with The British Library, 2018). He is presently at work on other books about Thomas North and his plays.

June Schlueter, Charles A. Dana Professor Emerita of English at Lafayette College, is the author of several books on the early modern period, including *The Album Amicorum and the London of Shakespeare's Time* (British Library, 2011). The book she and McCarthy published on the George North manuscript anticipated the current volume, which also pursues traditional and emerging approaches to source study. For twenty years, Schlueter co-edited *Shakespeare Bulletin*.

www.ingramcontent.com/pod-product-compliance
Lightning Source LLC
Chambersburg PA
CBHW070828300426
44111CB00014B/2487